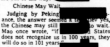

REPORTER

Jake Highton

Reporter

Reporter

Jake Highton
Editorial Writer
The Detroit News

McGraw-Hill Book Company

New York   St. Louis   San Francisco   Auckland   Bogotá   Düsseldorf
Johannesburg   London   Madrid   Mexico   Montreal   New Delhi
Panama   Paris   São-Paulo   Singapore   Sydney   Tokyo   Toronto

REPORTER

1 2 3 4 5 6 7 8 9 0 D O D O 7 8 3 2 1 0 9 8 7

This book was set in Press Roman by Intergraphic Technology, Inc. The editors were Donald W. Burden and John M. Morriss; the cover was designed by Suzanne Haldane; the production supervisor was Milton J. Heiberg.
R. R. Donnelley & Sons Company was printer and binder.

Cover illustration: © 1977 by The New York Times Company. Reprinted by permission.

Library of Congress Cataloging in Publication Data

Highton, Jake.
    Reporter.

    Includes index.
    1.   Reporters and reporting.   I.   Title.
PN4781.H5   070.4'3   77-10339
ISBN 0-07-028771-6

Contents

v

PART 2 ADVANCED REPORTING

Preface

Gene Fowler, newsman in the brawling and boozing Colorado journalism early in the century, had grumbled as an undergraduate about a required journalism textbook. "The book's insufferably dull," Fowler related in *A Solo in Tom-Toms.*[1] "If the newspaper world produces dusty-minded clods such as this author, I don't want any part of it."

Fowler's journalism professor admitted he had never read the book and reminded Fowler that he never referred to it in class. However, the professor said, his dean had insisted on a textbook for appearance's sake.

Perhaps this text will be more useful. It is designed for two fundamental classes in journalism schools, basic reporting and advanced reporting. Its stress is on practical application—doing—as opposed to theorizing about reporting. The book focuses on the basic, standard principles and practices of reporting that are universally accepted by good journalists.

This book will not make you a reporter. No book can do that. If you want to be a journalist, go to work for a newspaper. Journalism schools cannot teach experience. Still, good journalism courses and good journalism teachers can be invaluable to future journalists.

The book presents the foundation for good reporting and good writing. It offers students a better understanding of newspapers. It imparts a high ethical standard. It may foster an attitude of critical analysis of press performance.

The emphasis is on big-city journalism even though few graduates will begin their careers on metropolitan newspapers. But the skills of reporting and writing are as essential in Franklin, Pennsylvania, as they are in Chicago.

Judgments as to what is news will vary widely between the "big town" and the "small town." But every newspaper in America can strive for excellence and the highest degree of professionalism.

[1] The Viking Press, New York, 1946.

Thanks are due to the following for their help and suggestions: Neal Shine, managing editor of the *Detroit Free Press*; Dick Femmel, radio and TV professor at Wayne State University; Lou Prato, former Midwest bureau manager of NBC Radio News; Ed Bailey, Detroit freelance photographer; Tony Spina, chief photographer of the *Detroit Free Press*; Herschel Fink and Ken Murray, Detroit attorneys specializing in libel law; Al Phillips, former public affairs representative from the American Natural Resources Company; Judy Rose, public relations professor at Wayne State University; Rich Oppel, executive editor of the *Tallahasse* (Fla.) *Democrat*, on wire service journalism; Lou Heldman of the *Detroit Free Press* on court reporting; Neale Copple, University of Nebraska; John DeMott, Temple University; Wilbur Doctor, Rhode Island University; Warren Franche, University of Nebraska; James Howard, University of California; James Moore, Mt. San Antonio College; Daniel Reeder, University of Kansas; Wil Sims, Modesto Junior College; Donald Williams, Baylor University; and Betty Highton and Joyce Walker-Tyson, who typed the manuscript.

Jake Highton

Reporter

Part One

Basic Reporting

Chapter 1

Newspapering's Highest Law

There is no higher law in journalism than to tell the truth and shame the devil.

Walter Lippmann

Journalism demands a high degree of professionalism. But in a true sense, it is not a profession. It has no licensing and no disbarment procedures such as law and medicine have.

Although it has codes of ethics and credos, journalism really has no laws. Yet what Lippmann said in the 1920s remains true today: Telling the truth is the highest law of journalism.

Newspapers do not always *tell* the truth—leaving aside the philosophical question of what is truth. But most newspapers do *seek* the truth.

The law really doesn't seek the truth, although lawyers theorize about seeking justice. Lawyers try to win cases—which is far different from seeking the truth.

But let's not glamorize journalism. Newspapering is a business. It has blots on its escutcheon and it will always get new blots. Journalists aren't demigods. They love to make money even more than most of them love to drink. As a group, journalists may be the world's biggest gripers. But the fact is that for many people journalism is more than a job. It is a calling in the same sense that people feel called to the clergy.

READ NEWSPAPERS

So you want to be a journalist? Read newspapers. Read the metropolitan papers in your area. Read your community weekly. Read the *New York Times*, the closest America comes to having a comprehensive national newspaper.

One of the oldest complaints of newspaper editors is that their staffers do not read their own newspaper. Student journalists should not make that mistake.

Read newspapers for information and content. Journalists must be informed. They must be knowledgeable. They must know what is going on in the world, nation, state, and community.

Students should read newspapers to study the techniques of the professionals. They should first play the sedulous ape, as Robert Louis Stevenson put it, copying the masters before they become individual stylists. Students can learn a great deal about writing and reporting by reading stories written by professionals.

Students should also read papers with a critical eye. Is the newspaper biased in its news columns? Is a story slanted? Is the reporting fair? The answers may be debatable. But it is important that journalism students develop the attitude of critical analysis of press performance.

Newspapers are put out by professionals. But these professionals are fallible. Anyone who has ever been involved in an event that made the papers can attest to that.

One caution is necessary, however, Do not let your own feelings or perceptions color your judgment of the reporting. Readers and listeners often let their biases determine what they call "slanted journalism." Journalists are trained to get the facts, to be objective. However subjective they are personally, most journalists strive for objectivity in news reporting.

It is not necessary to read everything in a newspaper. It might take two hours to do that. But you should develop the habit of reading the major stories and scanning all headlines. Then look at the lead and development of stories. If you are interested—or you think you should know the contents of a story—read on.

LEARN TO TYPE

Typing is a must. No one should be allowed to take a basic reporting class without being able to type. Speed is not essential at the start. Speed will come with deadline stories in class.

ELECTRONIC NEWSROOM—News editors and copy editors are in the foreground in this view of the *Detroit News* electronic city room. Reporters are in the background. Poles throughout the newsroom are casing for the wires that link the cathode ray terminals with computers. *(Photo by the* Detroit News.*)*

Some journalists still type with two forefingers, hunting and pecking. But they type swiftly. To develop speed, practice typing the lead story in your local daily for about fifteen minutes a day. This will not only improve your speed but also help ingrain the style of professional news writing.

If possible, learn to type with an electric typewriter. Most newsrooms today produce copy with a technological system based on the sensitive touch of electric typewriters.

REPORTER'S NOTEBOOK

Get a reporter's notebook or a stenographer's pad. Use it for overnight assignments and deadline stories in class. It slips easily into pocket or purse.

Notebooks are more permanent. They are preferable to the old newsroom practice of reporters grabbing a handful of copy paper before going on an assignment. Was there an error in the story? Does someone say you misquoted him? A notebook is better proof and not so easily lost as scraps of copy paper.

Date your notebooks. After filling notebooks, save them until you are sure you will not need them. Long after you have written a news story, you may want to refer to the notes again.

"Naturally, you have a right to remain silent."

FIRST AMENDMENT—Editorial cartoon suggests one aspect of the eternal conflict between the press and government. It was drawn by Draper Hill of the *Detroit News* when he
was editorial cartoonist for the *Commercial Appeal* of Memphis, Tennessee. *(Source:
Commercial Appeal.)*

Suppose you want to compare a campaign promise with performance in
office. The dated notebook is helpful. Suppose you want to do a backgrounder
or Sunday piece. You may be glad to have kept that notebook.

A reporter's notebook gives you a professional look. Journalism students
should not be fumbling with three-ring notebooks either in class or on assignment. Appearances are important in this case. It is a step toward looking, acting,
and thinking like a professional. It is a start toward learning the reporter's job:
getting the facts and writing them well.

NOVELS AND CAUSES

Perhaps you yearn to be a novelist, a creative writer. Great. Newspapering has a
long tradition of writers first earning their bread and observing life while working for newspapers.

Hemingway was a reporter before he became a celebrated writer. Walt
Whitman, possibly America's greatest poet, was a newspaperman. And Charles
Dickens wrote: "To the wholesome training of severe newspaper work, when
I was a very young man, I constantly refer my first successes."

But newspaper writing is fact writing. It is not fiction writing despite the
fact that newspapering has a shady tradition of writing fiction in the guise of fact.

So, while you may prefer Joycean or Faulknerian stream-of-consciousness writing, that is literature. Newspapers have no openings for novelists. Editors insist on crisp and clear prose. This means you will seldom if ever write deathless prose.

Causes? Fine. Your instructor may share some of them. But reporting is not advocating free love, free pot, or free higher education. Leave that to the editorial writers.

Relevancy? Mercifully, that student cry of the late 1960s has been muted. seldom today do you hear a student say: "I don't want to write your obituaries, fire, and accident stories. I want to write about important things."

Someday students may write about what they consider important things. But it is advisable to learn to report and write about newspaper staples first.

ADVICE

Please keep the following in mind as you begin your work in journalism:

- Deadlines are important in all media work. Missing a deadline is traumatic at newspapers, raising blood pressure and snarling circulation schedules. Missing deadlines can cost you your job. Students should get that copy in on time. Delays cannot be tolerated.
- Newspaper experience is invaluable. Seize every opportunity to write for your campus or local paper. It will pay off in many ways in later life.

Freedom of the Press

Congress shall make no law ... abridging the freedom ... of the press ....

—First Amendment to the United States Constitution

Chapter 2

A Dirty Word: Discipline

Discipline became a dirty word while permissiveness was in vogue in the 1960s. Students craved self-expression. They were like Archy, the cockroach of journalist-poet Don Marquis. Archy couldn't work the shift key on the typewriter, but he wrote, "expression is the need of my soul."

The permissive-school students could see little need to spell properly or to know grammar. "You know, like, well, ya know, do I really have to, ya know, like?" It did little good to tell students that concert musicians practiced scales even after they had become renowned.

Perhaps this sermon is not necessary any longer. But here it is: Student reporters must learn the disciplines of a writer. They should study the language. They should learn to spell. They should build a vocabulary.

Words are the tools of a journalist's trade, just as a baseball catcher needs a mask, chest protector, and shin guards. If you see an unfamiliar word, look it up. Jot down the meaning. If it is a good word, squirrel it away for future use.

Despite the rise in functional illiteracy in the United States, reporters should use the apt word, the word that fits best. The simple word is better than the sesquipedalian. But never accept the lunatic saying in newsrooms that newspapers should be written for a sixth-grade mentality.

Spelling There are more important things in life than being a good speller. But no city editor will tolerate copy speckled with misspellings. Besides, the city editor might muse, "If Jones is this careless about spelling, I wonder how careless he is about facts?" Facts are sacred to good newspapers.

Neal Shine, managing editor of the *Detroit Free Press*, puts it this way:

I've worked with a number of fine newsmen and women who were nonspellers, but all of them recognized the failing and worked with a dictionary close at hand. I think that reporters who give hard-to-spell words their best shot and then hope the desk catches any mistakes are lazy and sloppy and that this is going to show up in other aspects of their work.

- Students should carry a pocket dictionary to class.

Journalists are not grammarians any more than the author of this text is. But reporting students should make a habit of checking references when in doubt about grammatical points. Get a basic grammar and review the parts of speech. Writers should be able to recognize a noun and tell a split infinitive when they see one.

All of this may be painful. Discipline means forcing yourself to do things that are not fun. Correct use of the language is part of the discipline of being a writer.

If you use language incorrectly, you call attention to yourself. Grammatical errors are like typographical errors—they distract the reader. Readers who recognize grammatical mistakes fuss over the errors and temporarily lose the thread of the story.

ADVICE FOR ASPIRING JOURNALISTS

Journalism students, like the philosopher Francis Bacon, should take all knowledge as their province. Cultivate an interest in history, politics, religion, literature, music, art, theater, and movies.

The more you know, the better you will be able to write on a wide variety of subjects. To write clearly on complex problems, you must understand them. How can you write well about the courts if you do not understand how the law works? How can you write intelligently about space if you do not understand the elementary principles of science involved?

You do not need to be a lawyer to cover the courts. You do not have to be a scientist to write science news. But knowledge of those subjects will make you a better reporter.

Reporters should be general practitioners of knowledge.

Aspiring reporters should be serious about reading and writing. Read, read, read. Read newspapers, magazines, and books.

Read the writers of your newspaper who impress you as stylists and re-porters. Read Anthony Lewis and Tom Wicker, *New York Times* syndicated columnists. They are among the best reporter-writers in America. Their copy will also challenge you intellectually.

Write, write, write. Write at every opportunity—news stories, letters, articles, and essays. Write letters to the editor. See how they are edited for space.

Keep a diary or journal. This doesn't mean recording sophomoric effusions about love or how tough life is. Instead, fill your journal with observations about people, thoughts about life, and notes on books and articles you read.

Sir Arthur Quiller-Couch, the British man of letters, used to recommend that writers dabble in poetry just to develop a feeling for words.

Ultimately you will teach yourself to write. Journalism instructors can be helpful. But once into a newsroom, you will find few editors with the time or inclination to teach you.

Writing can only improve through writing, experience, and maturity. While writing for a newspaper or journalism class, note the changes made in your stories, Ask why the changes were made if you are not told or if you do not understand them.

Sometimes you will disagree with the changes. Enter your protests, give your arguments, but remember that the editor is boss. Journalism is not a science. Opinions and policies vary. With deadlines in sight, someone has to make a final decision.

WHAT IS NEWS?

News is what is published in newspapers. Does that sound flippant? It isn't meant to be. By observing what newspapers print, you will get a better idea of what is news than by memorizing a textbook definition.

Circumstances alter cusses, as Mark Twain used to say, and circumstances have a great deal to do with why one event is news and another is not. Some factors in news are:

- **Importance**   Stories of consequence to many people: a tax increase, a rise in bread prices, a new minimum wage law.
- **Magnitude**   Wars, disasters, hurricanes, earthquakes, jetliner crashes.
- **Prominence**   The President of the United States can cut his finger and it is news. You can break your leg skiing and it is not news. However, if you fall from a five-story building and *only* break a leg, it is news. A fender-bender accident is not news. But if the governor of your state is involved, it is news.
- **Proximity**   If three people die in a plane crash in Chile, it is not news. But if three die in a plane crash in your community, it is news. Or if one of the people killed in the crash in Chile is from your town, that could be news.

The fact that seventy-two people drown swimming off Japanese beaches on one summer day might make one paragraph in your local paper. That may sound calloused. But it simply is not news here. However, if seventy-two Japanese are swept away by a tidal wave, that is news.

• **Timeliness** If a metropolitan paper learns of a $500 burglary three days after it happened, it is not worth a story. But if the home of a VIP is burglarized, it is still a story even if reporters do not learn about it for three days.

The My Lai massacre in Vietnam was not reported until one and a half years after it happened. But it was certainly news.

• **Conflict** An old newspaper saying is that conflict makes news. That is why sports, court trials, and political races are news.

• **Oddities** An axiom set forth by John Bogart, *New York Sun* city editor, in the nineteenth century, still governs in news judgment: "When a dog bites a man, that is not news; but when a man bites a dog, *that* is news." If someone is left $25,000 in a will, it usually is not news. But if a cat is willed $25,000, that is news.

• **Human Interest** It is this kind of story: A woman dies in squalor with $50,000 under her mattress. Or this kind of story: A mother watching television sees her son wounded in Vietnam.

Those are the major factors that go into making news judgments. However, decisions on what is news vary widely from newsroom to newsroom.

A routine automobile accident in which two people are killed might be a page-one, banner-headline story in a community weekly or daily. A similar accident might get only a few paragraphs on an inside page of a large-city daily newspaper.

Good News versus Bad News

Guy de Maupassant, the French short story writer, was once asked why he had so many wicked women in his stories. "The honest woman has no story," he replied.

The same rationale operates in newspapers. Newspapers carry much good news. But "good news" often is not news in the newspaper sense. If a plane lands on schedule at your metropolitan airport, it is not news. But if it crashes on landing, it is news, albeit bad news.

NEWSPAPER PERSONALITY

Most newspapers fall between the personality extremes of the *New York Times* and the New York *Daily News*. The *Times* is sober, dignified, and restrained. The *News* is flamboyant, gaudy, and saucy.

This is a typical *Daily News* headline on a story about Mafia figure Joseph "Joe Bananas" Bonanno: "Banana's Back, Feared Ripe for Killing." Such a headline will never, never, appear in the *Times*.

Similarly, the tone and style of the writing reflects the personality of the newspaper. A story in the *Daily News* about a stripteaser had such words as "goody," "mobster," "hubby," "the pokey," and "big house." It was a light story—perfect for the *Daily News*. The *Times*, if it deigned to run such a story, would never use such colloquialisms.

"Painful Labor"

One of the secret resentments held by professional writers is that, while nobody can become a musician without patient years of practice, and nobody can enter medicine or the law without a long period of study, anybody who owns a typewriter feels qualified to set up shop as a "writer. . . ."

Writing . . . is difficult and painful labor, involving hard thought and the skillful use of professional tools that must be sharpened through years of apprenticeship.

—Sidney J. Harris
Syndicated Columnist

REFERENCES

Lure and Lore of Newspapering

City Editor. By Stanley Walker. Frederick A. Stokes Company, New York, 1934. Dated today, as you would expect from a book published in 1934. But the color, flavor, and character of yesteryear are here. Besides, the book contains information that is still good for students.

A Treasury of Great Reporting. Edited by Louis L. Snyder and Richard B. Morris. Simon and Schuster, New York, 1949. Probably as much literature as journalism. It features famous writers covering famous—and not so famous—events.

The Craft

All the President's Men. By Carl Bernstein and Robert Woodward. Simon and Schuster, New York, 1974. It tells more about Watergate than you will probably care to know by now. But it is excellent on revealing how good reporters work—their tenaciousness and doggedness—and the caution of their editors in wielding the immense power of the press.

The Boys on the Bus. By Timothy Crouse. Ballantine Books, Inc., New York, 1974. Humorous look at the Washington press from the *Rolling Stone* viewpoint. What it says about pack journalism is valid.

Style

The Elements of Style. By William Strunk, Jr., and E. B. White. The Macmillan Company, New York, 1962. Pound for pound, the best book on writing ever written. Every student eager to be a writer should get a copy. Professionals can profit by rereading it once a year.

Language

The Careful Writer. By Theodore M. Bernstein. Atheneum Publishers, New York, 1967. Tainted by *New York Times* persnicketiness, but good for settling arguments about grammar and language—and putting your own mind at ease.

English Grammar and Composition. By John E. Warriner. Harcourt, Brace and Company, Inc., New York, 1957. Parts of speech and grammatical niceties laid out understandably.

Strictly Speaking. By Edwin Newman. The Bobbs-Merrill Company, Inc., Indianapolis/New York, 1974. A humorous view of our foibles in writing and speaking.

The Critical Side

The Fading American Newspaper. Doubleday & Company, Inc., Garden City, N.Y., 1960. By Carl Lindstrom. Some of the things Lindstrom complained about may have been set right. But he is still right about so many newspaper shortcomings.

The Wayward Pressman. By A. J. Liebling. Doubleday & Company, Inc., Garden City, N.Y., 1948. Just about everything about the press by Liebling, the champion press critic, is worth reading. He wrote well. He had wit. He was often right.

Columbia Journalism Review and *MORE.* Best of the journalism reviews. *CJR* is outstanding. It is sober and reliable—which sometimes means stuffy. *MORE* is brasher and livelier.

Journalist's Library

Stylebook of your newspaper and postal guide.

Any good dictionary, abridged and unabridged versions.

The latest *World Almanac.*

Telephone and city directories; state manual; *Congressional Directory.*

Bartlett's Familiar Quotations. Little, Brown and Company, Boston/Toronto, 1968.

Any one-volume desk encyclopedia.

The Reader's Encyclopedia. By William Rose Benet. Thomas Y. Crowell Company, New York, 1965. Invaluable for allusions to literature, art, music, mythology, and the Bible.

Who's Who in America.

A world atlas.

The Bible (preferably King James version).

The above list is hardly definitive. Every instructor will have additions—and subtractions. The important thing is to start now to build your own library of useful books.

Chapter 3

Stylebook and Copy Preparation

Follow style out the window.

Old Newspaper Saying.

Parts of your stylebook may seem wrongheaded and foolish, but you must follow it. Publications need style consistency.

It really does not matter which way you write "a.m." But a paper would look silly if one reporter wrote "4 a.m.," and another "4 A.M.," and a third "4 AM."

A newspaper story once appeared with three references to a tunnel. One was "Tunnel Number One," another "Tunnel No. 1," and a third, "Tunnel #1." Stylebooks help avoid such inconsistencies.

Some newspapers are cavalier about stylebooks. Some papers don't even have stylebooks, reasoning that "everybody here knows our style."

Some stylebooks are elaborate and lengthy. The *New York Times* stylebook, published in hardback, is the most comprehensive. The *Detroit News* stylebook prints eleven pages of genealogy of the family owners—which is ridiculous.

Your journalism department might have a stylebook. If it does not, your instructor will give you style rules.

COPY PREPARATION

Newspaper technology has advanced so rapidly that typewriters are obsolete for copy production in many newsrooms. Still, you need to know how to prepare copy. Procedures vary from newsroom to newsroom.

Every story needs a *slug* or, as it is sometimes called, a *guideline*. The slug is one word with no more than six letters. Typical slugs are "fire," "slay," and "rob."

In the upper left of the first *take* (or page), write the slug and your last name: fire/jones. Start a third of the way down on the first take. This leaves space for bylines, headlines, and instructions to the printer.

Triple-space all copy. Leave wide margins so there is room for insertions. Don't crowd takes at the bottom or sides. At the end of the first take, write MORE under the center of the last paragraph. Start the second take at the top with 1st ad/fire. Continue this as long as necessary on subsequent takes: 2d ad/fire, and so on.

At the end of the story, sign off with #. A few romantics may cling to "30" as a signoff.

Don't worry about English-class neatness. Journalism is literature in a hurry, as Matthew Arnold once put it. You will often write under deadline, so forget the sensibilities of a stenographer.

Scratch out words, phrases, and whole sentences and start them again. But copy cannot be too raw. It must be readable. Besides, clean copy puts editors and instructors in a good psychological frame of mind to handle your stories.

Edit your copy carefully before turning it in. Use basic copy editing marks (see page 18). Pencil in words and phrases neatly. Check your copy for spelling, grammatical errors, and accuracy. Make sure you have accurately transcribed facts and figures from your notes.

WRITING TIPS

Charles Martin Hall was a brilliant young chemist but a poor writer. At twenty-two he discovered an electrolytic process that made commercial production of aluminum possible. Hall wrote a paper for a scientific journal to announce his breakthrough. But the article was so muddily written that a wag quipped, "Hall nearly succeeded in keeping the discovery to himself."

The point should not be lost on journalism students. Much failure to communicate stems from a lack of clear writing. The watchwords for writers are *clarity*, *crispness*, and *simplicity*.

Good newspaper writing is crisp and clear. Short sentences and short paragraphs are its benchmarks. This sometimes gets journalism students into trouble with their English professors who have an addiction to long paragraphs.

Newspaper paragraphing is arbitrary. Paragraphs are intentionally kept short to permit easier reading and to allow more white space on the printed page. Note the first three paragraphs of an Associated Press story:

STANFORD, Calif.—(AP)—Surgeons at Stanford University Hospital transplanted the heart of a marine into the chest of a retired Oregon postal clerk today.

The donor, Cpl. Larry B. Smith, 20, of Stockton, Calif., suffered what physicians termed irreversible brain damage in an automobile accident Aug. 14 near Stockton.

The recipient, Leonard Drake, 43, of Eugene, Ore., has suffered from a heart ailment for 12 years.

One idea to a sentence. Follow that rule to enhance readability. Look at this sentence: "Authorities at the ancient school located 35 miles north of Chicago and founded as a nondenominational college the year Lincoln was first elected president said they would let the demonstration run its course."

That is bad writing. Make it: "School authorities said they would let the demonstration run its course." Then put the background into another paragraph.

Hemingway has been justly praised as a writing stylist. His use of the simple sentence is masterful. Beginning writers can profit by reading his prose, absorbing what columnist Henry J. Taylor called Hemingway's "disciplined brevity." But in the hands of imitators, the technique becomes a silly mannerism. For example, this appeared in a metropolitan newspaper:

The door opened.
Parsons entered.
The door slammed behind him.
The other patrolmen threw their weight against the door but it held.
No voices were heard.
Five shots were fired.

Reporters should strive for economy of language. This is not mere word counting. It is heightening the impact of copy. It is going to the heart of the matter.

Don't write "he stated that." Make it "he said." Avoid using terms like "the former and the latter." That forces readers to double back to see who is the former and who the latter.

Don't play paired-negative games with readers. Don't write "not infrequently." Make it "frequently."

Use the active voice rather than the passive voice when possible. Say "police identified the body" rather than "the body was identified by police."

However, reporters sometimes use the passive voice to get the most important point in a sentence first, for example: "Zubin Mehta was named yesterday as the new director of the New York Philharmonic to succeed Pierre Boulez."

Since Mehta is widely known in music circles, it is better to use the passive than to write: "The New York Philharmonic named Zubin Mehta as its new director yesterday."

Write things positively, not negatively. Say "the mayor rejected a proposal to ban handguns," rather than saying "the mayor said he would not accept the proposal."

Architect Mies van der Rohe used an axiom in architecture that can be applied to writing: "Less is more." Strive for maximum effect with minimum means.

One of the barriers to economy of language is elegant variation, a noxious grammar school precept that still lingers. If you wrote an essay about Shakespeare, you could not repeat the word Shakespeare on the rest of the page. Students were forced to write, "the sweet swan of Avon," or "the noble bard." Use the word Shakespeare twenty-five times in the same story if you must.

Another bar to good writing is pedagogese. Russell Baker, humor columnist for the *New York Times*, once recounted the story of Little Miss Muffet as told by a sociologist:

We are clearly dealing with a prototypical illustration of a highly tensile social structure's tendency to dis- or perhaps even de-structure itself under the pressures created when optimum minimums do not obtain among the disadvantaged. Miss Muffet is nutritionally underprivileged, as evidenced by the subliminal diet of curds and whey. . . .

Baker concluded his column with a child's version: "This story is about a little girl who gets scared by a spider."

The child's way is a model of simplicity and directness. That is the reporter's way.

SUGGESTED CLASSROOM DRILL FOR INSTRUCTOR

• Dictate a story from a newspaper. Pretend you are a reporter dictating to a newsroom dictationist. Check the students' copy to see that they followed copy preparation instructions and your style rules.

Copy Editing Symbols

Symbol	Meaning
a̲ (underlined, double underscore)	capital letter
A̸	lowercase letter
⌐ or ¶	paragraph
⊙ or x	period
(fifteen)	reverse (15)
(Sen.)	write it out
=	hyphen
⊢	dash
how‿ever	close up
the ~~the~~ way	delete
⩊	caret for emphasis with insertions

Chapter 4

People Business

Newspapering is a people business. About 99 percent of news stories are based wholly or in part on *interviewing*—asking people questions.

Reporters depend on sources. Indeed, it has been said that a reporter is no better than his or her sources. But sources must be cultivated. One way to begin cultivating sources is by small talk. Chit-chat about sports and the weather may seem unimportant to you, but reporters need to do a lot of it.

Once sources get to know and to like you, they will volunteer stories. Sometimes sources will get so confident in you that they will call you at inconvenient hours. That is one part of newspapering you should not complain about.

No two reporters are exactly alike. Some are outstanding writers and mediocre reporters. Some are excellent reporters and poor writers. Some are just adequate as reporters and writers. Yet some attributes are useful for all reporters:

Cynicism   Reporters should be skeptical of the motives of most people and certainly public officials. From the White House to the courthouse, officials often serve their own interests first and the public's second. As a reporter you represent the newspaper and the public.

The height of reporter's cynicism has been expressed by I. F. Stone, one-time Washington gadfly, with his publication *I. F. Stone's Weekly*. "Every government is run by liars," Stone said. "Nothing they say should be believed."

Aggressiveness   Newspapering is no business for milquetoasts. Reporters should be hard-nosed and assertive. Naturally you should be polite. But reporters need a firm, cocky confidence that they have a right to get a story.

Curiosity   The newspaper cliché is having a nose for news. This means being alert about sniffing out good stories.

Observance   Like a detective, a good reporter notices details. Illuminating details can lift a story out of the ordinary and give it a "you-are-there" authenticity. Perhaps it is a little girl dragging a doll through the debris of her home that was destroyed by a tornado. Perhaps it is professors picketing with signs written in Latin. Take readers to the scene, make them see it and feel it.

Digging   Reporters should vacuum up facts. Maybe you will not use half your notes, but you have more information to choose from when writing your story.

Ask every conceivable question. Leave no holes in a story. One reporter did that by failing to ask what was the name of a phonograph record that led to a quarrel in which a man shot his wife. On the other hand, there is the story—probably apocryphal—of a reporter who measured the exact distance that someone jumped off a bridge by dangling string to the water below.

Pursuit   On a football team with good pursuit, defensive players get knocked down and still get up to help with the tackle. Reporters need this dogged quality. Follow up your questions. Don't let sources dodge.

A campus reporter once quoted a professor as saying he was a victim of the "university's oppression." How? The reader was never told.

MAJOR DIVISIONS OF A NEWSPAPER

Editorial, business, and mechanical departments are the three major divisions of a newspaper. Obviously all three are necessary to put out a paper. But the heart and soul of a newspaper is the editorial department. The editorial product is the raison d'être of a newspaper.

Still, students should be aware that without advertisements daily newspapers would cost about 75 cents. Few people would buy papers at that price. (Even if you pay 25 cents for your daily newspaper it is the best bargain in

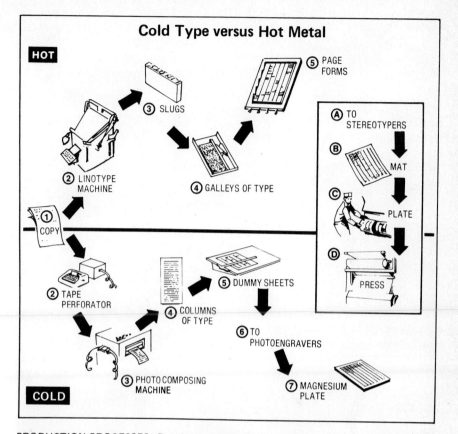

PRODUCTION PROCESSES—Drawing contrasts the hot-metal production process with the cold-type process used by most newspapers today. The last four steps (A through D) are used in both processes. (© 1974 by the New York Times Company. Reprinted by permission.)

America. A newspaper provides the news, sports, stocks, weather—and much more—for the same price as a cup of coffee.)

NEWSPAPER TECHNOLOGY

After 100 years with few fundamental changes, the newspaper industry today is undergoing a technological revolution. No end of that revolution is in sight.

The hot-metal printing process is being replaced by cold-type printing that features photocomposition. The industry is moving toward plateless and pressless production of newspapers.

A newspaper scientific advisor was quoted in *Publisher's Auxiliary* as saying that newspapers were moving rapidly to remove what he called a millstone around the necks of newspapers—the printing press.

PUNCHING OUT STORY—A reporter types his story on a cathode ray terminal, which is hooked up with a computer. *(Photo by the* Detroit News.*)*

Many reporters no longer pound out stories on typewriters. They are quietly typing stories into a television-type console that is hooked up to a computer. This device is called CRT—cathode ray tube—or VDT, video display terminal.

Other reporters are writing stories on sensitized paper with electric typewriters. This process is called OCR—optical character recognition. Reporters' copy is scanned by a machine that produces tape. The tape is then fed into a

COMPUTER BANK—Row of computers forms the electronic heart of a modern metropolitan newspaper. *(Photo by the* Detroit News.*)*

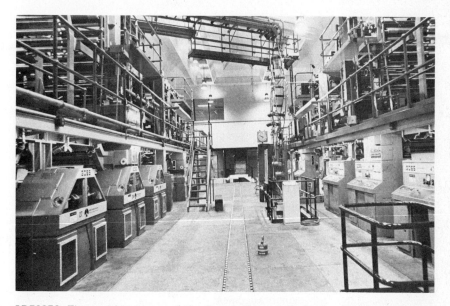

PRESSES—These mighty presses of the *Detroit News* are in Sterling Heights, Michigan, a suburb of Detroit. The *News'* production facilities at its "North Plant" are electronically linked to the downtown Detroit newspaper building. *(Photo by the* Detroit News.*)*

system that produces strips of printed copy ready for photocomposition pasteup.

However it is done, a newspaper is a miracle of production to anyone familiar with the process. Familiarity breeds admiration that so many parts mesh with so relatively few errors.

While production techniques are constantly changing, the reporters' skills are not. Students need not fear that they are preparing for an obsolete craft. Even if the day comes when you can receive a facsimile of your daily newspaper via home television, reporters and editors will always be needed to produce it.

"GET THE CLIPS"

Most newspapers have dignified their *morgues* (reference departments) by calling them "libraries." There is justification. Some newspapers have so many books and reference works that they need head librarians.

For reporters, the indispensable part of morgues is the *clips*. These are the envelopes containing everything the newspaper has ever published about an individual or an event.

Reporters working a story or doing research for an assignment glean background from the clips.

"COPY!"

Copy boys and copy girls—usually summoned by the cry "Copy!" in metropolitan newspapers—are in a good position to break into newspaper work. They observe firsthand the newspaper business, rub shoulders with professionals, and get good pointers.

Some newspapers give their copy "messengers" six-month tryouts as reporters after they have worked for two years. Other young people use those jobs as springboards to reporting. They do it by enterprise—showing their worth and determination by doing more than they are asked. This often means voluntarily writing stories and doing statistical chores for reporters and editors.

Terminology

Newsroom or city room—Heart of newspaper operation; where reporters work
City editor—Boss of city-side reporters
Managing editor—Chief of news operation
General assignment reporter—One who covers anything that turns up
Beat or run—Reporter's regular assignment
Copy desk—Where reporters' copy is edited and headlines written
Slot person—One in charge of copy desk
Proofreading—Correcting printer's errors
Future book—File of upcoming events to cover

The Role of Journalists

Journalism leads to everything—provided one gets out of it.

French Proverb

Journalists are lucky. They get paid for doing what—on good days—is fun and exciting. Not many people on factory assembly lines or clerking in stores can say that.

Reporters are eyewitnesses to important and exciting events. They cover space shots, political conventions, big trials, big fights, and big games.

Some even play influential roles in government policies. The Walter Lippmanns and James Restons can influence Presidents. Statehouse reporters can prod governors to take action. City hall reporters may nudge mayors in decision making.

One Canadian newspaperman, now working for a paper in the United States, had earned such respect from a judge in a Canadian province that the judge asked—and took—the newsman's advice about a judicial appointment. It is flattering when people in power take a reporter's advice. But that kind of respect does not come easily. It must be earned by scrupulously fair and accurate reporting.

Most reporters don't get that heady feeling of influencing the powerful. But nearly all reporters can influence the lives of ordinary people they write about.

"You meet such fascinating people." It is a cliché often uttered to reporters. They do interview fascinating people—actors, writers, and celebrities— but they also interview bores. That is part of the variety of newspapering. One day you may interview skid-row derelicts and the next day cardinals of the Roman Catholic Church.

Students should be warned, however, that newspapering has its drab side: writing routine obits, taking dictation, rewriting handouts, and gathering weather-table information. On some days newspaper work can be as dull as toiling in a factory.

WATCHDOGS

The public is often annoyed by the press. Like a messenger with bad news, the press is naturally disliked. The public also tends to get tired of a story like Watergate that goes on month after month.

But when the public tires of that kind of journalism, it is admitting it gets tired of democracy. An informed public is essential in a democracy. And no role is more important than that which the press plays as a watchdog over public officials.

Former Supreme Court Justice William O. Douglas, dissenting in the 1972 Caldwell case, wrote:

The press has a preferred position in our constitutional scheme not to enable it to make money, not to set newsmen apart as a favored class, but to bring fulfillment to the public's right to know. The right to know is crucial to the governing powers of the people. . . . Knowledge is essential to informed decisions.

As Mr. Justice Black said in *New York Times Co. v. United States*, "The press was to serve the governed, not the governors. . . . The press was protected so that it could bare the secrets of government and inform the people."

JOBS

Jobs are plentiful in newspapering—if you have talent, drive, and determination. There is always room in newspapering for genuine ability.

However, jobs are scarce at the *New York Times, Los Angeles Times*, and *Washington Post*. Those papers usually will hire only people with experience at other metropolitan newspapers.

Most big papers insist on three to five years' experience. This means starting at the bottom. Newspapering, in fact, operates somewhat like the minor leagues in sports. The typical progression is something like this: Students graduate from journalism school, work two years for a weekly or a small daily, move to a larger daily, and then three years later land on a metropolitan newspaper.

Editors ask at job interviews: What experience do you have? Do you have a scrapbook, a stringbook of clips? This often presents a *Catch 22* dilemma: You need experience to get a job, but you can't get experience without getting that first job.

Robert Woodward and Carl Bernstein did the nation a great favor with their relentless investigation of Watergate for the *Washington Post*, but they did journalism schools no favor, helping to push journalism school enrollments to their peaks. Journalism school rolls are padded with people not cut out for media work.

Still, there is always plenty of room for talented people in journalism. If you are good and determined, don't let the number of potential competitors scare you away. If your primary motivation for going into journalism is getting a job, try another line of work.

It is not necessary to have a college degree to succeed in the media. One $40,000-a-year writer with a national magazine never finished sophomore year in college. But that is rare. You should get a degree if you are going into the media.

However, it is not necessary to have a *journalism* degree. If you do major in journalism, it is advisable to have a second major or at least a minor. By specializing in political science, history, English, or economics—or whatever you are interested in—you will bring a special knowledge to newspapering along with the skills of a journalist.

As for the French proverb quoted in the epigraph, it contains a great deal of truth. Reporters often leave journalism to go into public relations. The money is better. Reporters also leave newspapering for television, where the money is also much better.

Many journalists wind up in politics, landing jobs as administrative assistants or taking jobs in city and state government agencies they once covered.

The point to remember is that all media are solidly based on reporting.

NOTE TAKING

"I live by two laws," author-journalist John Gunther remarked. " 'Never take notes on both sides of the paper' and 'all happiness depends on a leisurely breakfast.' "

You may not have time for a leisurely breakfast, but you should take notes on one side of note paper. It is easier to flip the pages to read your notes over the phone or to write a story. When you reach the end of the notebook, start back the other way to save paper.

Write large. Don't crimp your notes. Leave plenty of space between jottings. Print names and addresses to avoid errors.

Reporters develop a personal shorthand, omitting articles, abbreviating things like U.S. and U.N. and writing "culd" and "wuld" for "could" and "would," or "mtg" for "meeting." After the first reference to Jimmy Carter, they may simply write "C." They often must take notes quickly, not having the luxury of a careful library researcher.

In a controversy a few years ago about judges subpoenaing reporters' notes, *New York Times* columnist James Reston wrote:

Have you ever seen a reporter's notes? Would any serious judge really accept most of them in evidence? They are a jumble of phrases, home-made shorthand, disconnected words, names, wisecracks made by press-table companions, lunch dates, doodles, descriptions of somebody's necktie or expression, and large and apparently significant numbers, probably reminding the reporter of nothing more than his next deadline.

Neal Shine, managing editor of the *Detroit Free Press*, offers some advice on note taking learned in the University of Painful Experience:

I once interviewed an accused murderer, took voluminous notes and wrote a long story about him and the crime. I saved and dated my notes, like a good re- porter.

When the accused came to trial, the prosecutor called me to testify and told me to bring my notes of the interview. It was a sensational case. The court- room was packed.

The prosecutor asked me to read from my notes the parts about my ques- tions to the prisoner and about how he was treated during his interrogation and early incarceration.

I couldn't read my writing. After five stumbling, embarrassing minutes the prosecutor asked for my notes and he couldn't read them. The defense attorney tried his luck—same result.

I was excused as a witness.

Since that time I go over notes while they are still fresh in my mind and write a legible translation over all the parts that I might have trouble deciphering at a later date.

SUGGESTIONS

• Rather than hand out mimeographed notes to students from which to write news stories, instructors are urged to play roles. Tear stories out of a news- paper. Have students question you as if you were the police officer or other official from whom they get news stories.

In that way students will learn to ask questions. No matter how well students learn to write, if they do not learn to ask good questions they will be poor reporters.

• Have students write some stories requiring datelines. Most papers use datelines on stories originating outside the metropolitan area. Everything without a dateline is considered a local story.

• Students should do deadline and overnight stories. The deadline stories can be done in class before the period ends. Overnight stories can be assigned for the next class meeting.

• Working under deadline, students should compose stories on their typewriter or VDT. They should not write a draft or rough out the story in longhand first.

They should think while the typewriter or VDT keys are clicking. They will have no time for draft writing under deadline at a newspaper.

• Students: Whenever you call a source, identify yourself and your newspaper immediately. You are training for newspaper work, not the Central Intelligence Agency.

• Newspaper practice is to use the day of the week one week in the future and one week in the past. Outside that two-week cycle, use the date.

The yesterday, today, and tomorrow cycle for the time element is preferable. It has more immediacy and avoids the confusion of "Tuesday Weld Wednesday signed a contract." However, the style at some A.M. (morning) papers is to use the day of the week for yesterday and tomorrow.

• Do not pad a story, writing to reach a certain length. Always write a story the length it is worth—and no more.

Chapter 6

Accuracy above All Else

Accuracy! Accuracy!! Accuracy!!!

Joseph Pulitzer

A newspaper in the Southwest, reporting on a Detroit mayoral election, said that "Roman S. Gibbs, a black, was elected ... in a close fight with incumbent Richard Austin."

The facts: The winner's name was Gribbs, the white incumbent, and the challenger was Austin, a black. This was not a world record for newspaper error, but it epitomizes the most recurring sin in journalism—inaccuracy.

It hardly seems necessary to make a case for accuracy. It is enough to say that inaccuracies damage credibility. A story in a campus newspaper about pornography began: "Nine old men on the U.S. Supreme Court recently decided that a movie graphically portraying oral-genital relations and sexual intercourse (*I Am Curious–Yellow*) was not obscene." Anyone who followed court decisions knew the justices never ruled on that film. No matter how well written and accurate the rest of the story may have been, it was ruined by that false first sentence.

Probably the chief source of newspaper error is names. The *Hartford Courant* once sent out clippings to people who had been mentioned in its news stories. On the first batch, 30 percent of the names were misspelled; on the second batch, 47 percent.

In some cases reporters are defenseless. Police misspell names. Even relatives of victims sometimes misspell names. But reporters can cut down errors greatly by checking. "Brown" is sometimes "Browne." "Smith" is sometimes "Smyth." Errors can be avoided by spelling out unfamiliar names letter by letter. Check to see if you have transferred names correctly from notes to copy.

NEVER ASSUME ANYTHING

Another maxim: Never assume anything in the newspaper business. *AP Log*, the wire service's newsletter, related how reporters wrote that a human heart had been transplanted in a man. Actually, it was a chimpanzee heart. The hospital announcement referred only to a donor heart. Journalists wrongly assumed it was a human heart.

Rumor and gossip are rampant around journalists. Print no story without verification. Go to the source. Pick up a phone. Check it out.

A campus reporter once wrote that the *Detroit News* had barely devoted a line to an antiwar march. It was simply not true. The newspaper had given extensive coverage to the march, including an eight-column, 12-inch-deep picture on page one. How had the reporter made such an egregious error? "A friend told me that," she said. She was publishing hearsay as truth.

Much the same thing happened in a more serious situation. A representative for the Black Panthers, trying to make a case for genocide of blacks, said that twenty-eight Panthers had been murdered by police. Soon the charge was picked up and reported as fact by newspapers across the country. But a writer for *New Yorker* magazine thoroughly investigated the twenty-eight cases and found that only one conceivably could have been a police murder.

Ask. Don't guess. Check things out. Check sources, the morgue, references. Don't trust your memory. Even look up quotations you think you know—phrases, words, punctuation may be different.

"Careless Reporter"

Gene Fowler in *A Solo in Tom-Toms** tells of a Colorado newspaper editor examining a story written by a reporter:

"Suddenly he exploded. He seized a pair of long-billed scissors and began to snip the air with them. 'Can't anyone on this damned newspaper spell names correctly?'

"Now he turned his fierce eyes upon me, as though I were reponsible for the misspelling. 'A man works year after year to make his name mean something.

*Viking Press, New York, 1946.

Then along comes a careless reporter to misspell the man's name, and we have another enemy for life."

THIRD-PERSON RULE

Reporters write most stories in the third person. Reporters should be anonymous because readers generally do not care about their problems. Using "I" is intrusive. Leave the "I" to critics and columnists.

However, there is an exception to the third-person rule. That is the eye-witness story. The use of "I" heightens the impact in eyewitness accounts of dramatic events.

Reporters also use the "I" for humorous effect in feature stories. For example, a *Detroit Free Press* business writer started a story:

If Detroit's salesgirls don't talk or smile during the entire month of January, forgive them.

They're just sell-shocked. They're prattle-fatigued.

And I can understand why, because for four hours last week I served with the best of them, manning the men's toiletries counter during the Christmas rush at the J. L. Hudson Co.'s downtown store.

PAST TENSE

Use the past tense in hard-news accounts of events that have happened: "The President said," "the governor announced," "the mayor proposed."

In some features or analytical stories it is all right to use the present tense: "The governor says he'll run again." In statements not tied to specific events, the present tense is okay: "McLuhan says the medium is the message."

NEWS-STORY IDENTIFICATION

Everyone should be identified in news stories. Even if a council member's name appears regularly in the newspaper, you cannot assume everyone knows who he or she is. You must identify the person as a council member.

Newspapers identify people in several ways:

- Occupation—Northern High School biology teacher, Baton Rouge plumber.
  - Title—Street commissioner, county auditor.
  - Reputation—Playboy, reputed Mafia leader.
  - Relationship—Niece of movie star Katharine Hepburn, Kennedy cousin.
  - Link to event—Accused slayer of an Atlanta socialite, man sought in the slaying of a University of Texas student.
  - Address. Last resort. Use only if no better identifier is available.

Sometimes reporters have to go with qualified identification: "a man believed to be," "a woman tentatively identified as." But never write "an unnamed man." He has a name.

It is much better to start stories with a broad identification: "A Corvallis carpenter was charged today with first-degree murder of his wife on Jan. 14." Then work in the age, address, and other details in subsequent paragraphs. That way the story flows better and does not get bogged down at the start with details.

The ancient style of newspapering was to jam everything into the lead, like this example from the long-dead *Detroit Journal* in 1911:

With no word of warning, Frank Brady, aged 30, a brass molder, living at 433 Fifteenth Street, entered the store of his brother, William E. Brady, 45 Larned Street West, shortly after 8 o'clock Friday morning and fired three shots into his brother's body.

Many papers insist on the first name and middle initial with names in the first reference. With perhaps hundreds of Smiths in your town, you should write Richard X. Smith.

Some editors argue that a middle initial is not necessary. Edwin Newman in his book *Strictly Speaking* criticizes the print and electronic media for insisting on middle initials. However you feel about middle initials, always get them unless your editors tell you not to bother.

One exception to the middle-initial rule: Follow the usage preference of the individual. Write "H. L. Hunt" or "G. Mennen Williams."

The style on most papers is to use just the last name with titles of incumbent Presidents, governors of your state, and mayors of your city. Out-of-state governors and out-of-town mayors need first name and middle initial.

RACIAL AND ETHNIC TAGS

Use racial and ethnic designations only if pertinent to the story. It is all right to write "a black civil rights leader," but you should not write that "John W. Jones, a black dock worker, was charged today with armed robbery."

A racial or descriptive tag is used by most papers if a suspect is sought by police. Although there is some disagreement about this practice, most editors feel it is not racist in this context.

Avoid nicknames unless widely known and commonly used. You should write "Yogi Berra" instead of "Lawrence Berra" and "Bing Crosby" instead of "Harold Crosby."

Often with underworld figures the nickname is better known than the real name. In that case use the nickname in quotes if that is your paper's style— William "The Greek" Demetrius.

Avoid using such obvious nicknames as William "Bill" Groman or Anthony "Tony" Lenzo.

AGES

Get ages automatically for certain kinds of stories: police stories, obituaries, and stories about youngsters or oldsters where age is pertinent.

Sometimes stories do not need ages. It depends on the kind of story. If Sen. Edward M. Kennedy makes a speech, you do not need his age in the story. But if he announces that he is running for President, you need his age.

Age is a help in identifying people. If you say a man is fifty, for example, you are placing him in a narrow category. You are helping to "pin him down" for the reader.

Newspaperman's Prayer

Dear God, may I be fair. . . . Give me the drive that will make me check and countercheck the facts. . . . Remind me to be kind to copy boys, for I'll meet them on the way back down—when they are editors. . . . Make me use my legs and eyes, the better to track down and see the truth. Deafen me to the Lorelei song of rootless hearsay, rumor, and . . . gossip. . . . If word that could cause great harm comes to me, even from sources far above reproach, let me have the . . . decency to pick up a phone and ask the subject about it.

—Bob Considine

Chapter 7

Handouts and Deadline Writing

Newspapers are deluged with press releases from the mighty to the humble, from General Motors to your local garden club. The more professional releases come into newspaper offices with letterheads, headlines, and copy broken into short paragraphs—tailored for newspaper use. They are a perfect invitation to slap your own head on the copy and rush it into type.

Don't. You are journalists, not press agents. PR people are honest people doing an honest job. But they represent a company or an institution. As reporters, you work for the newspaper and the public. The difference in point of view is vast.

Your job as a reporter getting handouts is to pare them down, trim the verbiage. Cut out puffery and flackery. Space is valuable in newspapers. Department editors sometimes pound the table to get more space.

When you are trimming a handout, rout all the glittering promises like "gala event" and "exciting affair." The gala event may be a dud. The exciting affair may be boring. But more important is the fact that journalists report the news, not offer their opinions.

It is not your business to urge everyone to attend a meeting. Just report that it will be held. As for promises that "a world-renowned poet" will talk, remember that few if any poets are ever renowned while they are alive.

Suspicion, if not cynicism, should be your attitude toward press releases. Suspicion is especially necessary when dealing with any government handouts. As columnist Joseph Alsop has written: "All government handouts lie. Some lie more than others."

If you get a release from any government or a company, never simply rewrite it. Look into it. Call a company official for more detail, for elaboration, for fresh quotations.

The press release information may be sound. But the viewpoint could be the company's, not the public's. Sometimes an important angle is buried in the final paragraphs of the story. That could be the real story.

Always rewrite releases in your own words. The Christmas Club once put out a release that began: "Those tuneful chimes that will be sounding out all over America during the next few weeks won't be jingle bells—they will be cash registers ringing as 16,015,000 . . . members of the country's largest club, Christmas Club, begin spending a good portion of their savings ($2,218,672,000) for a better Christmas for their families and loved ones."

Under the byline of the business editor of the Syracuse *Herald American*, a column began:

Those tuneful chimes that will be sounding out throughout Greater Syracuse during the next few weeks won't be jingle bells—they will be cash registers. They will be ringing because more than 62,000 members of Christmas clubs will begin spending a good portion of their savings—$8,631,952—for a better Christmas for their families and loved ones.

It is embarrassing because the writer let his newspaper be used by a PR firm. Besides, as a matter of pride, journalists should write their own stuff, not fob off another's words as their own.

Always read handouts all the way through before starting to rewrite them. On releases worth a good story, look through them for the hidden or masked angle. But even on routine inside-fill stories, first read the entire release. Having started your rewrite without reading the whole release, you may get to the second page of the release and discover a better, more important lead angle.

Releases that come in without a person's name and phone number should be tossed into the wastebasket. Releases should list a contact person.

Watch out for hoaxes. A metropolitan newsman used to delight in making up phony press releases, sending them out to the weekly papers, and then roaring with laughter when they came out in print verbatim.

A final point: Don't trust the accuracy of spelling and names in news releases. As any women's editor can tell you, some prospective brides cannot spell the names of their husbands-to-be.

FIGHTING THE CLOCK

"I was a flop as a daily reporter," E. B. White once wrote. "Every piece had to be a masterpiece—and before you knew it, Tuesday was Wednesday."

Newspapers live by deadlines. Every story does not have to be a masterpiece. Often you must write speedily under deadline. Moreover, it must be speed that retains accuracy.

Sometimes the story flows more smoothly under deadline. You are in a hurry. The copy just flows. You don't have time to fuss over your copy. As a result, it is often better.

William L. Ryan, foreign news analyst for the Associated Press, made this point in *Reporting/Writing from Front Row Seats*:

The most difficult thing about news writing is the organization of thoughts. It seems that the more time one has to fiddle around with a story, the harder it is to get on paper. I have found over the years that pressure, far from being something to fear, is a boon. When the hot breath is on the back of the neck, when the competition is keen and the deadline is the next minute, the story moves and almost organizes itself.*

REWRITING: YES AND NO

Jean-Jacques Rousseau in his *Confessions* complained of the extreme difficulty of writing: "My manuscripts, scratched, smeared, muddled and almost illegible, bear witness to the trouble they have cost me. There is not one of them which I have not been obliged to copy four or five times before I could give it to the printer."

For many writers, good writing is rewriting. But journalism is usually not literature. Much of it is produced in haste. The output of some reporters is prodigious. This is not to alibi for poor writing. But the fact is that with most news stories, reporters simply do not have the time for draft writing.

Undoubtedly much newspaper copy would be improved by rewriting. Newspapers produce plenty of sloppy copy, not all of which can be blamed on deadlines.

On magazine-type pieces—analytical and interpretive articles and long features—do a draft first if you have time. Rewriting will greatly improve your copy, allowing you to polish it, crispen it, and tighten it.

However, reporters seldom have the luxury of being able to rewrite.

---

*William L. Ryan, *Reporting/Writing from Front Row Seats*, Simon and Schuster, New York, 1971.

WRITING THE NEWS STORY

Reading a story in a newspaper might suggest that there's nothing to *writing* one. Indeed, most hard-news stories (as opposed to feature or non-hard-news stories) are written in an unvarying formula. The lead (first paragraph) tells what happened.

The lead is followed by facts, further details, and quotations in descending order of importance. Readers can quit the story any time they have read as much as they wanted to.

Newspaper writing may look deceptively easy. But as many beginners in Newswriting 101 ruefully discover, it "ain't so simple." A novice might take fifty or sixty words to write a one-paragraph short—something a professional could write in twenty or twenty-five words.

Beginners must learn conciseness and directness. They must learn to eliminate verbosity. They must get to the heart of matters. They must master the simple declarative sentence. Writing for a newspaper is a craft.

You can't learn to write a news story by reading a "how-to" book—this book or any other. Experience is essential. The only way you can learn to write is to write constantly. The nature of the newspaper business is such that practice seldom leads to perfection. But practice does improve newswriting skill.

Your instructors will be most helpful to beginning news writers. Your writing—and their ruthless editing and stern suggestions—will help you to learn the trade.

Sure, *you* know what you meant to communicate to the reader. But if your instructor-editor can't understand what you meant, how can the reader?

No flat commands can be given on writing news stories. Most stories are different in some ways but alike in many ways.

This book is full of hints and advice on writing news stories. It carries many examples of published news stories. Even the stories printed in the book are not perfect. Your instructors may find flaws in some of the examples. Many stories are routine and undramatic. But many of the stories you will write for a newspaper will be routine and undramatic—and flawed, too.

"Begin at the Beginning"

" 'Where shall I begin, please your Majesty?' he asked. 'Begin at the beginning,' the King said, gravely, 'and go on till you come to the end: then stop.' "

—Alice in Wonderland

From phone calls, personal interviews, morgue clips, and press releases, you will gather many facts for news stories. Your job is to decide what to put into a story and what to leave out. You must present the information in a coherent, readable fashion.

Before you start a news story, read over your notes. Underline or check the main points. Then write the lead (first paragraph). The lead is usually the most important paragraph in a hard-news story. It must be interesting and/or convey information succinctly. It is the prelude to your whole "symphony."

The story needs continuity. It must flow smoothly and logically from beginning to end. Transitions are important to avoid "bumps" between paragraphs.

Your story must present facts interestingly. After the lead, the story should march from detail to detail. Beginning news writers may have trouble learning to organize their stories, something that becomes routine with experience.

Quotations are an important part of most stories. They are like dialogue in a novel. Quotes make copy come alive. They make a story "move." (A student once wrote a news story about a "heated" council meeting. Yet in three pages the student did not have a single direct quote to *reveal* the temperature of the meeting.)

Good reporters know what to quote, what to paraphrase, and what to leave out of a story.

"Direct quotes enliven a story and add authority, but just because a news subject says something doesn't make it worth quoting," the Associated Press house organ, *AP Log*, has suggested.

"You can't make a windy platitude, a burst of muddled bureaucratese or a tedious affirmation of the obvious more palatable by putting it between quote marks," *AP Log* advised.

"It's one thing to quote a flood victim as saying, 'This will ruin me,' which is concise and punchy. It's another to quote a relief official saying that 'the flood had a deleterious impact on the community's viability.' That calls for a short paraphrase—if it's used at all."

Well, still more words *about* writing a news story. The best thing to do is to write news stories. But note the solid construction of this AP story:

BRUSHY MOUNTAIN, Tenn.—(AP)—James Earl Ray was run to earth early today by a brace of bloodhounds named Sandy and Little Red, ending a desperate 54½-hour flight for freedom from life in prison.

[*The lead sums up the news event. It has drama. It has impact. It makes the reader want to know more.*]

At the end of a three-hour, three-mile run through a wooded creek valley and up thickly covered mountain slopes, the assassin of civil rights leader Martin Luther King Jr. was found hiding in a pile of leaves.

[*More dramatic detail. Note how the reporter used the phrase "the assassin of civil rights leader" as a substitute for Ray.*]

Driven and exhausted, covered with mud and sand, the 49-year-old Ray offered no resistance to his captors.

[*More information. More strong writing: "Driven and exhausted. . . . "*]

His first words, according to prison guard Sammy Joe Chapman, Sandy's handler and the first officer on the scene, were: "I feel good."

Chapman, 33, petted Sandy after returning with Ray and said: "She's the prettiest dog in the world."

[*New element. Prison guard with good quotes.*]

The location was only five miles from the Brushy Mountain State Prison where Ray and six other felons escaped over a wall with a makeshift pipe ladder on Friday evening.

[*Background information. This is the "old news" woven into the new story. Readers need a brief reminder of what happened earlier.*]

Two escapees—Douglas Shelton, 32, and Donald Caylor, 24—remained at large after Ray's capture.

"We started with seven, we're down to two," said Joel Plummer, state public safety commissioner.

[*More information followed by quote.*]

Two others were captured yesterday. They were: Larry Hacker, 32, of Hamilton, Ohio, serving 28 years for armed robbery and safecracking, the reputed ringleader of the escape, and Earl Hill Jr., 34, of Erwin, Tenn., convicted of murder and rape, a former cellmate of Ray's.

[*Note transition—"two others were captured"—pushing off quote in the previous paragraph.*]

Another fugitive, David Lee Powell, 27, of Chicago, was recaptured Saturday. He was serving 100 years for murder.

[*Good transition: "Another fugitive."*]

Plummer said Gov. Ray Blanton was "extremely pleased with Ray's capture."

Blanton said earlier he had kept U.S. Atty. Gen. Griffin Bell briefed on the search and that Bell had kept President Carter informed.

Ray's capture "concludes one of the largest manhunts in the history of Tennessee," Plummer said.

The capture, at 2 A.M., was reported at 2:35 A.M. Ray was returned to the prison soon afterward in a squad car driven swiftly through the gate to the administration building.

[*Note how the exact times give the story preciseness.*]

Ray appeared tired but alert and wide-eyed. His hair was wet and matted and his clothes, a black sweatshirt and black pants, were covered with sand and mud. His face also was smeared with mud.

[*Color and description. The reporter has figuratively taken readers to the scene.*]

It was not known whether Ray had eaten during the weekend chase, warden Stoney Lane said.

Ray was examined by a medic and placed in a prison hosptial. Lane said this was routine procedure.

Lane said Ray would be placed in "administrative segregation" for three days while a hearing on the escape is conducted.

"It is not solitary confinement, but his movements inside the prison are sharply restricted," the warden said.

[*More information. The story has a "oneness" about it. It is "buttoned up"; that is, it has answered readers' questions about the news event. The story is written "upside down" in the inverted-pyramid style. The most important things are written at the top of the story. The story can be cut from the bottom up without losing anything essential.*]

Lane, riding with Ray, said bloodhounds pursued Ray until they found him in a wooded area, lying on the ground covered with leaves in an attempt to conceal himself.

Ray's capture came a few hours before 160 Tennessee national guardsmen were scheduled to join the expanding search.

Gov. Blanton, who at one point speculated that Ray might even have escaped the country, later canceled the order calling up the guard.

The search had been broadened to a 25-mile radius encompassing the towns of Wartburg, Oliver Springs and Caryville. Caryville was the scene early yesterday of the theft of a car and of clothes and money from a second vehicle.

Prison officials had noted that money, clothes, food and a car would be tops on an escapee's want list.

Warden Lane said that in the last leg of his run for freedom, Ray fled down a heavily overgrown bank of the shallow New River and crossed it.

[*Note how the reporter dropped in a reminder that Lane was the warden.*]

Ray followed a logging road for some distance, then climbed a slope across a logging road before burying himself in the leaves.

Authorities said heavy thunderstorms that raked the Cumberland Mountains earlier in the day, the first rain since the escape, helped in the search.

The fugitives' scent adhered to damp earth better than on dry ground. Dogs sometimes become confused on dry ground.

[*Good interpretive detail.*]

Earlier, State Corrections Commissioner C. Murray Henderson said speculation that authorities at the maximum-security prison helped Ray escape was "absurd, irresponsible and absolutely untrue."

"We'll make a full investigation," Henderson said. "If I'm wrong, the evidence will prove it."

[*Quotes break up the narration of events, keep the story driving forward.*]

Henderson said that people seemed to think that maximum security means that the man would be locked up 24 hours a day in his cell.

"A few years ago, a federal court ordered Ray released from his cell, from lockdown," Henderson said. "It shouldn't surprise anyone he is not in isolation."

The escapees and their sentences were:

[*Several more paragraphs of information about the escapees concluded the story.*]

SUGGESTIONS TO INSTRUCTOR

• Periodically give students a surprise news quiz. Ask them ten questions about people and events in the news for the past week. Pleading with students to read newspapers does not work. Quizzes help.

• While role-playing, set traps for students. Give them the name of a well-known person like columnist William F. Buckley, Jr. Deliberately give him a wrong middle initial. See if anyone catches the error.

Sweating for Simplicity

At the typewriter, Boyle was a study in concentration and terror, taut, silent, intense, measuring out each word carefully for content and sound, writing, X-ing out, rephrasing, sweating out the sentences until finally they emerged with shining simplicity.

> —Saul Pett, AP feature writer, in a *Reader's Digest* tribute
> to the late AP columnist Hal Boyle. *Reader's Digest*,
> Pleasantville, N.Y., October 1974.

Chapter 8

Obituaries

Obituaries are essential newspaper stories. It gets dull writing routine obits day after day. But reporters can console themselves by remembering that obits are among the best-read items in the paper. Besides, the older you get, the more obituaries will interest you.

Cub reporters are often stuck with them. One practical reason is that obits follow a formula and newcomers can easily write them.

Neal Shine, managing editor of the *Detroit Free Press*, acknowledges that obits are the most formula-written material in the great majority of American newspapers. But he advises:

If editors would make a reporter take the time to make a few phone calls on one or two obits a day, the result would be astounding and we'd get less of the leads that are almost computerlike: "Marvin Green, an unemployed handyman and civic leader, died Friday at Grace Hospital."

Another kind of obituary is a challenge to the writer in every reporter. It is the personality obit. These obits about widely known people can produce lively copy.

43

In the hands of Alden Whitman of the *New York Times*, writing obits is an art. Whitman, facetiously called "Mr. Bad News" or the "ghoul writer," writes advance obits. These biographical sketches are written before a person dies and kept in the morgue (library) so they will be ready for print instantly. Whitman often gets two stories out of one. Before writing his morgue obit, he visits elderly famous people. From that visit he writes feature stories for immediate use. When Whitman visited an eighty-three-year-old Harry S Truman in Independence, Missouri, Truman cracked, "I know why you're out here."

The device enables newspapers to make editions under deadline with a full obit. Some journalists argue that in an age of instantaneous radio and television coverage, morgue obits have a questionable value.

Still, most major newspapers find it well worth the expense and trouble to update morgue obits. If obits are prepared in advance on important people, it enables newspapers to meet deadlines with stories that have been given the thought and care that writing under deadline sometimes precludes.

EUPHEMISMS

An ancient newspaper taboo still prevailing in some offices is refusal to print the cause of death in obituaries. In such offices, obit euphemisms can be gems. Some country weeklies may report hanging suicides as "death of asphyxiation under circumstances being investigated."

If readers know the code, they can at least guess at the cause of death. For instance, for long illness or lingering illness, read "cancer"; for sudden death, read "heart attack."

The argument is that newspapers do not want to upset survivors. Fine. What about the readers? Newspapers should inform readers, not mystify them. The first thing many readers will ask is, "What killed old Joe?" A woman of twenty-eight with three children dies. Readers wonder what she died of. They should not have to guess.

The American Cancer Society has long urged newspapers to publish the fact that cancer is the cause of death.

Newspapers are guilty of other nonsense with obits. Some write "passed on" or "passed away," just as some people cannot bring themselves to say "died." Write "died." Write "burials," not "interment"; "Mr. Jones," not "the deceased."

OBIT FORMULAS

Obituary styles vary from paper to paper. Basically there are two kinds: first-day obits and second-day obits. The paper that runs the story first generally uses a first-day lead. The paper that runs the obit second follows with a second-day lead.

The first-day formula is as follows:

- Name, identification, time, place, and cause of death: "Peter R. Fedor, editor of the *Boating News*, died today in Beaumont Hospital of cancer."
- Age and address: "Mr. Fedor, 58, of 33376 Woodward, had been ill for nine months." The "Mr." is used in second reference in obits. The age is sometimes given at the end of the first paragraph: "He was 58 years old." Addresses are less frequently used. Newspapers discovered that literate burglars showed up at a dead person's house when the funeral was scheduled. Now addresses are usually given simply as "of Highland Park."
- Biographical detail. The amount varies by the importance of individuals.
- Survivors. Immediate survivors only. "Surviving are his wife, Pauline; a daughter, Sarah Anne; a son, Peter; and a brother, Samuel."
- Services. "Services will be at 11 A.M. tomorrow at St. Paul's Catholic Church in Royal Oak."
- Burial. "Burial will be in White Chapel Cemetery in Troy."

On the second-day formula, the structure is the same except that you lead with the services: "Services for Benjamin M. Rose, co-chairman of Wayne State University's Board of Governors, will be at 2:30 P.M. tomorrow at the Ira Kaufman Funeral Home, 18235 West Nine Mile, Southfield."

In the second-day format, the burial should still be the last line.

One caution on second-day leads: Avoid overdoing the Churchill-is-dead approach. With Churchills, perhaps it is all right. But do not use it for obscurities like Joe Schmedlap.

ADVICE ON WORKING OBITS

The following advice can be very helpful:

- Do not be squeamish about calling families for obituary information. It is your job. Just be professional.
- Even though you get the clips, check funeral homes and families for more information, accuracy, and clarifiction. Also call former associates and friends of the dead person.
- Never tear an obit from another newspaper and rewrite it without checking it out. It is amazing how many errors one reporter will find in a rival paper's obit.
- In checking out obits, be alert for a crime story that perhaps the police reporter missed.
- Observe the canons of good taste. This lead, while sparkling, violated the rule: "Winnie Ruth Judd walked into the Arizona State Prison death house yesterday and sat down in the only unoccupied chair in the house."

FUNERAL STORIES

Newspapers run funeral stories on prominent people or events of public interest. Here is the start of a funeral story in the *Detroit Free Press*:

For at least a few hours Saturday love and grief broke through the walls of race.
    It took the life of a policeman to do it.
    Police officer Robert Moore was buried after a service in a small Methodist church in Dearborn.
    The three-year police veteran, married just one year, was shot to death Wednesday in the backyard of a Carol Street home in northwest Detroit as he pursued three fleeing men.

WILLS AND ESTATES

Newspapers report one other kind of obituary-connected story: the filing of wills and disposition of estates for wealthy or widely known people.
    Here is the "top" of a will-filing story in the *Detroit Free Press*, written by Jim Neubacher and Julie Morris:

In her will, filed Friday, the late Mrs. Edsel B. Ford instructed that her great Gaukler Point mansion in Grosse Pointe Shores be kept alive with a $15 million endowment from her estate and "used for the benefit of the public."
    It was the major bequest in Mrs. Ford's 23-page will filed in Macomb County Probate Court by a family attorney.
    The Detroit Institute of Arts, Mrs. Ford's grandchildren and her employes were the only other major beneficiaries of the estate.
    Attorney George D. Miller paid a $16 filing fee, accepted a Dec. 1 hearing date to admit the will to probate and thus began the process of disbursing an estate that family attorneys estimate to be worth $85 million to $90 million.
    About $45 million, they estimated, will be paid for state and federal taxes and the cost of administering the will.
    There was a ripple of uncomfortable consternation but no public comment Friday afternoon in the office of some charitable and cultural institutions that had expected to benefit from Mrs. Ford's estate but did not.
    Mrs. Ford had been a dedicated patron of the Detroit Institute of Arts, a major supporter of the Detroit Symphony Orchestra and a mainstay of the Merrill-Palmer Institute.
    The art institute received five paintings—roughly valued at $4 million— from Mrs. Ford's personal collection. There were no other bequests to cultural organizations.

PERSONALITY OBIT

A good personality obit brings the subject "to life" in death. Certainly you need career highlights and the summation and evaluation of a life. But every effort should be made to bring out character and personality.

Quotation and anecdote are two of the best ways for writers to show character.

In getting quotes, get not only what the person has said, but what others have said. ("He was a bastard to work for," his secretary said.)

Anecdotes support character judgments. Don't just say someone was conscientious. Back it up by describing a specific incident.

An obit in the *New York Times* about Yale swimming coach Bob Kiphuth revealed how exacting he was. One anecdote told how Kiphuth donned a diving helmet and descended to the bottom of the pool to get a better look at one of his stars he suspected of having a swimming flaw.

DE MORTUIS NIL NISI BONUM

An old Latin expression tells us to "speak no ill of the dead." It should not apply to obits, but it often does. Newspapers tend to deodorize the dead.

The mayor of your town dies and the obit will say: "The city mourned today the death of Mayor Smith." He may have been universally disliked.

Newspaper handling of obits recalls the story of a Jewish funeral. The rabbi launched into oratorical flights, extolling the dead man's greatness. As the rabbi reached a crescendo, the man's son threw himself across the coffin and cried out: "Oh, Dad! Dad! I didn't know you were so great."

Newspapers are beginning to show more candor. When actress Tallulah Bankhead died, most obits properly indicated that she was "a bitch" and "a boozer."

Famous-person obits, like a good biography, should be black and white, showing warts and halos.

Try to give an honest appraisal. For instance, after President Lyndon B. Johnson died, many obituaries suggested that his domestic record was outstanding, but that his foreign policy was a disaster because of Vietnam.

Here is the start of a personality obit in the *Los Angeles Times*, written by Dorothy Townsend:

Madame Lotte Lehmann, the grande dame of opera, died Thursday morning in her sleep at her Santa Barbara home.

She was 88 and had been in ill health for a long time.

Memorial services for the acclaimed German-born dramatic and lyric soprano will be held at 2:30 P.M. Sunday at the academy in Santa Barbara.

Mme. Lehmann has been described as one of those rare artists who generate love from the stage.

At her farewell recital at New York Town Hall in 1951 those in the audience wept openly.

Conductor Maurice Abravanel, who shared with her some memorable performances at the Metropolitan Opera in New York, said Thursday that "for half a century she has become a symbol of artistic humanism."

Abravanel said "her approach to music and the arts was a completely humane one, emphasizing the deepest impulses of both composer and performer."

Mme. Lehmann sang a broad repertory in her early years in German and Austrian opera houses, scenes of still unforgotten triumphs, but in America she was most celebrated as an interpreter of the operas of Wagner and Richard Strauss.

She was most closely identified with the complex role of the Marschallin in Strauss' "Der Rosenkavalier" in which she was said to have conveyed unique elegance without artificiality.

She made Austria her homeland shortly after Hitler came to power in Germany. Having refused Hermann Goering's offer of the position of prima donna assoluta on condition she perform only in her native land, she was consequently forbidden to sing in Germany.

MORE ADVICE

Here are other helpful hints that will help your writing:

• Try to include something in personality obits that gives them an extra dimension. The *New York Times* enhances its outstanding obit coverage by including diagrams of unusual bridge or chess games, receipes of famous chefs, and samples of a poet's work.

• Follow up the lead of a personality obit with a summation of career highlights and an evaluation. Perhaps follow with anecdotes or quotes before reaching that inevitable paragraph, "Born in Kokomo, Ind., she. . . ." Too many students insist on putting that paragraph right after the lead.

SUGGESTION FOR INSTRUCTOR

• Have students tear a routine obit from a local paper. Have them rewrite it, doing the reverse of the original. If the paper used a first-day lead, have the students write a second-day lead.

"A Minor Masterpiece"

The *Free Press's* Shine calls the following personality obit from his paper "a minor masterpiece mostly because the reporter who wrote it didn't have to work hard to get the information—it took place in front of him for years."

"A little work and there are a dozen more obits like this waiting to be reported," Shine said.

Services will be held Monday for Roy Myers, a near legendary figure around the Free Press Building for a quarter-century and one of the last of a species known as newsboys regardless of their age.

Mr. Myers, known simply as "Roy" to a generation of Free Press reporters, editors and other employes, died earlier this week at age 67 in a nursing home where he lived out his last few years.

Until a few months ago, when failing health finally stopped him, he delivered the New York Times and other out-of-town newspapers to the desks of his regular customers and hawked those papers and the Detroit News on the sidewalk outside the Free Press.

He tried retirement for a month last year but soon returned to his paper-hawking.

All but blind, he wore spectacles thick as the bottoms of shot glasses, tilting his head back in an effort to see.

A frail wisp of a man, white-haired, ailing, he struggled under the weight of a canvas bag heavy with papers, the strap cutting deeply into his bony shoulders. But the frail image belied a fierce independence. He was all business. Small talk rolled off him like rain.

"How you doin' today, Roy?" a prospective customer would greet him.

"Wanna buy a Times?" he would reply, in a rough rasping voice that sounded as if it were tumbling out over gravel.

Roy once stepped from a Free Press elevator into the middle of a news staff meeting. Either because of his bad eyesight or his dogged persistence, he made his deliveries to the assembled reporters anyway. The meeting stopped till Roy finished.

"A quarter?" a reporter once protested when Roy told him the price of a Chicago Tribune. "Hell, Roy, I can get one for 15 cents."

"Yeah, but you'd have to go to Chicago," Roy replied.

Reporters short of money on collection day were known to hide from Roy. That was easy, because Roy collected by braille. Whoever sat at a customer's desk was dunned. Roy once mistook a female reporter for the male, bearded reporter who usually sat at that desk.

Another reporter was surprised to find a New York Times at his desk each day when he first joined the Free Press, but decided it came with the job. At the end of the month, though, he found out how the system worked. "That'll be $6.25," Roy told him gruffly.

Roy is survived by a daughter, Mrs. Delores Tahlman, one sister and one grandchild. Services will be at 2 P.M. Monday at the Girrbach Funeral Home, 10783 West Jefferson, River Rouge. Burial will be in Ferndale Cemetery, Riverview.

Handling Quotations

Please observe the following in handling quotations:

- Don't fake quotes. If you do not catch a full quote, put quote marks around only the words you do catch. The *Detroit News Stylebook* ridicules improbable quotes such as these: a three-year-old quoted as saying her "mother was morose" and a man saying, " 'So I went into a drugstore at 5804 Hamilton and called my buddy, Peter J. Maginnis, 26. . . .' "
- Periods and commas always go inside quotes. When you have a quote within a quote, periods and commas go inside the single quote. Always use single quotes for a quote within a quote.
- Use subject-predicate word order with speech tags: He said. An exception. To avoid abruptness of "said" following a long identifier, you can write: "I don't care," said Sen. Russell P. Long, chairman of the Senate Finance Committee.
- Put speech tags at the end of a sentence if the speaker has already been introduced. Do not put speech tags at ridiculous places: "I have suggested before," he said, "that I welcome an investigation." Put speech tags at natural breaks.
- Introduce new speakers first. It is common courtesy. Reporters will quote someone. They give another quote, but readers do not realize it is someone else speaking until they get to the end of the paragraph. Quote the first individual. Then throw in a transition line: "Sen. Robert P. Griffin disagreed." Follow with a Griffin quote in a new paragraph with the speech tag at the end.
- With two- or three-sentence quotes, put the speech tag at the end of the first sentence. Do not make readers wade through three sentences to find out who is speaking.
- Always start a new paragraph for a direct quote.
- Avoid speech tags by implication. For example: Smith was pessimistic "We'll never survive four days." Quotes need speech tags even when it is obvious Smith is speaking.
- One speech tag is enough. "We were robbed," the coach said. "The officials ruined us with idiotic calls," he added. You don't need "he added."
- Use of a colon can be an effective device for quote variety: Some called it a poor trade, but Houk said: "We wanted experience—and we got it. We traded an untried youngster for an established pro."
- Avoid run-on quotes. Magazines use them, but most newspapers do not. This is a run-on quote: Major Beckwith called the enemy troops the finest soldiers he had seen "in 30 years of combat experience. I wish we could recruit them."

The preferred usage is:

Major Beckwith called the enemy troops the finest soldiers he had seen "in 30 years of combat experience."

"I wish we could recruit them," Beckwith said.

- Open quote. You quote a sentence and put a speech tag at the end. You quote another paragraph and go on to a third paragraph of quote. Leave off quote marks at the end of the second paragraph. For example:

"Now is the time for all men to come to the aid of their country," Smith said.

"For too many years the American public has sat idly by and let someone else do the difficult things that need to be done. [No quotation mark needed.]

"But if we would all pitch in and do the things that have to be done, this would be a far better place in which to live."

- Ellipsis. The ellipsis mark should be used when part of a full quotation has been omitted. In quoting a long passage, reporters often select only the key parts. Any omission should be indicated by an ellipsis (. . .). For instance: "Fuel shortages . . . make it essential that we rely more on mass transportation," the governor said.

Chapter 9

Leads: An Invitation to Read On–Or Quit

The *lead* is the first paragraph of most hard-news (breaking or spot news) stories. It is this from the *New York Times*: "Semon E. (Bunkie) Knudsen was fired today as president of the Ford Motor Company."

But a lead can also be several paragraphs, particularly in a feature approach to a story containing description and dialogue. It is this from the *New York Times*:

LOS ANGELES—Sen. Robert F. Kennedy stood on a street corner in the heart of Watts today and looked out at a sea of black faces.

"How many of you want the kind of leadership you have had for the last two years?" he asked.

A chorus of boos arose from the crowd.

"How many of you would like to have Richard Nixon as President?" he asked.

A louder chorus of boos arose.

"How many of you will help me get elected President?" Kennedy asked.

A roar went up from the crowd.

The story went on like that for three more paragraphs until it got to the news peg: a Kennedy campaign rally in Watts.

Sometimes reporters write leads that combine elements of a hard-news and a feature lead. Here is one from the Los Angeles Times-Washington Post News Service:

SAIGON—Daniel J. Monaco has come to Vietnam to solve a most pressing personal problem—Shirley Temple.

Monaco, a 45-year-old attorney, is a Democratic candidate in the Dec. 14 special election in San Mateo County, California, for a vacant seat in Congress.

The former child movie star, now Mrs. Charles Black, also has announced her candidacy for the seat on the Republican ticket.

Although Monaco, graying, bespectacled and baldish, cannot match Shirley Temple in glamor, he hopes to make up for what he lacks in chic by an informed view of Vietnam.

The reporter might have written that one straight, saying that Shirley Temple's opponent will make Vietnam a major issue. But that would have been much duller than the approach the writer took.

No flat rule can be given as to what approach to take on a story. It depends on the kind of story. It is a judgment that reporters sharpen through experience.

THE INVERTED PYRAMID: "FORM FOLLOWS FUNCTION"

The *inverted pyramid* is the newspaper technique of writing hard news "upside down." You start stories with the most significant things and end with the least significant. It has these virtues:

- Fast writing—It permits reporters to write under deadline, moving a take at a time.
- Fast editing and cutting—While the reporter is still writing a story, editors can handle the lead and write headlines. The story can also be cut from the bottom up in the composing room without losing anything vital.
- Fast reading—Readers can quit the story any time they want. They do not have to read it all to get the point.
- Fast telling of news—Although the inverted pyramid is not literary, it is a natural way for people to pass on news: "The Red Sox won"; "Nixon has resigned"; "It's a girl."

The inverted pyramid perfectly fits the dictum of architect Louis B. Sullivan: "Form follows function."

Critics of the inverted pyramid have complained that it is a bad way to write. They say it is archaic, breathless, nonliterary, and anticlimactic, ending in a whimper instead of a bang.

Others argue that with television and radio, everyone knows the news by the time it is read in the paper. That is not true. About three-fourths of the stories in daily newspapers are unreported by radio and TV.

Because of criticisms of the inverted pyramid, some papers tried to develop the news-magazine feature approach to hard-news stories—stories opening with wheeling hawks, steaming jungles, or limousines arriving at an embassy.

One paper tried a narrative approach to police stories. A lead would start with two gunmen entering a bank. In the fifth paragraph readers learned that $175,000 had been taken. Then, perhaps in the ninth paragraph, readers discovered that two tellers were slain.

The problem with this approach is reader exasperation. Who wants to read ten paragraphs of a routine news story to find out that two tellers were killed? The reader would rightly complain of having wasted his or her time.

In short, the inverted pyramid is not dead nor is it ever likely to die. The inverted pyramid is a must for most hard-news stories. However, the inverted pyramid is dead—if it ever was alive—for feature stories, background, analytical, and interpretive stories.

THE FIVE Ws

The five Ws—who, what, why, when, and where—and the H—how—should be answered in a news story if possible. But the five W's and H should not be answered in the lead. Trying to do that, you wind up with sixty-three-word jaw-breaking leads that occasionally turn up in the *New York Times*.

Write your lead crisply, in broad outline. Then fill in the five-W and H details later.

IMPORTANCE OF LEADS

A lead demands your best effort. It is a lure to the rest of your story. If the lead is dull and uninviting, the reader may quit.

The lead should seize the reader's interest. If it has punch, good. Some stories do not have impact, but they must be reported. In such stories, your lead should inform readers pointedly and quickly.

Leads must be honest. They must be supported by the story. You cannot throw razzle-dazzle at the reader in the lead if the story does not support it.

A *Detroit News* story had this lead: "Indonesia's playboy President Sukarno is remembered in Detroit chiefly because he spoke of brotherhood but seemed more interested in sisterhood."

That lead was supported by quotes from talks he gave about brotherhood and details of his request that police provide him with a harem.

Do not overreach for a dramatic lead that tortures logic as this one does: "A black cloud of Aberdeen Angus steers hovered over Chicago during the 81st annual International Livestock Exposition Saturday night."

Marching Leads

The best start for most hard-news stories is a straightforward lead that capsulizes the whole story. Here is one from the *Los Angeles Times*:

BEIRUT—The Lebanese government began distributing 10 tons of free food in a Beirut slum Friday in an appraent effort to obtain freedom for a kidnaped U.S. Army colonel.

One newspaper had a twenty-word limit on leads. The principle is sound. Leads should be kept tight. But never lock yourself in with silly rules that inhibit good writing.

Good leads can come in thirty-nine words, or twenty-one words as in this lead: "NEW YORK—A New Jersey Garden of Eden turned out to be just another weedpatch of discrimination, a black woman nudist complained today."

Kinds of Leads

Do not memorize textbook names of leads. Never ask, "What kind of lead did I write last time?" Always write a lead that best fits the story at hand. Here are some dos and don'ts about leads and some lead varieties you might use:

• Summary lead. A sum-up of what happened. Sometimes there are several factors, each of which standing alone would be worth a lead: "NEW YORK—An explosion designed to 'kill and maim' blasted a baggage area at La-Guardia Airport into a mass of rubble last night, killing at least 11 people and injuring about 75 others."
Here is a summary lead from the *Philadelphia Inquirer*: "Heavy thunderstorms swept across the eastern half of Pennsylvania Thursday night and yesterday morning, causing one death, knocking down trees and causing some minor flooding."
• Participial swing. All from the *New York Times*: "MOSCOW—The Soviet Union has again turned to Canada for wheat and flour, purchasing 336 million bushels at a cost of $800 million"; and, "Reeling like a dazed boxer, the stock market stumbled through periods of price drops and advances yesterday before closing in a thoroughly confused state."
• Apposition lead. "ALGIERS—(UPI)—Algeria and Morocco, embroiled in a dispute over Spanish Sahara, have massed troops at the frontier and brought home their ambassadors, diplomatic sources said Tuesday."
• Quote leads. Okay if they have impact. But too often they are a lazy way for a reporter to start a story, just digging into notes for a quote. Here is a good quote lead from the *Detroit Free Press*: "WASHINGTON—'I will not work for Henry Kissinger. He is a liar and a cheat.'"
• Question leads. They carry the same danger as quote leads. If they lack impact, if they do not raise another question forget them. Here is a good one

from the *Detroit News*: "How do you thank someone for the gift of life?" Here is one from AP: "Does an ambassador's dog have diplomatic immunity?"

- Direct versus broadside. This story is from the *New York Times*:

WASHINGTON—Ralph Nader, the crusading auto safety expert, turned his guns on the luxurious Rolls-Royce today.

"The overrated and overpriced Rolls-Royce has poor door latches," he told the House Interstate and Foreign Commerce Committee.

A pinpoint approach would have been Nader's attack on Rolls-Royce door latches. But the reporter took the sweeping approach and had a better lead.

- Freak leads. Usually in the form of a classified ad: "WANTED: Six-foot-two, 195 pounder, excellent forward passer; leadership qualities; salary in five figures. Apply to the Detroit Lions, Pontiac Stadium."
- Spoke leads. "Governor Milliken spoke today to the Economic Club." Bad. What did he say?
- Topic leads. "President Carter discussed the economy today." Same problem.

Many other lead possibilities exist, including analogy and literary allusion. Read the newspapers, paying special attention to leads. Good leads can be found in newspapers every day.

BLEEDING AND SWEATING

"Every journalist who has ever struggled with one knows why it takes so much effort," British writer Henry Fairlie has written about leads. "It is as important to him as to the reader. Writing it concentrates the mind wonderfully, forcing him to decide what in the story is important."

Many journalists have angrily yanked five, six, and more abortive leads from the typewriter, cursing because none was said just right. They can appreciate the stage business in the musical *1776* when Thomas Jefferson is struggling to express a thought while writing the Declaration of Independence. The stage Jefferson makes a few scratches with a quill pen and throws away his parchment. He makes a few more false starts and finally is crumbling his parchment without having laid a pen on it.

Deak Lyman of the *New York Times* wrote thirteen versions before settling on a lead on the story of Lindbergh's decision to live in England in 1935.

Feature leads in particular provoke much bleeding and sweating. Most hard-news leads, particularly those written under deadline, are rapped out straight.

Still, even with hard-news stories, be alert for good leads such as this from the *New York Times*: "Massachusetts, which has seen almost all manner of hats tossed into its political ring, saw for the first time today the biretta of a Roman Catholic priest added to the lot."

STORY DEVELOPMENT

Having started with a good lead, a reporter cannot let the story die. A story should flow easily. The connecting links must be smooth. Development must be logical. The story should "sing."

Transitions should be skillful, the story gliding easily from one paragraph to another.

Stories need background. But background should be brought in unobtrusively so the flow of the story is not interrrupted.

Note the following story that appeared in the *Detroit Free Press*. The second two paragraphs, while necessary background, bog down the story before it is barely under way:

Law professor John Mogk announced his candidacy for mayor of Detroit yesterday by making a slashing attack on the policies, performance and life-style of Mayor Young.

This will be Mogk's second race for mayor. In the 1973 primary he finished fourth.

Mayor Young is seeking re-election to a four-year term.

The story would have been much better written this way:

Law professor John Mogk announced his candidacy for mayor of Detroit yesterday by making a slashing attack on the policies, performance and life-style of Mayor Young.

"Virtually nothing has been done to stop deterioration since 1973," Mogk said.

"The mayor touts the Renaissance Center, designed, financed, built and rented by Henry Ford. The rest of downtown is being drained dry."

Mogk said the restoration of the city's neighborhoods will be his central campaign theme as it was in 1973.

"How can the city talk seriously about spending $32 million for a downtown arena when for the same price it could buy all the HUD houses and rehabilitate them?" Mogk asked.

The arena has been a pet project of Mayor Young.

This will be Mogk's second race for mayor. In the 1973 primary he finished fourth. Young is seeking re-election to a four-year term.

Here is a hard-news story from the *Chicago Tribune*. Notice how the reporter, John O'Brien, has woven the key elements of the story in descending order of importance:

Two former employes of a Chicago burglar-alarm service were among three persons arrested over the weekend as police knocked out a ring of thieves believed to have stolen $150,000 worth of goods in a series of suburban burglaries.

A police spokesman said 115 pounds of dynamite, plastic military explosives and seven guns were confiscated from one suspect, reputedly a minor figure in the Chicago crime syndicate.

More arrests were expected, according to the spokesman, who said police worked on the case with the Federal Bureau of Investigation and sheriff's police.

Sgt. William Maloney of the Chicago police Central Intelligence Unit said police, acting on a tip, had infiltrated the gang, which allegedly included the two burglar-alarm experts.

The pair, both arrested Saturday night, were identified as John Johansen, 30, and his girlfriend, Linda Klod, 31, both of 268 Lippincott Dr. in northwest suburban Fox Lake.

Both had quit their jobs at the alarm service in December after working there four years, Maloney said.

But before they left, he said, Johansen became adept at disarming burglar alarms and Klod took more than a score of keys kept by the service for emergency checks on offices of their clients.

Police said two CIU undercover agents, who had infiltrated the gang, arrested Johansen in a Franklin Park jewelry store after he used a key to let himself into the building and then set about disarming the store's burglar alarm.

Instead of cracking the safe, Johansen's "partners" took him into custody. Klod was picked up about a mile away. Police said she had been standing guard outside the store.

Maloney said officers later arrested Leonard Valente, 46, of 510 Mackinaw Av., Calmuet City, owner of a television sales and repair shop at 1507 E. 142nd St., Dolton.

At Valente's shop, police confiscated the dynamite, plastic explosives, guns and other burglar tools and about $100,000 worth of stolen television components, Maloney said.

Johansen and Klod were charged with burglary. Valente was charged with theft, possession of explosives and possession of a silencer adaptable to a revolver.

Before dawn Sunday, police bomb experts detonated explosives in a rock quarry in south suburban Bloom Township because investigators were jittery about storing the evidence in the station house.

All the explosives were photographed before they were ignited.

Maloney said the trio was suspected of being involved in at least eight suburban burglaries in the last year.

The crimes included thefts at a lumber company, a television warehouse, an auto-parts business and a department store. They took place in the suburbs of Elk Grove Village, Franklin Park, Melrose Park and Westmont.

Valente is under investigation as a possible receiver of stolen goods, Maloney said.

Police speculated that the explosives had been intended for safecracking or for possible intimidation of store owners or other local businessmen.

According to Maloney, police and the FBI were seeking three other possible members of the ring, including another woman.

SUGGESTION FOR INSTRUCTOR

- Have students clip five leads from a newspaper, asking them to label each as hard-news, feature, or combination lead. Then ask for a brief comment as to whether the lead is good or bad and why.

Matching Words with Feelings

The intolerable wrestle with words and meanings.

> —T. S. Eliot in *Four Quartets* on a writer's struggle to match words to feelings. Harcourt, Brace and Company, Inc., New York, 1943.

Chapter 10

Police Reporting

Newspaper veterans spin yarns about two police-reporting legends: the dumb cop and the dumb reporter. Today police officers and reporters are better educated and better paid.

Police are people, not pigs as it was fashionable for some people to call them a few years ago. Like reporters, police are fallible human beings. Whatever your feelings about police, as a reporter you need them.

Police are a source that must be cultivated. The better they like you, the more trust and confidence they have in you, the more helpful they will be as a source.

Sometimes you must play on their vanity, working their names into stories. Sometimes you have to use psychology such as Norman Vincent Peale once did. Peale, doing a stint as a police reporter, tells about a gruff desk sergeant who would not volunteer any information. Peale found out that the man had a granddaughter he doted on. The next time Peale saw him he said, "Say, Sarge, how's that cute little granddaughter of yours?" Peale had a good source from then on.

BASIC TRAINING

The police beat is the traditional starting point for reporters. It is a basic training in which reporters learn to get the facts.

You want to be a Washington correspondent? A critic? An editorial writer? You covet the Paris bureau assignment? Wonderful. Before you get those jobs, however, you will probably have to start with cop-shop reporting.

Police coverage varies from paper to paper. Some papers do most of it by phone, reporters seldom visiting a station house. Other papers insist that their reporters go to station houses regularly.

If you go to the station house, get reports from the desk sergeant. Check with officers who worked cases you are interested in. Check teletypes, twenty-four-hour reports of crime. Check readout files or blotters, listings of everything that happened overnight. See the commanding officer for possible follow-ups on stories you worked earlier.

If you are covering police in a big city, keep constant touch with your desk as you make your rounds. Most police reporters today have police radios and telephones in their cars. The telephone link can be useful on breaking stories, especially in remote areas, with desk people directing you to the scene of a crime.

Editor-reporter communications today are even better because of "people beepers"—electronic paging devices. Reporters sometimes hook the little gadgets to their belts. When they start beeping, reporters know they should call their office.

The car phone is valuable for calling in details from a crime scene. If you ever find yourself without a phone and without a public phone nearby, knock on the door of the nearest house. Usually people are delighted to let the press use their phone.

POLICE REPORTING TIPS

Look for angles. Perhaps the police captain's son has been caught violating a curfew the captain imposed. Look for patterns of crime: cat burglars, slayers of female students, silk-stocking stranglers. Sometimes polite gunmen or kissing bandits will give you a new angle.

A minor incident that is not worth a story could be a good one if politicians, athletes, or VIP's are involved. A drunk-and-disorderly case involving a major league baseball manager is news.

Look for off-beat, noncriminal police news: rescued animals, unusual injuries in the home, police using a breeches buoy to haul a fat person from a third-floor apartment to go to the hospital.

Not all police stories need to be serious. UPI moved a story with this lead: "Sometimes a guy just can't make a dishonest buck." The story told of a bandit who, after robbing a night club, had nothing but bad luck. First he shot himself in the leg. Later his gun jammed as he whirled to fire at pursuing police. He wound up in a hospital in police custody.

The comedy-of-errors treatment fit. However, if someone had been killed, the light approach would have been wrong.

Sometimes stories must be dug out because the police do not recognize them as news. A policeman once asked a reporter where he got so many story ideas. "There's a story there," the reporter said, pointing to the blotter. When the policeman said he saw nothing but stolen-bike cases, the reporter said that if he had time to check each one out he was sure he would find a story.

The managing editor of the *Detroit Free Press*, Neal Shine, says it is a good rule on the police beat—and courts and city hall beats—to know "just exactly what information you are entitled to by *right*, what documents you are allowed to see."

"It saves a lot of hassle when a precinct commander decides suddenly that maybe he better not let you look at the preliminary complaint report log," Shine adds.

TRIAL BY NEWSPAPER

Two amendments to the United States Constitution clash: the First and the Sixth. The First guarantees a free press. The Sixth guarantees a fair trial.

Journalists should respect the Sixth as much as the First. Do not convict suspects in the newspaper. Leave trials to the courts.

Newspapers too often have been guilty of a knee-jerk reaction, crying that the public has a right to know. The public does. But defendants have a right to a fair trial. The press must be restrained and responsible in its pretrial coverage.

Ultimately this is a matter for newspaper editors to decide. No government or judge should ever decide what a newspaper can print. That is suppression and censorship. Newspapers must constantly fight battles for freedom of the press.

Most newspapers today are more careful about suspect's rights than they used to be. Many papers have set up guidelines for what to print in pretrial stories. (These are guidelines—fortunately not laws.)

The *Toledo* (Ohio) *Blade* guidelines bar publication of the following:

1   Any previous criminal record of the accused
2   Any so-called confession the accused may have made other than the fact that he has made a statement to police
3   Any statements by officials construed as detrimental to the accused
4   Any statements by attorneys detrimental to the accused

Newspapers are free to ignore these guidelines in special cases. Most newspapers do not even use the word "confession" in police stories any more. They refer to statements as in this lead from the *Detroit Free Press*:

Two young Ann Arbor men have told police that they kidnapped 13-year-old Timothy Stempel, according to a sworn statement presented Saturday in U.S. District Court in Detroit.

ATTRIBUTION

One of the biggest failings of student copy is lack of attribution. You must attribute all charges, accusations, and viewpoints. This applies not just to police stories. In police stories, "police saids" are essential: "He ran the red light, police said"; "he fired three shots, police said."

This may not absolve you from a libel suit, but it shows that you got the information from police. Your newspaper is not making the charge, the police are.

POLICE-PRESS COOPERATION

Two major changes have occurred in police reporting. First, newspapers devote far less time, money, and space to crime reporting than they used to. The change is for the better. Newspapers are stressing social problems, providing interpretive and investigative reporting to a much greater extent.

The other major change is a greater reluctance by the press to accept the police version of every story. This has chilled that cozy relationship in which reporters were half-cop and half-journalist.

The buddy-buddy arrangement saw reporters look the other way when suspects were being clubbed and saw cops tear up reporters' traffic tickets. Although they got scoops and the inside story on certain events, they were more police officers than reporters. So this change, too, has been for the better.

However, police and press should and do cooperate on certain stories. In kidnappings, for instance, papers have often voluntarily withheld news that might endanger the life of the kidnapped.

After the *Detroit Free Press* had withheld a kidnapping story, executive editor Kurt Luedtke said, "At any point where it is a question of jeopardizing somebody's life or safety we will hold it."

SOCIOPOLITICAL STORIES

The last decade has seen the emergence of stories that are more than just crime stories in the old sense of ax murders and mayhem. They are stories of attempted assassinations of the President, the Patty Hearst case, the Charles Manson case.

These stories are as much social and political stories as they are crime stories. As such, they warrant every bit of the extensive coverage the press has given them.

Slaying Story

Here is the top of a homicide story from the *Milwaukee Journal*:

A North Side Milwaukee man was arrested as he stepped off a bus in Chicago Tuesday night on charges of slaying a 17-year-old Shorewood girl Saturday.

Chicago police said Arthur L. Botany, 26, of 3868 N. 23rd St., was arrested on a complaint of first-degree murder and armed robbery issued by Milwaukee County.

They said he offered no resistance and agreed to his extradition to Milwaukee.

Botany is charged with shooting and killing Rebecca Ann Inman, of 2501 E. Stratford Ct., in a holdup at the Great Things store, 1932 E. Capitol Dr., Shorewood.

The girl had worked as a clerk at the store since last December.

Her body was found by a younger sister and a friend. The holdup and fatal shooting occurred about a half block from the Shorewood police station.

Shorewood police refused to discuss the arrest.

At a news conference, Dist. Atty. E. Michael McCann said five rings taken from the store were recovered at a home the suspect visited after the slaying.

Several persons, some from that home, contacted police and helped authorities track Botany to Chicago.

The cash drawer at the store had been emptied of bills but change and checks totaling $465 were left, police said.

The store owner said that about $200 or $300 in cash should have been in the register.

Botany was expected to appear in court here later Wednesday.

Multiple Sources

Often as reporters you will have to work a story through multiple sources. Some stories will require five, or ten, or more phone calls. All stories cannot be wrapped up by a single call. If you still need more information as you are completing calls to sources, ask sources if they know of anyone else that they would suggest calling.

Terminology Pitfalls

Lacerations and contusions—Write "cuts and bruises."
Not expected to live—Make it "grave condition."

Completely destroyed—Redundant (one of the most frequent misusages in news-papering).

Lone bandit and lone gunman—You figure it out.

Armed gunman—Ditto.

Rushed to the hospital—How else?

Criminal assault—Write "rape," as ugly as it is, if that is what it was.

Murder—Use the terms "homicide" or "slaying" until a murder charge is filed.

Alleged crime—Usually the crime took place; it is an alleged criminal.

Arrested for burglary—Editorializing. Make it "a charge of burglary."

Chapter 11

Fires, Accidents, and Suicides

Fire and accident stories are basic in daily journalism. Most are routine, a few spectacular. They must be reported because human lives are involved.

The space devoted to fire stories varies greatly with circumstances—the personality of the newspaper, the amount of news on a certain day, and whether the fire is in a hospital or a garage.

A house fire with no injuries, no serious damage, and no human drama will not make a paragraph in your metropolitan newspaper. But the same fire might make a couple of paragraphs in a community weekly.

On slow news days—days in which little newsworthy is happening—a routine fire might rate six paragraphs in a large daily. The same fire on a day in which everything seems to be happening might get one paragraph.

The following factors will not be involved in all fire stories, but they are things to look for:

- What and where—Location, name, nature of structure; home, bank, warehouse?
- Dead—Names, ages, addresses, occupations. How they died.

- Injured—Nature, extent, condition, hospital?
- Damage—Extent, monetary value? Adjacent buildings?
- Cause—Where did it start? How? Why? Attribution essential.
- Time—When did it start? How long did firefighters combat the fire?
- Weather—Zero temperatures? Wind hampering firefighters?
- Evacuees—Number from home, school, hospital, nursing home?
- Rescues—Who? By whom? Drama? Circumstances?
- Owners—If factory, what does plant make? How many employees? How long will they be out of work?
- Arson—Attribution essential.
- Traffic—Rerouted? How long tied up?
- Insurance—Do not suggest fire was deliberate without attribution.
- Quotes—From firefighters, police, evacuees, rescuers, eyewitnesses.
- Other questions—Previous fires at site? Discoverer? Number of alarms? Number of firefighters? How many pieces of equipment?

SOURCES

On a routine fire you might get everything from one source without having seen the fire. On big fires a reporter might work from multiple sources—police, fire fighters, emergency units, hospitals, owners, eyewitnesses.

Some newspapers cover spectacular fires with several reporters, perhaps two at the scene and one covering hospitals. Such fires usually merit a main story and a feature sidebar (companion story).

This typical fire account appeared in the *Houston Post*, written by Larry Troutt:

A bolt of lightning struck a large crude oil tank at the Crown Central Petroleum Corp. Pasadena terminal Monday night, sparking a spectacular fire that injured fire fighters and threatened gasoline storage tanks near-by.

At least five Pasadena fire fighters were treated at local hospitals for smoke inhalation and heat exposure during the blaze, Pasadena Fire Chief Sam Hemby said.

The terminal at 1319 Red Bluff is adjoining State Highway 225, across from a drive-in theater.

No structures outside the terminal were endangered.

Liz Boyd, a 19-year-old fire security guard at the terminal, said she was only 150 feet from the tank as she made her rounds in a truck when the lightning struck at 6:43 P.M.

No other employes were present.

"I saw a big flash of lightning and half the tank just blew up," she said. "Flames shot more than 300 feet in the air and I ran. That's all I could do, was run and shake."

Boyd said the tank, which fire officials estimated was capable of holding about one million gallons of crude oil, had about three feet of oil in its base when the fire erupted.

Chief Hemby said fire fighters from Pasadena and Deer Park, aided by equipment and personnel from nearby refineries, had the blaze under control within two hours.

However, he said the fire was impossible to extinguish because of intense heat and an excessive amount of oil which was flowing from the melted tank in a surrounding safety reservoir.

He said fire fighters could only cool surrounding tanks, which were filled with gasoline and in danger of exploding, and continue spraying foam on the fire.

A hospital official said three fire fighters were treated at Southmore Medical Center for smoke inhalation and heat exposure.

One of the men, the official said, complained of chest pains and was under observation. All three were listed in good condition late Monday.

Two other fire fighters were treated for similar problems at Pasadena General Hospital, a hospital official said.

AUTOMOBILE ACCIDENTS

As with fire stories, circumstances can change the amount of coverage. Some accidents are handled as "shorts." Other auto accidents are handled in a roundup story in which only the barest details are given. A single fatality that gets only a couple of paragraphs in a large daily might be a big story for a local paper.

These are some of the factors that could be involved in accident stories:

- Where—Pinpoint location.
- Dead and injured—Names, ages, addresses, occupations; nature and extent of injuries; condition of injured; what hospitals; cause of death, although often that is obvious.
- Number of vehicles—Direction of each; driver of each; passengers; names, ages, addresses.
- Cause—How? Attribution a must. Police charges?
- Speed—Miles per hour if a factor.
- Time—When did it occur? Rush hour?
- Traffic—Tieups? When to when?
- Weather—Condition? Icy? Visibility?
- Seat belts—Did they save a life? Attribution needed.
- Destination and purpose—Driving to work? Starting vacation? A block from home? Returning from honeymoon?

OLD TABOO

Some newspapers refuse to print names of cars in accident stories. Their editors argue that that would be free advertising. Rather than say Volkswagen, some papers will write "a foreign, bug-shaped car." It is difficult to understand how it is free advertising if you report that a five-ton truck has demolished a Volkswagen.

But then newspaper coyness has gone to ridiculous lengths. Rather than say a Gulf station would be built along with a Holiday Inn, one paper noted plans to build "a gas station that customarily accompanies Holiday Inns."

The specific, brand name is better than the general, generic name. But your editor will have the last word about this.

Here is an automobile accident account that appeared in the *Boston Globe*:

Three young children were among six people injured last night in a three-car accident on I-93 northbound in Somerville near the Charlestown line.

Trooper Gerald F. Tully said a pickup truck "drove up and onto a small Chevrolet sedan, rolled over and hit another car about 8:20."

The driver of the truck was charged with driving under the influence of liquor and with other vehicle violations.

Tully said five members of a Wakefield family in the Chevrolet were taken to Massachusetts General Hospital for treatment of cuts and bruises.

He identified them as Martin Ammer, 32, of 8 Lakeview Ave., his wife, Marie, 30, and their children, David, 6, Tim, 5, and Laura, 3.

Hospital officials said they would not be held overnight.

Admitted in serious condition was an unidentified man riding in the pickup truck with the operator.

Arrested was Wesley E. Aben, 25, of Ashland Street, Melrose. Tully identified him as the truck driver.

Tully said no one in the third vehicle was injured.

SUICIDES

Newspapers have never given much space and attention to suicides unless they involved people newsworthy in themselves. But a few things should be said about suicide coverage.

Always let the police, coroner, or medical examiner say it is a suicide. If you have no confirmation, phrase it this way: "Jones plunged to his death from his fifth-floor apartment." Let police speculate as to whether he jumped or was pushed.

Here is an example: "NEW YORK—(UPI)—Eli M. Black, chairman and chief executive officer of United Brands Co., plunged to his death yesterday from the 44th floor of the Pan American Building in what police call an apparent suicide."

Do you print the motive of suicide? If possible, give a hint or a suggestion of why. You can quote family, friends, or authorities: "He was despondent over the death of his wife"; "he was fearful of a grand jury investigation"; "he was losing money in the stock market."

The second paragraph of the UPI suicide account read: "Associates said Black, 53, was depressed and under great strain in recent weeks because of business pressures."

Families are sensitive about suicides. Some families of suicides possibly feel guilty. Some individuals may feel that if they had done things differently, the relative might be still alive.

Still, if newspapers do not make an effort to tell why persons committed suicide, they are doing a disservice to the reader, leaving a gaping hole in the story.

This is a suicide story from the *Detroit Free Press*:

The daughter of a prominent Grosse Pointe physician was found dead in the family garage shortly after noon Monday, an apparent suicide.

Diane Goodman, 16, daughter of Dr. and Mrs. Virgil Goodman of 762 Bedford, Grosse Pointe Park, was a junior at Grosse Pointe South High School.

Dr. Goodman is an anesthesiologist at Cottage Hospital, Grosse Pointe Farms.

Miss Goodman's body was discovered by her mother in the family car, a 1974 Buick.

The car was parked in a garage attached to the house. The garage door was closed and the house permeated by carbon monoxide fumes.

Mrs. Goodman was treated for shock.

According to police, Miss Goodman left several notes addressed to her parents and to friends.

Police declined, however, to reveal the contents of the notes.

Miss Goodman, an only child, was described by friends as a quiet girl who was close to her parents.

Friends described Miss Goodman—who was small and thin, with short dark hair—as cute, popular and an average student. She had a new boyfriend, but preferred horses to people, they said.

She rode her own horse in competition at the Grosse Pointe Hunt Club last summer.

DISASTERS

Many stories essentially similar to fire and accident stories appear constantly in newspapers: plane crashes, explosions, mine disasters, terrorist bombings.

Each story is different but alike in many ways. The techniques involved in covering fire and accident stories—getting the facts—are also used in covering tragedies and disasters.

SUGGESTION FOR INSTRUCTOR

• On successive days have students write a fire, accident, suicide, and homicide story under deadline. Get these stories from a newspaper. Have the students quiz you for the facts. Then give them fifteen to twenty minutes to write each story.

Overattribution

A woman giving the name of Mrs. James Jones, who is reported to be one of the society leaders of the city, is said to have given what purported to be a party yesterday to a number of alleged ladies. The hostess claims to be the wife of a reputed attorney.

—Mark Twain

That is a jocular look at overattribution. Many news stories need attribution throughout. But everything you write does not need attribution. For example, you do not need to say, "it snowed yesterday, according to the weather bureau" (unless you have a tongue-in-cheek reason for writing it that way).

Time Element

Usually place the time element in the lead right after the verb: "Thousands of Luo tribesmen gathered today"; "President Carter announced today"; "Mayor Young said today."

But place the time element where it sounds best. Sometimes it fits best before the verb, sometimes after the verb with several words intervening. Write by ear.

For instance: "The Federal Trade Commission adopted Tuesday a rule." It sounds as if the FTC adopted Tuesday. Make it: "The FTC Tuesday adopted," or, best of all, "The FTC adopted a rule Tuesday."

Exact Time

The exact time of unscheduled events should be in news stories. The lead may say "early today," "today," "last night," or "yesterday." (Newspapers generally call 12:01 A.M. to 6 A.M. "early today," 6 A.M. to 6 P.M. "today," 6 P.M. to midnight "last night.")

If your lead tells of a fire "early today," later on specify that it broke out at 2 A.M. Exactness enhances reporting. Besides, many readers like to figure where they were and what they were doing at that time.

For scheduled events, obviously you do not have to say, "The kickoff, which took place at 2 P.M." However, if a speaker is scheduled to talk at 8 P.M. but does not arrive until a half-hour later, your story can note that.

Advance stories need the exact time of scheduled events: "The meeting begins at 8 P.M."; "The kickoff is at 1 P.M."

Exact Place

You need the exact place in news stories. Do not just say "a press conference in Washington," but specify later that it was in the White House.

Similarly, you need to tell readers the exact form, forum, or outlet for stories: a Senate speech, a TV address, a news conference, a telephone interview, a press release, a statement from a press secretary.

• Caution: Do not clutter your leads with such details as exact time, place, and form. Work them into your story later.

Abbreviations with Titles

Stylebooks on some newspapers insist that all-cap abbreviations must follow the first reference to the names of organizations and departments. That style is: "The Department of Housing and Urban Development (HUD)." Since HUD is widely known, it really is not necessary to include the initials with the first reference.

However, with less familiar groups and things it is a good idea to include all-cap initials in parenthesis. For instance: "He passed the Scholastic Aptitude Test (SAT)."

It is perfectly all right to use all-cap initials when you are making a second reference: HUD, FDA, CIA, etc.

Chapter 12

Second-Day Leads and Follow-ups

Newspapers constantly try to get the latest news to the public. That is why they seek to come up with a second-day lead or follow-up angle to an old story.

The last edition of yesterday afternoon's newspaper reported a big fire. Television news last night showed films of it. The morning newspaper tries to find a new angle or follow-up.

It works vice versa. If the morning paper had the story first, the afternoon paper comes up with a second-day angle.

Here is a first-day lead in the morning paper: "An assistant fire chief died and 13 people were injured yesterday in an explosion at a Roseville plastics plant."

The afternoon paper followed up with this lead: "Investigation opened today in the explosion and fire in a Roseville plastics plant that killed an assistant fire chief and injured 13 people."

Reporters working a second-day story look for a new angle, a new development. Perhaps it is an arrest, perhaps an investigation. They start their story with the newest information. Then they go into the earlier details, eventually recapping the whole story.

Here is a first-day story in an A.M. paper: "BEIRUT—(UPI)—Two Palestinian guerillas hijacked a Lufthansa airliner with 17 people aboard Sunday, tricked West German authorities into releasing three Arabs charged in the murders of 11 Israeli Olympic team members, then escaped to Libya."

The P.M. paper led with new information before backing into the first-day details in the third paragraph. This is a combined account from UPI, AP, and *Washington Post* dispatches:

Israeli Foreign Minister Abba Eban today summoned the West German ambassador to make clear Israel's anger at what it considers a surrender by Bonn of three Arab prisoners to Palestinian guerilla hijackers.

Ambassador Jesco von Puttkamer made the trip from Tel Aviv to Eban's office in Jerusalem as the nation's newspapers joined Israeli officials in condemning the release as a "terrible deed" that cannot be condoned and a "spectacular surrender."

The government assailed West Germany's action in surrendering three jailed Arab guerillas to hijackers who yesterday seized a Lufthansa jetliner over Turkey and threatened to blow it and its passengers up unless their comrades were freed.

In writing second-day stories, do not assume that readers have read or know the earlier details. You must tell the whole story. Actually, a second-day lead is telling an old story with a fresh angle.

Metropolitan dailies are constantly updating stories. Let's say you are working on an afternoon paper with four editions. Your first edition might have a story about a holdup. Your second edition story might lead with the fact that the suspects are trapped. Your third edition story might lead with a shootout between police and suspects. The final edition might lead with the capture of the suspects.

Reporters usually dig up some second-day approach to stories. Sometimes they have to stretch for it, however, as in the classic second-day lead on a police story with no new developments: "Police today are seeking a gunman who. . . ."

Some editors feel that having "yesterday" in the lead dates their paper. So they bar "yesterday" in leads. This sometimes results in contrived absurdities such as: "Pope Paul is on record today as having appealed for peace."

Suggestion: Say "yesterday" outright in the lead, or mask the time element by saying in the lead that "the Pope has appealed anew for peace" and put the time element into the second or third paragraph.

Sometimes reporters take a bright or feature approach to a second-day story. The morning paper might report this: "City Council killed an ordinance last night that would have limited city households to two pets."

The afternoon paper cannot write the same thing so it might take a second-day, feature approach that backs into the news peg:

"Dogs are better behaved than many children," said Harvey Carse, an owner of four dogs.

"I'll buy that," said a voice at a crowded hearing last night before city Council.

"Your real animal lovers are not going to part with their animals," an older woman said.

After many other citizens complained in the same vein, City Council killed an ordinance that would have limited city households to two pets.

Issue versus Edition

Students should distinguish between *issue* and *edition*. Each daily newspaper has one issue a day: say, the June 15 issue. But for that issue it may have three or four editions.

TIEBACK

All second-day and follow-up stories need continuity, a link with an earlier story. The reader needs a *tieback*, the aspect that connects the new story to the earlier story.

A campus newspaper once ran a second-day obituary about a student slain in his apartment. Nowhere did the story have a tieback, the link with a story that it had bannered the day before.

Newspapers reject the argument that everybody has seen yesterday's paper. Even if everybody had—and everybody never does—you still need the tieback. Readers must have that background information.

The *UPI Reporter*, the wire service's bulletin, has expressed it well: "The art of good editing (and reporting) is to blend the background or synopsis of previous chapters into the presentation of today's news without diluting the excitement of what is fresh."

Here is a second-day lead in an A.M. paper: "INDIANOLA, Miss.—Dr. Martin Luther King Jr. said today that he and other civil rights leaders will return to Philadelphia, Miss., this week with their Mississippi marching force to 'straighten the place out.' "

The story followed with some quotes from Dr. King. Then the reporter dropped in the tieback: "The march in Philadelphia led by Dr. King in honor of three slain civil rights workers erupted yesterday in a stone-throwing and fist-swinging battle."

FREQUENT FOLLOW-UP FAILURE

One of the biggest neglects of newspapers is failing to follow up on stories. For instance, papers report a shooting in which the victim is in grave condition. Does he or she live or die? The next day's paper often neglects to tell.

Perhaps the paper will carry a story about a family facing eviction for failure to pay the rent. Was the family evicted? Sometimes papers forget to tell.

The managing editor of the *Detroit Free Press*, Neal Shine, admits the problem: "Too often we forget a story the day after we write it. Good reporters file things in a tickler [future reference file] to come up in six months or a year so they can check and see how things are going."

Shine tells a story from his own reporting experience that illustrates that a follow-up story is often better than the original:

In the 1950s I covered a nice fairy tale feature about a polio-stricken couple who, despite their crippling disease, were married with the help of a community which pledged, among other things, to refurbish the home in which the couple lived, pay the mortgage and see to it that all their needs would be attended to.

A year later I checked and found out that the community had forgotten about the couple. They were living as virtual prisoners in a house without furniture and barely able to keep up the mortgage payments. The second story was much better than the first.

EXPLANATORY DETAIL

Reporters never assume that readers know as much as reporters know. They know their job is to inform readers, not puzzle them. They know the importance of explanatory detail. They define technical and unfamiliar terms. They anticipate questions readers might raise.

If reporters refer to the second black elected mayor of a city, they tell who the first was. If they mention the second Jew elected governor of a state, they tell who was the first.

If reporters refer to the Eighth Amendment, they tell what it covers. If they refer to Mark Hanna, they tell who he was. Until an organization such as NOW becomes well known, they say that the National Organization for Women is a women's liberation group.

Explain, explain, explain. Don't make readers guess. The AP once quoted President Lyndon Johnson as saying he knew what it was like to be a school teacher. It then gave a one-sentence reminder of when and where Johnson used to teach in Texas.

The *New York Times* does a good job of backgrounding unfamiliar detail. But occasionally it goes too far as when it quoted someone as saying that "man doesn't live by bread alone" and then followed with the exact quotation and citation from the Bible. Another time it wrote: "You'd have to look it up in Webster (dictionary)."

The principle is sound, however. If you report that the GOP captured 187 seats in Congress yesterday, you must tell the reader how many seats it had before the election. You cannot do as a campus newspaper once did. It reported that "Wayne is now the second lowest-paying institution of higher education in Michigan," but never told what college was lowest.

HOLES IN COPY

Reporters should leave no unanswered questions. In a story about striking service workers at a university, the *Detroit News* gave this information: "The local has asked for a 32-cent-an-hour increase while the university has offered 25 cents." Fine. But nowhere in the story was the important information: What are the workers making an hour? What is their weekly pay?

The same newspaper's TV critic once wrote a page-one article accusing Johnny Carson of using bad taste in a show in which he joked about an earthquake in California. The critic never cited a single example of alleged bad taste. Without some examples, the reader who had not seen the show could not form an opinion about whether Carson showed bad taste.

ADVANCE STORIES

Newspapers often write about upcoming or expected events. They certainly cannot be cautious in every routine story. For example, they do not write: "The Garden Club of Highland Park is expected to meet tomorrow in Barber School at Woodward and Buena Vista." Papers simply say the club will meet even though a snowstorm or some other unforeseen circumstance may prevent the group from meeting.

However, on bigger and more important stories, newspapers protect themselves with cautionary words. They write that "railroad workers are expected to walk off their jobs tomorrow," or that "phone workers were set to strike at 12:01 A.M. tomorrow." (The conditional past is used in cases where the paper must go to press, but an action could be taken by the time the reader sees the story.)

Professionals do not need to be told perhaps, but students should be wary of predicting the outcome in advance stories. A UPI Washington reporter once wrote confidently that Sen. Edward M. Kennedy was a cinch for election as Senate whip. Kennedy lost, leaving the reporter highly embarrassed.

If your interpretation leads to the conclusion that something is a cinch, you still should leave yourself an out: "Kennedy is expected to win," or "is heavily favored," or some other phrasing that will not leave you out on a limb if the unexpected happens.

Perhaps the most painful incident in this regard was the *Chicago Tribune* streamer in 1948 proclaiming "DEWEY DEFEATS TRUMAN." Truman gleefully held aloft a copy of the paper. Students should remember the lesson.

SUGGESTION TO INSTRUCTOR

- Have students do a second-day or follow-up story that backs into and includes the pertinent details of the first-day story.

Odds and Ends

- If you write that a town is 40 kilometers east of Paris, provide the equivalent—25 miles. If you refer to a kilogram, make it "kilogram (2.2 pounds)."
- Differentiate between a hyphen and a dash on the typewriter. A hyphen is: -. A dash is --. Does it matter? Yes. If you use a hyphen where a dash is intended, or vice versa, the sentence doesn't read right. For instance: "The injury—plagued Minnesota Vikings defeated the Los Angeles Rams." Clearly a hyphen was intended.
- Most newspapers avoid italics. So while you would write *The Sun Also Rises* for books or magazines, you would use quote marks in a newspaper: "The Sun Also Rises."
- The *New York Times* is probably the only English language newspaper in the country that still uses accent marks. (It still writes communiqué.) Accent marks are not needed.
- Be wary of calling anyone elderly in your stories. Editors will get objections even if you call people in their sixties elderly.

Definitions

Developing story—One in which new angles or leads are constantly turning up throughout the edition cycle.

Continuous or running story—A major story that runs day after day in newspapers: Watergate, the Patty Hearst story, celebrated trials such as that of Angela Davis. (Don't forget to throw in a paragraph or two of background from yesterday's stories.)

Chapter 13

Leg Person-Rewrite

The rewrite person is one of the most revered figures in the newspaper business. But he or she seems to be a member of a dying craft, the victim of changing newspaper practice and technology.

The reasons vary. Most newspapers are publishing fewer editions today. They have fewer "makeovers," or changes, between editions. Most papers will make over only for major stories.

With less concern for frantic deadline-racing, newspapers have much less need for city desk rewrite batteries.

Papers simply are not following news stories so closely for edition time as they once used to. Instead, reporters are writing their stories as overnighters—aiming for the next day's paper.

A major reason for the change is radio and television. No matter how much a newspaper is on top of the news, it simply cannot compete with the electronic media in reporting most stories first. Listeners can hear a story on the radio two hours before any newspaper carrying an account of the story is in their hands.

Newspapers are also placing more emphasis on analytical reporting, much less on that old newspaper staple—the crime story. More stories are coming into newspaper offices via teletype and telecopier. Indeed, some papers no longer use rewrite people.

For newspapers that still use them, rewrite people are invaluable. The best of them are cool, swift, efficient, and talented. Hugh Hough of the *Chicago Sun-Times*, who won a coveted Pulitzer Prize for local reporting in 1974, is one of the best rewrite people in the country. He has described a good rewrite person as one who can write about a jazz concert, a symphony, and a triple murder— and do all three in fifteen minutes.

That is an exaggeration, but it gives you an idea of the value of good rewrite people to newspapers. The leg person-rewrite setup works this way: The leg person gathers information from the scene of the story and phones the facts to the rewrite person in the newspaper office.

The leg person does not come in to the office to write the story because that would take too much time. For another reason, the leg person must stay at the scene and work the story until it is buttoned up.

Why doesn't the leg person dictate the story? That is, why doesn't he or she telephone the story in news form as the beat person does? Because the leg person often has only part of the story. Sometimes two or more reporters are at the scene. Sometimes a reporter is covering hospitals. The rewrite person takes information from all of them.

Other reporters in the office may work a story by phone and give their notes to the rewrite person. The rewrite person often works the story by phone.

Even if the leg person has the whole story, he or she seldom dictates. One reason is that the rewrite person may be doing a roundup story, combining several burglaries or holdups into one story.

Rewrite people are workhorses of the city desk. They are busy, busy, busy. Some days they do more than thirty stories, working under deadline pressure for multiple-edition newspapers.

SPEED ESSENTIAL

Speed is one skill all rewrite people must have. They must produce copy swiftly. Rewrite people also must recognize holes in a leg person's notes, asking and obtaining answers to key questions.

Most rewrite people write a crackling story out of drab detail. To be sure, some have strayed from nonfiction writing, but that is neither condoned nor recommended.

Robert B. Peck, rewriteman for the old New York *Herald Tribune*, once put it this way: "The rewriteman doesn't even have to get the facts. Somebody else digs them up and sends them in. All the rewriteman has to do is to marshal them, dress them up and let them march."

Peck made it sound easier than it is. Between editions, rewrite people are busy but under less pressure. They may rewrite a story from another paper, seeking a possible second-day angle, checking it out for errors.

Sometimes they take dictation from beat reporters. Sometimes they rewrite handouts, doing overnighters for inside fill copy. All the time they are getting notes from leg people and working stories by phone. On rare occasions they rewrite stories written badly by staffers.

LEG PEOPLE

Basically the role of leg people is that of police reporters. After they wrap up a story, they call the city desk. They tell either the city editor or an assistant the story in a nutshell: "I've got that East Side holdup. The gunmen got $15,000." Then the leg person is switched to the rewrite person who takes the details of the story.

Most rewrite people work with headphones while taking notes from leg people. Headphones make it easier to type without awkwardly cradling a phone between ear and mouth.

Leg people use their own phone code to spell unfamiliar names: "s as in Sam," "f as in Fred," "b as in boy." S's and f's are easily confused over the phone.

Figures, too, are given in two ways by leg people: "two million dollars" and "dollar mark 2,000,000."

LOCALIZING

Newspapers localize stories if they can. Generally, readers have more interest in local matters than news across the county line. The scale runs in decreasing order of interest: local, state, regional, national, and world news. Naturally, wars and disasters are exceptions to the rule.

But even with exceptions, the principle is at work. A story about twenty-seven people being trapped in a West Virginia mine might make page one in Chicago. But no matter how a Chicago paper handles it, it is an even bigger story in West Virginia. The auto industry is big news nationally. But in Detroit, the motor capital, it is even bigger news.

As a rule, the further you get from an event, the less play newspapers give it. A shooting took place at a Socialist meeting hall in Detroit. A gunman went berserk, killing one person and wounding three others. The story made page one in Detroit. The Lansing, Michigan, paper, about ninety-five miles away, carried the story on page two. Still further away in Michigan, Bay City, the story was worth page five. A Cleveland, Ohio, newspaper put it on page thirteen. The *New York Times* carried it on page forty-four. Yet, if one of the victims had been from Bay City, the paper there might have put it on page one.

If a press release comes in announcing a new dean at the nearby law school, the newspaper in the town where the person lives usually gives it a local angle. If a wire service story tells of someone's appointment to the governor's staff, the individual's hometown paper will write the story from its perspective.

If the local paper gets a wire service dispatch from Washington saying that 300 hospitals are in noncompliance with federal antibias regulations, the local paper checks out the situation at area hospitals.

Sometimes editors might run the national story as a sidebar to the local story. Or a local story might be used as a sidebar to the Washington story.

For instance, the *New York Times* Washington bureau moved this story: "WASHINGTON—Governor Rockefeller of New York proposed today the outlay of at least $150 billion in public and private investment over the next decade 'to save and rebuild the cities of our nation.' "

It then ran a local sidebar with this lead: "Mayor Lindsay said yesterday that the kind of massive urban construction programs proposed by Governor Rockefeller would not solve the problems of American cities."

Editors scan casualty lists in disasters for a possible hometown angle. If there is a naval disaster off California, an Ohio editor looks for names of Ohio sailors. If he or she finds any, the editor assigns reporters to do the clips and call families, friends, and acquaintances for background interviews and quotes.

Leg Person-Rewrite Collaboration

Here is a product of the collaboration between a leg person and a rewrite person. This holdup story appeared in the *Phoenix Republic*:

A gunman took about $1,800 Friday afternoon from the motor bank office of the Arizona Bank, 390 N. First Ave.

Detective Sgt. William Fleming said the robber entered the bank, approached one of the tellers and produced a derringer-shaped handgun.

He then handed her a note demanding money and claiming to have killed three people.

The robber, described as a Mexican or Indian about 35 years old, 5-feet-5, 130 pounds, took the money in a bank bag and walked out the front door.

A witness told officers that the robber apparently circled a few buildings, then ran north along the alley behind the bank and dashed into the back door of an apartment house.

Police and Federal Bureau of Investigation agents surrounded two apartment buildings on Second Avenue but a room-to-room search failed to locate the gunman.

Breaking News Reporting Tip

If you are covering a fire, holdup, accident, slayihg, or other breaking news, make sure you have wrapped up the whole story before you leave the scene or hang up the phone.

It helps to recap an event mentally from beginning to end to make sure you have covered all the angles, asked all the questions.

Definitions and Recommendations

News peg—What the story is hung on. You cannot write a story in a vacuum. Here is a lead: "C. Northcote Parkinson, the British lawgiver ('Work expands so as to fill the time available for its completion') came to town yesterday for the debut of his latest book, 'Mrs. Parkinson's Law.'" The fact that he came to town for the debut of his book is the news peg, the reason for writing a story about him.

Rambling titles—Avoid long titles before names. "Playwright Tennessee Williams" is okay. But do not write "Secretary of Housing and Urban Development Patricia Harris." It is much better to put the title in apposition: "Patricia Harris, Secretary of Housing and Urban Development." The Soviet news agency Tass once vied for a spot in the *Guinness Book of World Records* with this title: "First Vice Chairman of the Council of Ministers of the Peoples Republic of Bulgaria Zhivko Zhivkov."

Delayed identification—Often it is better to identify a speaker by title in the first reference. Then bring in the name in the second paragraph. In the lead you could write: "The president of the National Bank of Detroit denounced today a proposal to raise interest rates." The second paragraph might begin: "Jerome W. Franks, NBD president. . . ." You could start with Franks and his title in the lead, but it would be cumbersome.

Similarly, with widely known people you can start with their names and delay identification until the second paragraph. Thus: Benjamin L. Hooks accused the building trades today of blatant discrimination." Start the second paragraph: Hooks, executive secretary of the National Association for the Advancement of Colored People, ..." To write the title out in full would make an awkward lead. The problem is worse on papers that do not abbreviate NAACP on first reference.

SUGGESTIONS FOR INSTRUCTORS

- Give the students a real press release and have them localize it for a community newspaper.
- Clip news stories that are badly written from area papers. The stories may be wordy or written with lead angles buried in the third or fourth paragraph. Look out, too, for examples of editorializing—opinion in a news story without attribution. Have students rewrite just the tops of the stories, sharpening the focus and tightening the story by boiling it and going to the heart of the matter.
- Divide class into leg-rewrite teams. Send rewrite people out into the hall while leg people pull information from you for a story. Then call the rewrite people back in to take notes from leg people. Reverse the roles next class period.

Chapter 14

Feature Stories

Some journalists insist that there is no such thing as a feature story. They will say that there are only news stories. Perhaps. But the term "feature story" is useful to differentiate a hard-news story from a nonhard news (feature) story.

If a Kansas teenager scoops the Weather Bureau on a tornado warning, it is a feature story. It is not hard news. It is not a "must" story. Papers could go to press without it. Yet that kind of story contains human interest.

The hard-news story is essential. It deals with fires, speeches, elections, and jury verdicts. The feature story is nonessential. It deals with the little old lady in Dubuque who has collected so much string she has a three-ton ball.

A feature can have pathos, humor, the unusual, the oddity. A feature can inform. It can entertain. A feature can be a color story from a political convention with sights, sounds, and vignettes. A feature story can be a sidebar to the main story. If fire destroys the city marketplace, a reporter may write a feature about merchants whose businesses have been wiped out.

Usually feature stories are written in the third person. An exception is the first-person eyewitness account that lends a see-it-now feeling to events of high drama in which a reporter had personal involvement. Another exception is the dear-boss letter that reporters sometimes use to write a humorous feature. Here is one from the *Detroit News*:

Dear Boss:

I can explain everything.

I can explain why I was missing from the office for several hours and why, when I did return, my eyes were slightly bloodshot and I tripped over the cigaret butt.

I was drinking. But it wasn't because I wanted to drink.

It was strictly scientific—solely for research purposes.

As you know, boss, Michigan's new implied consent law goes into effect exactly one minute after midnight tonight.

Newspapers run features on religious and secular holidays; about the weather, from Groundhog Day to forecasts in the *Farmer's Almanac*; about parades; and about disappearing landmarks such as the old Met, Madison Square Garden, and Penn Station in New York.

Many city editors are suckers for animal stories—stories about dogs, cats, zoos, birds. A *New York Times* reporter once wrote a clever feature in the form of an obituary about the death of a zoo giraffe.

Reporters work features by "doing the clips," researching library references, and interviewing.

WRITING FEATURES

Some reporters prefer to write features rather than hard-news stories. Features can be more fun to write. They have fewer restraints. They are more literary. They require more imagination.

Features allow reporters to break away from the inverted pyramid formula. In features, more of you as an individual stylist and writer comes through. Features can be impressionistic, presenting facts filtered through the prism of an individual's personality. Feature writers can have a point of view, but one that always stops short of editorializing.

Unlike a hard-news story which trails off into nothingness, a feature needs a good ending as well as a good beginning. Features need a good opening, a good body, and a good close. Most features are written this way. Some are pure narratives in which a reporter unfolds a tale like a short story writer.

Indeed, feature writers can use all the techniques of the fiction writer. The only difference is that journalists deal with facts. Feature writers use narrative, description, dialogue, and flashback.

Sometimes a story is not important enough for a bang-bang hard-news treatment so reporters give it a combination hard-news-feature approach. Here is a tongue-in-cheek approach to such a story taken by a *New York Times* reporter:

The United Nations asked the city for a cease-fire yesterday to stop a police action too close to home—the towing away of illegally parked diplomatic vehicles.

The midtown towaway program was extended for the first time yesterday to the diplomatic corps.

By early evening the Police Department had established relations of a sort with six foreign countries.

It was then that a special committee of the United Nations on host-country relations met hurriedly and formally petitioned Mayor Lindsay for a moratorium.

WRITING THE FEATURE STORY

Feature writers have two major problems: getting into a story and getting out. They must get into a story in a way that arouses interest. They must get out skillfully, leaving the reader with an end-of-journey feeling.

Feature writing comes down to a formula, too, although it is not so rigid as the inverted-pyramid formula. The formula is this: opening, transition to body, body, and close.

Openings—or leads—should seize the reader's interest. Here are some kinds of openings:

Striking statement—A *New York Times* lead on a story about old people waiting in a bus terminal: "Two kinds of people wait in the Port Authority Bus Terminal near Times Square. Some are waiting for buses. Others are waiting for death."

Quote—Here is a lead from *Newsweek* about an archeological dig: "I knew something was there. I started to dig with my hands. I always dig with my hands to avoid maiming the marble. I feverishly pulled away the soil and there it was—a beautiful head of Apollo."

Anecdote—An almost sure-fire way to start a feature. Here is one by a *Toronto Star* reporter:

OTTAWA—The comely young Ottawa housewife was atwitter with anticipation. She was about to meet Pierre Elliott Trudeau, Canada's swinging Prime Minister, a man whose picture, she blushed to admit, was pasted to her refrigerator door for inspiration.

At a political garden party, she would shake the Prime Ministerial hand, receive the Prime Ministerial voice in her own shell-like ear, gaze into the Prime Ministerial gray-blue eyes. The moment arrived, the presentation was made, the housewife gasped.

"Oh my God," she told the startled leader, "you're an old man!"

Description—Use description sparingly. It can be static. Here is a UPI lead:

JOHANNESBURG—A crudely-lettered sign tacked to the gate of a drought-ravaged Transvaal cattle ranch is scribbled with a harsh and bitter blasphemy: "No Rain, No Grass, No God."

Nearby, a battered milk pail hangs from another gate. A sign above it says: "Throw your pennies in the bucket so we can buy a pair of spectacles for God, that he may see the sufferings of man and beast."

Question—From *Newsweek*: "What do Nahum Tate, Colly Cibber and Henry J. Pye have in common? They were all poets laureate of England."

Joke—A joke may illuminate a situation so it can be an effective opener. Here is one from the *New York Times*:

ALLENWOOD, Pa.—A visitor at the federal prison here walked into its little library the other day and began to inquire about its books.

"And do you have 'All the President's Men'?" he asked.

"No," said the inmate-librarian, looking up slyly from his desk, "not all of them."

Narrative—Another feature start that is guaranteed to hook the reader if it is gripping. Here is one from the *Lincoln Parker* in suburban Detroit:

Hunched over his transceiver, a citizens' band radio operator heard only the sound of subdued static.

Then suddenly, a voice broke through: "KEN 8383 to any base station— stand by for a 10-33 on 11."

The listener flipped a dial to "11" and in a moment made contact with the "voice."

"There's a bad accident on the westbound I-94 near the Southfield exit in Allen Park," the voice said. "I'm pulling over. Looks like you'd better send the rescue squad, too."

Epigraph—A quote preceding a feature that sets the mood and tone of the piece. The UPI's Doc Quigg wrote a story about a University of Texas tower slaying. He began with a quote from Thornton Wilder's *The Bridge of San Luis Rey*: "It was a very hot noon, that fatal noon."

Literary allusion—Here is a lead from the *New York Times* that paraphrases a Mark Twain quip: "PARIS—The reports of the death of Marcel Cerdan Jr.'s boxing career have been greatly exaggerated."

TRANSITIONS

Now you have baited the reader. The next trick is to make a smooth transition or glide into the *news peg*, the point or reason for the story.

After a description-narrative opening of a priest saying mass, a *New York Times* writer used this transition paragraph: "The scene was the dining room of a private home in northern New Jersey on a recent Saturday evening. The occasion was one of the rapidly increasing number of home masses being conducted by Roman Catholic laymen and priests."

THE BODY

The bulk of a feature is development and support for the story. You can use incident, quote, anecdote, vignette, exposition, narrative, and description.

Whatever you do in the body of a feature, show—don't tell exclusively. Illustrate your points by showing examples rather than just telling about them.

Keep to the theme. Do not let the story wander, even if this means ignoring two-thirds of your notes. Good writing requires picking the relevant from the irrelevant in your notes.

The piece should keep moving. One of the best ways to assure this is to use quote and anecdote.

Daniel Gilmore, reporting from London for UPI, kept the body of a feature story moving with anecdotes. Here is a "mid-section":

British driving examiners are tough.

Take the case of Mrs. Margaret Hunter, probably the world's most famous learner-driver.

This 67-year-old retired schoolteacher had her first driving lesson 27 years ago and is still trying to pass the test.

You probably first heard about her in 1962 when one of her instructors abandoned her in the car in the street with the cry: "This is suicide!"

Miss Hunter's last try at driving in England was a secret side trip to the Republic of Ireland where she wangled a license.

She returned proudly to England last year to drive—right into a tree.

A sports writer for the *New York Times*, Robert Lipsyte, wrote a feature about a competitive eater named Bozo Miller. Lipsyte kept his story from sagging in the middle by sandwiching quotes around an incident:

"Now, some of these pro football players think they're pretty good eaters," Bozo said. "Some gamblers are trying to match me up with one of the Buffalo players, a fellow with good size.

"Height means nothing. I'm about 5-foot-7, down to about 275-280 right now, but that's a good proportion. You get one of these ballplayers, 6-7 or 6-8, even one who weighs close to 300 pounds, he doesn't have a properly stretched stomach."

The waitress returned with the drinks, and Bozo said: "My friend here is getting hungry, how about eight club sandwiches?"

The waitress was new and blinked twice before she understood.

"Even if one of those ballplayers could handle, say, a few three-pound steaks, I'd switch to ice cream sundaes on my turn." Bozo said.

"No athlete could handle something that rich and if he could I'd destroy him with hot sauces or minestrone soup. Fluids is one of my strengths."

THE CLOSE

Feature closes should sum up the story. You can use the same devices you used in feature openings: quote, anecdote, striking statement, question.

A good closing device is the *comebacker*, a return to the opening theme. A *Detroit News* reporter opened a story with the quip about a Michigan secretary of state having only one tough decision—choosing the color of license plates. The reporter's close: "The secretary of state would be much happier if his only task for 1973 was the selection of a new color for next year's license plates."

You can end features with a tag line, a one-sentence wrap-up like this from *Newsweek*: "Howard Hughes is the most unforgettable man almost everybody never met."

Some good advice on "getting out" of features comes from Neal Shine, managing editor of the *Detroit Free Press*. Shine says he learned it from Lou Cook, *Free Press* editorial writer, and has "found its wisdom in years of practice": "When you're sitting at the typewriter staring at the paper and struggling for that last beautiful paragraph to end your story, chances are you've already written it. Just end it right there."

- Caution on closes: Avoid the apocalyptic, end-of-the-world, cosmic statement. Also avoid the fictional cliché: "Suddenly he felt tired." Do not force endings. It is better to write them straight than have them fail by being strained.
- Another caution: Writing a feature is no license to editorialize. You can have an attitude, a point of view toward events you are writing about, without editorializing.

THE NARRATIVE

The exception to the feature formula is the pure narrative. Your copy flows like a short story. It is a fictional convention you can use in newspaper writing.

You may start with suspended interest. You build the whole story to a denouement, an unraveling at the close. Sometimes the ending is an O. Henry surprise.

The formula is a foreshadowing, a period of rising suspense, the climax, and the denouement. The opening foreshadows what is to come, perhaps with an air of mystery. You increase the suspense until you reach the high point or climax.

UPI once moved a narrative feature with foreshadowing and increasing suspense. It was full of description and dialogue. It was as masterfully told as a good short story. But this was fact. Here is the story:

WASHINGTON (UPI)—Flying saucer reports may be exciting table talk for most of the nation but for the World War II crew of the battleship New York they can only bring back an embarrassing memory.

The incident occurred while the ship was headed for the Iwo Jima campaign.

The New York had had a series of bad-luck mishaps which had kept it out of action in the Pacific.

It was continuing toward Iwo Jima despite loss of a propellor blade which slowed its speed.

The day was calm, the skies clear. Suddenly, officers on the bridge sighted a strange object overhead.

They studied it but couldn't determine what it was. It was round, silver-colored and seemed about the size of a two-story house.

The commander, Rear Adm. Kemp C. Christian, was summoned.

The object could be seen with the bare eye but the admiral called for his binoculars. He focused them on the strange object which seemed to be following the ship.

The officers recalled reports of Japanese balloons sighted over the northwestern United States—balloons intended to set forest fires.

The consensus on the bridge was that the object was an enemy balloon.

But whatever it was, it didn't seem to be bothering them and they weren't bothering the balloon. So the battleship continued on its way.

The officers were confident that, even with a damaged propellor, the ship could outdistance any balloon.

An hour later, however, that big silver object was still hovering over the ship. It appeared to be about a mile away, directly overhead.

By this time the commander was getting annoyed—or perhaps worried.

He ordered: "Gunners give me a range."

The answer came back: "Seventeen hundred yards."

The same order went out to radar and the answer was the same.

Finally, the order went out: "Open fire."

The three-inch guns were brought into action and fired away but they couldn't touch the "silver balloon."

The commander ordered his destroyer escort to open fire with their five-inch guns. The effect was the same—all misses.

About that time, the navigator, who had been on night watch, came to the deck.

He studied the object in the sky and watched the shells zoom up and fall short of their mark.

His brows knitted. He hurried to his room, made some quick calculations and came back to report to the commander.

"Sir," he said, "If it were possible to see Venus at this time of day, you would see it at exactly the same position of the silver balloon."

The commander gasped. He signaled his destroyer escort to have navigators confirm the position of the planet Venus.

The answers all confirmed the reading of the New York's navigator.

The battleship New York had been firing at the planet Venus.

The one-sentence tag line at the end is yet another fictional convention that newspaper reporters can use in nonfiction pieces.

One warning: If you write a narrative story, ask the copy desk to write a teaser headline that will not give away the story. A Baltimore *Evening Sun* reporter once wrote a fine narrative story which was not unraveled until the last line. Unfortunately, the headline writer ruined the mystery with something like "Horseplayer Killed on Way Home from Track."

Subjective Narrative

"Subjective narrative" is a fancy term to describe a dangerous concept. It is dangerous because subjective narrative flirts with editorializing. In subjective narrative, writers impose themselves on their material. It is reporting from a personal viewpoint based on an individual writer's insights, experiences of life, and knowledge of human nature. However, subjective narrative does not mean philosophizing and editorializing.

The concept is probably best explained by illustrations. A *New York Times* reporter covered a speech that the late football coach Vince Lombardi gave to corporate executives. The reporter wrote: "The mostly paunchy and out-of-shape audience reacted at the end of the speech as if they were ready to go out and take on the Kansas City Chiefs."

Nothing really happened. But the reporter described his perception of the scene.

Another *New York Times* reporter, covering the opening of a new wing at the Detroit art gallery, concluded her story by mentioning that a sculpture got only a passing glance. "But that, in Detroit, was understandable," she wrote. "It's made of welded automobile metal and looks vaguely like a wreck."

After the assassination of Sen. Robert Kennedy, *New York Times* Pulitzer-prize winner Tony Lukas wrote a reaction story. One part was pure subjective narrative:

And the common thirst for every scrap of news, combined with the shock of the event, seemed to draw New Yorkers together in that particular kind of camaraderie that great disasters and great tragedies seem to inspire in this often cold and impersonal city.

In the early morning hours, families invited strangers off the streets and neighbors across the hall they had barely met to come into their apartments and listen to the news.

Somehow, people in the streets and the subways even seemed a shade more courteous.

BRIGHTS

Brights are short, short, short features, about two to six paragraphs long. They are not to be confused with *pluggers*, those short items that fill the bottom of a column ("China produced 50 billion tons of rice this year"). Brights are usually the lighter side of the news. They also are unusual or bizarre aspects of the news.

Brights need not be uproarious sidesplitters. In radio parlance, they are "kickers," something light to end a broadcast. Newspapers sometimes use brights in boldface boxes for special attention.

Sometimes they give readers a chuckle. Sometimes a reporter chuckles while writing them. Reporters try for a clever angle with brights. Sometimes they hit, sometimes they miss. Often they will make four or five false starts before hitting on the bright idea.

Brights must be honest and accurate. The feature angle must fit the facts. Reporters should not try to embroider with humor something that may be intrinsically funny, such as a police officer being robbed of a gun.

Aside from being apt, brights must be tight. You can leave out detail you ordinarily might include in a hard-news story. Here is a bright:

AUBURN, N.Y. (AP)—The management at Curley's Restaurant is fed up with the graffiti writers in its rest rooms.

Repainting the walls every three weeks gets a little expensive.

The solution? A blackboard in both the men's and women's rooms and an ample supply of chalk.

Here is another bright:

TOPEKA (AP)—Are you ready for the gnus, Weather and Sports?

The Gage Park zoo's two new gnus, a 4-year-old female and a 1-year-old male, have been named Weather and Sports.

Ex-Nun Is Hooked on New Profession

That headline appeared over the following feature story in the *Chicago Tribune*, written by Paul Weingarten:

When Cynthia Kane traded her nun's habit for a miniskirt and began strolling the streets as a prostitute, it wasn't just another tale of a good girl gone bad.

Officer Kane, 28, traded the peaceful life in a convent for work as one of nine policewomen masquerading as prostitutes during a five-week city-wide crackdown on streetwalkers, their patrons and pimps, in which scores have been arrested.

Her life now is a drastic departure from the two years she spent as Sister Mary Anthony of the Sisters of Our Lady of the Good Shepherd.

"Being in the convent was not my place in life," she said. "I needed more freedom. God had other things in mind for me.

"It was a beautiful, peaceful life, but not fulfilling. After two years of soul searching, I decided it was not the way I wanted to live the rest of my life."

So she quit the convent before taking her final vows and, after much traveling, she returned to Chicago and took a job as an executive secretary.

But she still wasn't satisfied.

She moonlighted as a volunteer counselor for runaway juveniles.

"I had to reach out more," she said. "I wasn't doing well going on promotional tours for books or sports teams."

So, with "nothing to lose," she set out to become a policewoman. She graduated in July and hasn't looked back since.

"I could never go back to my old job," she said. "I'm not degrading it. It's a great profession. But here, every hour is different from every other hour."

Since joining the vice division's prostitution unit in October, she has infiltrated call girl rings and other illicit operations.

"I never knew what vice was," she said. "I still couldn't explain it to you. There are just a lot of sad people out there."

Is Kane successful in her new role?

If last Saturday night was any indication, yes.

While her male associates created a minor spectacle searching one man who had tried to solicit her favors on a busy street corner, Cindy watched from across the street.

Before the first arrest could be completed, she was propositioned by another man.

She has little sympathy for the male motorists who invariably swoop down in droves when she saunters on the sidewalks of Uptown or New Town.

"The men are just as guilty as the women," she said. "I don't think we'll stop the women, but we do deter patrons. And that means a lot.

"The prostitutes are complaining that we're hurting business. I think we are putting a dent in the prostitution problem."

Jazzing Up a Row of Phone Numbers

As reporters, you will be assigned many routine features. Some will be so uninviting you will wish you were in public relations.

But features are a perpetual challenge to the writer inside the reporter. It is true that you cannot make a silk purse out of a sow's ear. But good writers try to "jazz up a row of telephone numbers." They try to make the most statistic-ridden story interesting.

Remember

Color touches can be included in hard-news stories. They are not exclusive to features. In a hard-news story about testimony before the House Armed Services Committee, a newspaper wrote: "Rep. Rivers, whose mellifluous voice and long silvery hair lent a touch of Southern grace to the occasion, praised General Hershey warmly. . . . Gazing benignly down on the committee room with attentive youths of draft age. . . ."

SUGGESTIONS FOR INSTRUCTOR

• Assign a feature story of an exhibit. Stress the need for people in the copy. Don't let students forget the news peg. Emphasize the need for a theme, urging them to discard what does not fit that theme. Remind students they are reporters, not critics or essayists.

• Assign a feature story on a tour of a newspaper plant. Stress a brisk journalistic approach with observations, quotes, and description, not a dull chronological account. Stories should be kept tight. No prizes are awarded for length.

• Tear a bright from a newspaper. Have students question you about it and then rewrite it, perhaps under deadline. Some of theirs may be better than the original.

• Assign students to visit a police station or police headquarters and write a feature story about it.

Chapter 15

Interviewing

You can be a darned good reporter without being a slick writer, but you can't be a good reporter without being a good interviewer.

Bob Foresman
Tulsa Tribune

The importance of interviewing should be apparent to journalism students by now. Without interviewing, newspapers would regress to the journalism of the 1770s.

Basically there are three kinds of interviews, although journalists might disdain such labeling. They are *spot*, *informal*, and *formal interviews*.

Techniques and uses overlap. For instance, if the Secretary of Defense comes to town, your paper might do a spot-news interview at the airport for today's paper. Later the reporter might meet the Cabinet member at a hotel for a formal interview, producing a feature story for tomorrow's paper.

SPOT-NEWS INTERVIEW

Spot-news interviewing means getting information for a hard-news story. It might be an accident, a slaying, a fire. Such stories are worked by telephone or in person.

These interviews are much more businesslike than a formal interview. In spot interviews, reporters ask brief, pointed questions. They want facts, figures, quotes, and details of what happened. They wrap up the story as quickly as possible.

While interviewing, speak up forcefully. You have a right to ask questions. J. Curtis Montgomery, Knight chain executive, once said that cocky kids are the best reporters, those who are not too "reverent toward authority." Be polite but persistent until you get all the information you want.

On unsolicited calls, get names and phone numbers for callbacks. You may need more information and clarification. You have a number for confirmation. Newspapers have been victimized by hoaxers before and they will be again. Sometimes a callback will foil a hoaxer.

A newspaper once ran an obituary of a woman after someone identifying herself as the woman's niece said her aunt had died. The "dead" woman got quite a jolt reading her own obituary. A confirming telephone call to the funeral home would have prevented the newspaper's embarrassment.

INFORMAL INTERVIEWS

Informal interviews are daily fishing expeditions by beat reporters, either done by phone or in person. If reporters run across something good, they work the story as they would a spot-news assignment and get it in today's paper. Much beat-round information is used on an overnight basis.

FORMAL INTERVIEWS

Formal interviews usually require appointments. After setting up an appointment, reporters should do their homework. By burrowing through morgue clips and library references, reporters can learn much about people to be interviewed and their specialties. Reporters can give some thought to the questions they will ask in an interview.

Sometimes a preinterview check in *Who's Who in America* will yield useful information for an interviewer. Lots of "good stuff" can be jammed into one tight paragraph of *Who's Who*.

The more you know, the more intelligent questions you will be able to ask. You will also be able to avoid such trivial questions as, "How old are you?" or "Where were you born?"

A reporter for *Newsweek's* Detroit bureau once was granted just fifteen minutes to interview the president of American Motors Corporation (AMC). But the reporter had prepared for the interview so diligently that an impressed AMC president extended the interview for forty-five minutes.

The late press critic A. J. Liebling has told how thorough preparation paid off with a good interview:

One of the best preps I ever did was for a profile of Eddie Arcaro, the jockey. When I interviewed him the *first question* I asked was, "How many holes longer do you keep your left stirrup than your right?" That started him talking easily and after an hour, during which I had put in about twelve words, he said, "I can see you've been around riders a lot."

Find out what other people—rivals and foes—have said about your subject. These quotes will be springboards for tough questions. How do they answer that charge?

The tougher the questions, the better. Columnist Carl Rowan once wrote: "There aren't any embarrassing questions—just embarrassing answers." Reporters need not apologize for hard questions. It is a reporter's job to put sources on the spot if the situation warrants it.

Some reporters will argue about it, but generally it is better to save your tough questions for last. In that way, if the source throws you out of the room, you still have a story.

As beginners, you might want to jot down questions in advance. (Most pros frame advance questions mentally.) Ask yourself: What is my line of questioning? What is my angle? Keep flexible. Let answers to your questions lead you to follow-up or related questions—or perhaps a new line of questioning.

Arrive on time for an interview. It is not only courteous, it gives you time to size up the place, perhaps even chat with a secretary or press aide. What you see or learn minutes before the interview could serve as a conversational icebreaker.

Go into an interview with confidence, aplomb. Be polite but firm. Show no undue reverence for the "Great One."

CONVERSATIONAL RAPPORT

Conversational flow helps formal interviews. But don't you do most of the talking. If the interviewee asks a question, answer it. But quickly come back with a question of your own.

Avoid lengthy questions that become speeches. Sometimes questions need a preface. But long-winded questioning, a habit easy to fall into in a TV age, is bad questioning.

Every interview subject is different. Size each one up and play it by ear. Athletes, actors, and politicians are usually easy to interview. Like a courtroom lawyer, fit your tone to the "witness." Be soft or aggressive as the subject's attitude dictates.

Some people talk too much. They may even filibuster. Politely interrupt with a question to get them back on the track. A few people will not be interrupted. William Ryan, AP reporter, tells of trying to interview Cuba's Premier Castro and listening to a monologue. "I asked one question and he went on for about four hours," Ryan said.

Some people are like clams. It is difficult to pry an answer out of them. With the reluctant ones, patient, gentle prodding helps. Pointing out the advantages of publishing information sometimes breaks down resistance.

Saul Pett of the AP has written: "The most difficult man I ever interviewed was Alfred C. Kinsey, who saw me at the precisely appointed second, pulled out a traveling alarm clock, wound it, set the alarm, pulled out the alarm, set the coffee table between us, checked the clock against his wristwatch, and, finally, looking up, said, 'Yes?' "

Pursuit is important in interviewing. Reporters should press, probe, and follow up until they get what they want or get a no-comment. Ask: "How?" "Why?" "Can you give an example of that?" A reporter sometimes has to act like a cross-examining attorney.

Impartiality? Yes, in principle. But many interviewers say they do better if they seem to be agreeing with the interviewee. You do not have to be a phony, agreeing with something you disagree with. You can nod or grunt "un-huh." There is no point in getting into a shouting match. You want to get information, not win an argument.

Avoid tendentiousness, asking loaded or slanted questions: "What do you think of our stupid Mideast policy?" The interviewee is entitled to ask whether you want an answer to your opinion or your question.

In short, the purpose of an interview is neither to make someone look good nor bad. It is to report what they say, portraying them for readers.

MANNERISMS

Note appearance, dress, voice, mannerisms. Such observations enhance interview copy.

Milton Berle, who once edited an actor's school newspaper, gave this advice on interviewing: "Don't talk. Listen and look. See if they chew their nails."

A *New York Times* feature about the late French writer André Malraux was interspersed with "bon," "alors," and "n'est-ce pas?" showing the flavor of the man's English.

NOTE-TAKING

In spot-news and on informal beat rounds, you definitely should take notes. Few reporters have total recall. But in formal interviews, some reporters do not take notes, or they take them sparingly.

Some pros find notetaking distracting, marring conversational rapport. They find sources more relaxed if they do not take copious notes. They can concentrate on what is being said, note mannerisms, dress, and gestures.

A reporter for *Newsday* prefers not to take notes during formal interviews. But as soon as he leaves the source, he jots down everything he can remember.

As beginners, take notes. Try to concentrate, jotting down key points and quotations. Just as in a history lecture, you will do much better to listen to and absorb the material, writing only the important points instead of trying to get down every word.

The disadvantages of not taking notes are obvious: faulty memory and inaccuracies. As a Chinese proverb has it, "The strongest memory is weaker than the palest pen."

In formal interviews, take notes unobtrusively. Write down key figures and phrases. Develop a note-taking cablese: "U shud see it." It is good to maintain eye contact while interviewing.

TAPE RECORDERS

Tape recorders produce an astonishing increase in accuracy. They leave reporters freer to concentrate during formal interviews without incessant scribbling. A tape recorder is optional for formal interviews. But in spot-news or informal interviews, reporters do not use them. The insurmountable barrier is playback time. If you are on deadline, you simply cannot use a recorder.

Sometimes reporters use tape recorders as a backup in talking with and listening to politicians, finding them useful to expose charges of misquotation.

Tape recorders are especially useful for the lengthy question-and-answer interview popularized by *Playboy*. However, most professionals do not use a tape recorder even for formal interviews. They feel that playing the tape back and transcribing it is like doing two interviews. Most reporters argue that if you cannot take notes you ought to be in another line of work.

Some sources do not like recorders. Others feel uncomfortable if reporters use them. However, if you do use a tape recorder, get the source's approval. In an age of electronic sophistication—with bugged martinis and bugged navels—reporters should be sensitive to an individual's concern about privacy.

Still, some hard-nosed journalists argue that using a hidden recorder is no different than having total recall.

MAN-ON-THE-STREET INTERVIEWS

The man-on-the-street (MOS) interview can be one of the most idiotic assignments in journalism. (This term refers, of course, to people of both sexes.) Sometimes the questions you are sent out with are less than burning. Sometimes the public is grossly uninformed and misinformed. A South Carolinian, once asked by a roving reporter what he thought of daylight-saving time, replied: "That sudden extra hour of sunlight really hurts my flowers."

The MOS interview is an old-fashioned, make-circulation kind of newspapering designed to get names in the paper. ("Why don't you print the phone directory?" some reporters grumble.)

Still, there are valid reaction stories when something big is happening or the public is talking about an event. Reaction stories can be worked by phone or in person.

In writing MOS stories, don't forget a disclaimer. Remind readers that this is just a sampling of opinion, not a Gallup or Harris poll. You might even joke about "a highly unscientific survey."

Leads are usually based on a summary of findings or reactions. Because you need to identify several people in an MOS, vary your phrasing to avoid a sing-song approach: name, identity, and quote.

One way good writers avoid the sing-song pattern is by using transistion. Push off the previous paragraph. Use one-paragraph transition sentences between quotes: "Not all plant workers were happy about the strike"; "A Louisville housewife disagreed." Then quote and name the individuals.

FOOTNOTES ON INTERVIEWING

Never promise to show your interview copy. You should not because: It is a nuisance, it is impractical, and you have deadlines. Besides, some people will insist on tampering with your copy to make themselves look better.

Henry Clay Frick, the coke baron, hated and mistrusted reporters. He once granted an interview on condition that he be allowed to see the copy. He pared the reporter's 22-inch story—a whole column—down to ten lines.

Agree to show the copy only if that is the sole condition of the interview. Few people are worth that concession—maybe the leaders of the Soviet Union and China.

However, it is all right to check with a source to see if you are correct about some point.

Finally, never promise when the story will appear. Stories are held up and crowded out for lack of space. Sometimes they are never printed.

In mass interviews, save your good questions to ask the source privately. It is not always possible to buttonhole someone afterward, but if you can, other reporters will not get your special questions.

Similarly, if you find yourself in a situation where you have done your homework but rival reporters have not, arrange for a private interview so they do not benefit from your diligence.

- Accuracy. Never hesitate to ask a clarifying question: "Did you say you did that in 1974?"

Ultimately, interviewing is a highly individual and personal art. What works for one reporter, may not work for another.

The AP's Saul Pett suggests trying the pregnant pause:

Interviewing for me is still a mysterious, elusive art. Few techniques provide generalizations. I once thought I had one . . . that is the value of the deliberate pause. You ask a question. He, or she, answers it. You pause before the next question. Sometimes, merely because of the lull, the subject will begin to think his or her answer was inadequate or inaccurate or dull, and he or she resumes talking.

Writing the Interview

- Write it while it is hot, before notes and impressions grow cold. If you see a movie and dislike it, the next day you probably could give five reasons why. Two weeks later you will be hard-pressed to give one reason.
- Find an angle, theme, thread, and develop it.
- Don't forget news peg, setting, time element.
- Work in sights and sounds, but don't overdo it. Rather than hanging description on speech tags—"he said, pulling on his beard"—work them into one-paragraph blocks. This way: "Maier is 50 years old but looks younger. During an interview yesterday, he was wearing a brown business suit, loafers, and suspenders."
- Quotes improve most stories, but they are essential for formal interview features.
- Formal interviews are written like feature stories. Here is the beginning of a *New York Times* story:

AMENIA, N.Y.—New York City is relentlessly strangling itself and it is probably too late to do anything about it by simple means, Lewis Mumford, a community-planning pioneer and an authority on urban civilization, said today.

Interviewed in his cozy frame house in Leddsville Road here, Mumford peppered these criticisms at the city in which he was reared and from which he has fled to Dutchess County:

- New York, with a population of 8 million, has 2 million too many people.
- It has far too many skyscrapers—"The newer ones are just glass-and-metal filing cabinets."

- It has far too many high-rise apartment buildings—"All they contain are filing-card people."
- It has far too much vehicular congestion—"There ought to be free parking spaces on the outskirts and efficient public transportation to bring people into Manhattan."

Here is the close of the same story:

Mumford prefers rural life even though he sometimes suspects urbanization may be creeping in. Three cars passed his house as he was bidding his visitor goodby.

"Look," he exclaimed with a chuckle, "we're getting congestion out here in the country."

'Playgirl Editor Exposes Philosophy behind Nude Male Photographs'

That headline appeared over a feature story in the *Minneapolis Star* that was based on an interview done by Marilynn J. Taylor:

Nude males and inflation have a lot in common.

Women are interested in them and they're featured in the pages of Playgirl.

Marion Scott Milam, a former free-lance writer who became editor-in-chief of Playgirl by being "in the right place, at the right time," admitted that it is the centerfolds of males, not the articles on inflation, that attract readers to the magazine.

"There's a sexual side to women," she said yesterday while in Minneapolis on a promotional tour." "Why not spotlight it?"

But she said she hopes there is some truth in the old "I-buy-it-for-the-articles" excuse some men's magazine readers used to use.

"I hope women don't need the same crutch," she said. "Of course we buy it to look at the photos."

She said the magazine is designed for the total woman.

"We attempt to treat women as innately intelligent and visibly sexual," she said.

Playgirl, which has more than a million readers, was called schizophrenic in the beginning, Ms. Milam said, because of an apparent contradiction between the women's equality theme it stresses and the sexually explicit photos of men.

She said, however, that there is no contradiction.

"Men are not in the same position as women," she said. "It's possible to reduce the woman to a sex object, but is it possible to reduce the male to a sex object?"

The 40-year-old editor said it is her belief that women won't do this. She cited a survey of women done for the magazine that showed they projected a personality onto the nude males they saw in photos.

Women see more than just a body, she said.

Monthly contests have encouraged men in a variety of careers to bare all before Playgirl's cameras.

Many enter for the prize of $2,000 and some because they have a "certain kind of ego," Ms. Milam said.

Others are seeking acting or modeling careers and want publicity.

"It works," she said. "It gives them good exposure."

Most of Playgirl's readers are women between 18 and 35 years old, most are working and about 50 percent are married.

Ms. Milam is proud that 40 percent of the magazines' readers are men, a figure about equal to the percentage of female readers Playboy has.

The magazine is not connected with Playboy. It was started in 1973 by Douglas Lambert, a Los Angeles nightclub owner.

Ms. Milam, who was raised in Nebraska and has been married for 14 years, identifies with the woman Playgirl is trying to reach: "the woman who doesn't identify with radical (feminist) rhetoric and is trying to cope with work, children, home, husband or lover."

She said she wants Playgirl to be the magazine for that woman. And she doesn't want to be remembered just as the editor of the magazine with the centerfold.

SUGGESTIONS FOR INSTRUCTOR

- Assign a man-in-the-street or reaction story. Have students ask a question about a controversy or public concern in the news. Don't let them forget the background and context of the question in their stories.
- Have someone come in to be interviewed by the class. In that way, you know what was said—checking on the students' accuracy—and can comment on their interviewing technique.
- Assign students an out-of-class formal interview with anyone who is "good copy"—someone who is a fascinating personality, has an interesting job, or espouses provocative ideas.

Chapter 16

Objectivity

It makes about as much sense to say a journalist can't be impartial as to argue that a judge can't dispense justice, or that a lawyer can't give a sound defense because he finds a prisoner or client personally obnoxious. . . ."

Wes Gallagher, former AP general manager

The fundamental difference between a news story and an editorial or personal column is this: In a news story you should have no opinion without attribution. In an editorial or column you do not need attribution. The reporter's job is to tell what happened without injecting personal opinion.

The writer of the following news story lead did not follow that rule: "The Columbus City Planning Commission added another of those peculiar actions dealing with the Olentangy River Road Thursday when it voted 3 to 1 to adopt plan 2B for the Olentangy Freeway." That is partisanship. A reporter taking sides in a news story loses credibility. A reporter owes it to the public to present a controversy fairly.

In a news story you must say: "President Carter is a joke, Sen. Barry Goldwater said"; "a national health insurance plan would mean this country has gone socialist, the American Medical Association said." Editorial writers and columnists do not need attribution to give those opinions.

Newspapers and reporters who use unattributed opinion in the news columns are little different from the Soviet press about which the quip is: "There is no news in Izvestia (news) and no truth in Pravda (truth)."

Ray Mungo, a New Left exponent of advocacy journalism, used to say, "Tell the truth, brothers, and let the facts fall where they may."

The problem with that is that you never can tell the truth if you let the facts fall where they may. Reporters, no matter how much they may be committed to causes and sympathetic to political views, remain neutral professionally. They give the facts in the news columns and leave the side-taking to the columnists and editorial writers.

Good reporters for good papers seek the facts for a story. Bad reporters on bad papers seek facts to support a preconceived idea of what the story should be.

ADVOCACY JOURNALISM

American journalism has improved enormously since the vilification and open advocacy of the party press organs in the Hamiltonian and Jeffersonian era. To move back toward that kind of journalism would be a demeaning retrogression.

Advocacy journalism should be left to the journals of opinion—magazines like the *New Republic* on the left and *The National Review* on the right.

The highest and best standard of newspaper journalism is nonpartisanship in the news columns. What good newspapers strive for is objective intent.

The best newspaper journalism is to handle major news events this way: Thoroughly blanket an issue—giving all sides—without bias and without polemics. Then the editorial page takes a strong position.

The *Michigan Daily*, one of the best campus newspapers in the country, covered a general strike planned at the University of Michigan some years ago. Page one carried a main story and three sidebars, all fair and objective accounts of the situation. On the editorial page two editorials and two personal columns blistered the university administration. It was classic newspapering.

Some supporters of advocacy journalism say: "But the Establishment press is not objective." Sometimes it isn't. But that doesn't make nonobjective reporting good journalism.

Finally, it is faintly amusing to observe how some of the country's socialist newspapers will quote facts from the capitalist press—the *New York Times* and the *Wall Street Journal*—before launching an attack against "the running dogs of capitalism." It shows the respect with which those two papers are held.

MYTH OF OBJECTIVITY

Newspapers display subjectivity every day. Editors can play up or play down a story. It is a matter of judgment. If you put a story on page one—or page eighty-eight with the girdle ads—that is subjective.

A jury convicted a Boston doctor of manslaughter after a major abortion trial. The *New York Times* carried the story on page one. The *Detroit News* ran it on page four. The *Times* was right, the *News* was wrong—another purely subjective judgment.

Newspaper reporters are also subjective in that they select facts and quotes for a story. A Vietnam war correspondent once spoke on the Wayne State University campus. Students who supported the war wrote leads declaring that the speaker supported the war. Students who opposed the war wrote leads declaring that the speaker opposed the war.

Professionals would not have let their perceptions get in the way of the facts. Reporters are trained to be objective. They have objective intent. They struggle to be neutral observers. They strive desperately to be objective in the news columns. Most reporters would subscribe to the view of the Italian philosopher who said, "Impartiality is a myth, honesty is a duty."

That is why the best general interest newspapers in the country—the *New York Times*, the *Los Angeles Times*, and the *Washington Post*—all may give the administration hell on the editorial page but treat it with scrupulous fairness in the news columns. They let readers make up their minds on the basis of facts.

Charles de Gaulle once said he was neither of the left nor of the right—but above. It was quintessential de Gaulle with his Olympian conceit. But the statement captures the aspiration of most journalists.

Paul Poorman, editor of the *Akron Beacon-Journal*, once spoke about objectivity at a Wayne State University journalism workshop. "In a world filled with special pleading, no one else is even trying to be objective," he said.

One of the reasons the *New York Times* is so respected is its great integrity. It strives to be fair, balanced, and objective in the news columns. It is a paper that you can trust to give you the facts on an issue no matter where it stands editorially.

Pleasing Diogenes

Our job is to please no one except Diogenes.

—Walter Cronkite

To the extent that a reporter is a liberal reporter or a Communist or a conservative or a Republican reporter, he's no reporter at all.

—H. L. Mencken

I've always hated the Vietnam War. . . . But at no time did my animus mean that I would deliberately alter or consciously distort facts in order to buttress my personal beliefs. And that . . . is what the much-agonized debate over objective reporting . . . is all about.

I think it's possible to say that I have committed view about something and can still report honestly on it.

—Seymour Hersh, *New York Times*

Writing Tips—And Pitfalls

The following comments should prove helpful:

• Analogy—Comparing the unfamiliar to the familiar: "The military cargo giant, only 18 yards shorter than a football field"; "The Apollo rocket is as tall as the Fisher Building"; "The congressional district is shaped like a thin slice of pie"; "Like some gigantic bathtub, Lake Erie sloshes back and forth whenever it storms."

• Simile—Comparison using "like" or "as." From one *New York Times* story: "The hearing room was jammed like market day in Algeria." "Each word that filters out from the hearing room is picked over like fruit in a stall."

• Metaphor—Comparisons without "like" or "as": "Vietnam's Red River, a warm can of tomato soup."

• Danglers—When fully developed, Miss Roberts said the community will have 10,000 people." "Sipping a cup of coffee, a note was dashed off on an envelope."

• Misplaced modifiers—"He was identified as the latest victim in the chain of murders by police." "Smith was hit by a car while crossing Woodward Ave. driven by Jones."

• Surprise paraphrase—Reversing a cliché, making something fresh: "Failure went to his head." "It was a trade that could hurt both clubs."

• Transitions—Overlapping paragraphs. Pushing off the previous paragraph. One paragraph: "They said it couldn't be done." The next paragraph starts: "But Jones did it. . . ." One paragraph: "The newspaper's headline crowed: 'World's tallest building.' " The next paragraph begins: "It was. At 280 feet it towered. . ."

• Direct address—Direct address is often a good technique, especially in leads. It immediately involves readers in your story. It is a good way of "hooking" them. This sort of thing: "Have you rummaged through your attic lately? You may have a valuable stamp on an old envelope." One caution with direct address: Watch out for making it too exclusive. For example, this lead: "Take heart, fellow Twinkie addicts." It is a safe bet that that kind of lead excludes three-quarters of your readers. Finally on direct address, do not insult the intelligence of readers by asking a question that many may know the answer to. For example: "Did you know that the population of New York City is 7.8 million?"

Stories from Memos

Reporters must often dig up a story on the basis of a memo from the city desk. Something like this:

Pat Ellis, director of a project called Educational Leadership Laboratory sponsored by the Model Neighborhood Agency, has a possible story on her lab and the 26 councils in the model neighborhood area.

The lab is new, funded for 12 months to work with the councils. The operating agency is Shaw College.

We can call Ellis at 378-2079, ext. 222.

A call to Ms. Ellis netted the reporter much information. The reporter also telephoned two other people whose names and information were used in the story.

It was an everyday newspaper story—no big deal—but the kind reporters constantly work up.

Chapter 17

Speech Reporting

When assigned to cover a speech, do the clips first if time permits. The research you do on speakers and their specialties will pay off in stronger speech stories.

The usual lead is based on the speaker's most important point or most striking idea. Exceptions would be riots, disturbances, or anything else that would take precedence over what was said.

Heckling, spitballing, tossing of marshmallows, or audiences walking out might be significant enough to include in a summary lead.

Speech stories should include the speaker, the speaker's identity, the setting, the occasion, and mention of the audience.

The setting: "The President said in a television address"; "the governor spoke at a $500-a-plate fund-raising dinner in the Jack Tar Hotel." The occasion: "Mondale spoke at the annual Jackson Day dinner in Cobo Hall." Audience comment should include size estimates and perhaps an indication of crowd reaction.

Be wary of crowd estimates, particularly in political situations. It is best to err on the side of conservatism. Trained reporters will not have biased perception, overestimating or underestimating on the side of their sympathies.

But they can be victimized, particularly in reporting political gatherings and speeches. Reporters often get their crowd estimates from police chiefs. Police chiefs often arrive at their figures through political advance people. *Newsweek* once gave the scenario:

ADVANCE MAN: "What do you estimate, chief, 40,000?"
CHIEF (startled): "I don't think that many."
ADVANCE MAN: "I don't know, chief, I've seen some big crowds before and this one's at least 35,000."
CHIEF: "That big? Well, maybe there's 33,000."
If all goes according to plan, five minutes later the chief will announce to any reporter willing to listen that the crowd—perhaps 12,000—is officially estimated at 33,000 people.

Always use attribution for your crowd estimates. But even then wear your reporter's cynicism.

The managing editor of the *Detroit Free Press*, Neal Shine, has a few more tips on crowd-counting:

Custodians or managers of halls where events are held can tell you the hall's capacity, how many chairs were set up, how many tables were set up and how many can fit at each table.

You'll probably get a better estimate of crowd from the guy who's running the hall or the facility and he's probably a uniquely unbiased source for such information.

One thing I learned over the years: Politicians will usually quote the crowd figure at a clambake or a fund-raising dinner by the number of tickets sold—not the number of people attending. Talk to the caterer. They get paid for the number of dinners served and the information is invariably accurate.

Background information should not clutter leads. Just be sure to work it in by the sixth or seventh paragraph.

As soon as you arrive at a speech site, get a text from the speaker or an aide. With most politicians you can depend on getting a text. If you get a text, read it and mark the important paragraphs.

Follow the text as it is delivered. Watch for departures from the text, deletions, and insertions. President Johnson's announcement in 1968 that he would not run again came at the end of a speech, totally by surprise. Hubert Humphrey once threw away a prepared text of a speech he gave in Paris and, according to *Newsweek*, spoke so movingly of the glories of France that de Gaulle was moved to tears.

Reporters working for morning papers often file a first-edition story before the speech is given. They report the speech just as if it had been delivered—

in the past tense—with the exception of a disclaimer line: "in a speech prepared for delivery."

You must get that disclaimer in. If for some reason the speaker doesn't attend, the newspaper is off the hook. Speakers stand behind their texts once they are released to the press.

Reporters update their speech stories for later editions either by dictating a new lead or, if a fresh top is not warranted, working with inserts to get in color, crowd reaction, and a substitution for the disclaimer paragraph.

EMBARGOES

Speeches, press releases, and texts of long reports are usually embargoed for release at a specified time: "Hold for release until 4 P.M. Friday." This is one way of dividing up news breaks fairly between A.M. and P.M. papers.

Embargoes also permit reporters to read lengthy government reports without rushing into print with a badly digested story.

The ethics of embargoes are plain: Observe release times and dates. A cheap beat or scoop is not worth breaking an embargo. However, once an embargo has been broken for whatever reason, other papers are free to go with the story immediately.

GETTING QUOTES

Covering a speech without a text is tougher. Listen for key words and phrases. Get accurate quotes. If you don't have the exact words, use partial quotes or paraphrases. Never put quote marks around something the speaker did not say. Roger Tatarian, former general manager of UPI, has written:

I think it is a cardinal sin, a capital crime to horse around with somebody's direct quotes. . . . If there is something missing you have got to indicate that. Just because a man used a word that makes a quote slightly awkward for you, you can't leave it out unless you indicate what you left out.

All a reporter has to do to indicate an omission is to use three dots— . . . — for an ellipsis.

While taking notes, underline, star, or use side-slashes to indicate major points. Some reporters use a three-star or a three-slash system to emphasize lead possibilities.

In writing speech stories, mix direct, indirect, and partial quotes. The lazy way, particularly if you have a text, is to use five or six consecutive paragraphs of open quote.

You need to break up the rhythm and pattern of the writing. You need to remind readers who is speaking. Probably no more than four straight paragraphs of open quote should be used.

Weave in some color. Make readers feel as if they were there. Did the speaker talk rapidly, vigorously, softly? Did he or she jab the air to emphasize points? What about the length? Was it twelve minutes or fifty-two minutes? How did the crowd react? Wild applause? Sitting on its hands? Twenty-seven interruptions?

Watch for incidents: militants chanting or little old ladies in tennis shoes stalking out.

UPI moved a speech story about former Sen. Mike Mansfield shortly after he had spent five days in a hospital for tests. After noting that fact, the UPI reporter threw in this phrase, "looking wan but speaking animatedly."

INTERPRETATION

Speech stories sometimes need interpretation, the whys and wherefores to place what was said in the context of world and national situations.

The *New York Times*, reporting a speech by Gen. William Westmoreland, noted that the general inserted a phrase not included in advance texts. The reporter added this interpretation: "The insertion appeared to soften a sentence that could have been interpreted as a threat of further escalation of the war in Vietnam."

That's why it is important to have knowledge of the speaker, the topic, and national and world events. You can tell readers how the President's position differs from the one he enunciated in Minneapolis six months ago; how his health care plan differs from the principal opposition plan.

It is not editorializing to point out contradictions with a previous stance. You cannot call a speech bad, the speaker stupid—that is editorializing. But it is fair to give background and interpretation.

SPEECH-LEAD PITFALLS

Full-quote leads are weak unless they have impact. "Spoke leads" are taboo. This sort of thing: "University President Robben Fleming spoke yesterday in Hill Auditorium." The biggest student failing is topic leads. This sort of thing: "The Eldridge Cleaver presidential campaign was the topic of discussion yesterday at the South End forum."

Delayed Attribution

The lead might be something like this: "The world is coming to an end tomorrow." The second paragraph contains the attribution: "That was the view of the Rev. John X. Weltschmerz of the First Cosmic Church in a speech. . . ."

Many papers bar delayed attribution leads because standing alone, such leads can be editorializing. This sort of thing: "Illinois should not get an atomic reactor because of its racist policies." Then the second paragraph follows with the attribution: "Vernon X. Porter, chairman of the Illinois Urban League, said that what he called the state's discriminatory policies disqualify it for consideration as a federal plant site."

Still, some editors do not object to their reporters using delayed-attribution leads.

Partial Quote in Lead

Whenever you use a partial quote in the lead, be sure to give the full quote later on. If your lead has someone calling a course of action suicidal or irresponsible, in fairness you should use the full quote in context.

A UPI lead quoted a congressman as saying that a 10 percent tax surcharge was a "bandaid on a hand cancer." Eight paragraphs later it gave the full quote: "What we've done is put a bandaid on a hand cancer. We've kept everyone from seeing that we have that skin cancer on our hand, but we haven't done a thing in the world about eliminating the cancer."

In that case the full quote may not have been essential. But it is necessary to avoid quoting out of context. After George McGovern lost the Presidential election in 1972, the *Detroit News* ran this paragraph under the credit of AP and the *Los Angeles Times*: "McGovern's concession came at 11:37 P.M. 'You have my full support,' he said in a telegram to Mr. Nixon."

The text of McGovern's statement ran as a sidebar. This is what the text said: "I hope that in the next four years you will lead us to a time of peace abroad and justice at home. You have my full support in such efforts." That is entirely different from what the partial quote indicated.

SYNONYMS FOR "SAID"

The best and safest speech-tag verb is "said." Sometimes reporters think they cannot repeat "said" so they resort to "opined," "declared," the stilted "stated," "asseverated," or some other silly avoidance. A single story in the *New York Times* once used "vouched," "confessed," "disclosed," and "lamented."

Synonyms for "said" are all right if they fit the context: "suggested," "urged," "explained," "implored," and "asked" are okay—if the speaker was really doing those things. Often students write something like this: "It's great to be alive!" he explained.

Two speech tags should be avoided in nearly all news stories: "pointed out" and "claimed." Those are editorial verbs. If you write "pointed out," it suggests it is true. It may be just opinion. Similarly, if you write "he claimed," the connotation is that that is what he says but it is not true.

SUGGESTIONS FOR INSTRUCTOR

• Tear a speech text out of the *New York Times* and deliver it in class, pretending you are the real speaker and the background is the same. Have students write the story under deadline—and without a text. Have them use a dateline if the story originated out of town.

• Get another speech text from the *Times*. Have it dittoed and hand it to the class as a text. Have them do the story as an overnighter.

Professional Speech Story

Excerpts follow from the top and middle of a *New York Times* story. Note the punchy lead. Note, too, how the writer, Jack Raymond, was careful to say the speaker criticized *what he said* was the incorrect use of air power.

Notice how the lead is followed quickly by a quote. See how the writer worked in the news peg, description, and background.

WASHINGTON—Gen. Curtis E. LeMay sharply criticized today what he said was the incorrect use of air power in Vietnam.

"We're hitting the wrong targets," he said.

The former Air Force Chief of Staff, usually taciturn, said that American air strikes in Vietnam were also "too little and too late."

As a consequence, he said, "we're getting people killed who shouldn't be killed."

He called for air strikes in North Vietnam that would hurt the Communist regime more than he said the bombings were, saying that the end of the war thus hastened, fewer people would be killed on both sides.

General LeMay's unusual public expression of his views came at a luncheon in the Waldorf-Astoria honoring him as the recipient of the 1965 Collier Trophy, one of aviation's leading awards. . . .

In his 35-year career, General LeMay, who is now 58, gained fame as a bomber commander in World War II and as creator of the Strategic Air Command in the postwar period.

He had a reputation as a "hawk"—an aggressive military man.

But except in Congressional appearance, General LeMay, a glowering figure who is seldom without a cigar, rarely spoke publicly in any but prudent terms about any differences with policymakers.

Chapter 18

The Weather

Everybody talks about the weather but nobody does anything about it.

Attributed to Mark Twain

Reporters can't do anything about the weather either, but they must write about it.

Weather is a news staple like obituaries, fires, and accidents. People are interested in the weather because they live with it all their lives. Everybody does talk about the weather. It is the number one conversational icebreaker.

To farmers and growers the weather is important news.

People are also interested in the weather because often their plans hinge on it. Picnics, football games, camping trips, and outings depend on the weather—whether to go or what to wear.

Newspapers use two basic kinds of weather stories. Let's call them "weather-weather stories" and "disaster stories."

Weather-weather stories deal with cold snaps, heat waves, wind, and rain. Records are often elements of these kinds of weather stories. For example, this lead:

The mercury plunged to 32 here today, frosting the suburbs and setting a record low for a May 16.

Here are the first couple of paragraphs of a *Chicago Daily News* weather-weather story:

A record low temperature was set Tuesday when the National Weather Service's official thermometer dropped to 48 degrees at Midway Airport.

It was the coldest mark for the day since the old record—52 degrees—was set 97 years ago.

It also was the second day in a row for a record low.

The temperature dipped to 49 degrees Monday, lowest for the date since the 54-degree reading in 1964.

Here is the start of a weather story from the *Los Angeles Times*, written by Tom Paegel:

The mercury climbed to a high of 99 degrees at the Los Angeles Civic Center Monday and past the 100 mark ⏤t several other Southland locations as the heat wave went into its second day here.

The National Weather Service said the sizzling weather, coupled with eye-stinging smog and high humidity, was expected to continue at least through the end of the month.

But cooler weather—highs in the mid 90s—is expected to mark the first day of September, according to forecasters.

Wind and rain of unusual intensity often provide weather stories. Here is the top of such a story from the *St. Petersburg Times*, written by Frank DeLoache:

The kids at Ninth Street near 85th Avenue N look forward to those big dark clouds that spill their contents quickly and in big drops, making rivers out of streets, because they can get $4 or $5 to push the unfortunate motorists out of the swamped intersection.

But the owners of the houses at the intersection of 14th Way N and 86th Avenue cross their fingers and hope the clouds will dry up.

One of many black clouds crowding the sky Saturday burst about 2 P.M. and less than an hour later Julius Hinton, 65, of 1391 86th Ave. N., was standing in 21 inches of water at the end of his driveway.

A few feet away in his carport, rain water backed up and came within one inch (of a cement ledge at the door) of soaking the wall-to-wall carpet and ruining encyclopedias at the bottom of a bookcase, a couch, a Wurlitzer organ and a grandfather clock.

But the rain stopped—this time.

Here is the beginning of one from the *Boston Globe*:

A line of thundersqualls extending about 155 miles from Portland, Maine, to Providence moved southwest across New England yesterday afternoon, knocking out electrical power and causing extensive flash flooding.

A half-inch of rain fell in a six-minute period in the Reading-Swampscott-Woburn area, where the most severe thunderstorms hit.

A total of .80 inch of rain fell in the Greater Boston area between 2:30 and 4:30 yesterday afternoon as the storms moved through.

COMBINATION LEAD

Sometimes reporters write a combination hard-news-feature lead on weather stories. Here are the beginnings of two such stories from the *New York Times*, the first by John C. Devlin and the second by Deirdre Carmody:

A hungry robin turned up in Connecticut yesterday, a red-plumed cardinal whistled a love call in Westchester County and in Manhattan a coatless woman licked an ice cream cone as she strolled on 42nd Street at Fifth Avenue beside the Public Library.

There was good reason.

At 2:25 the temperature had climbed to a spring-like 61 degrees, only one short of the record set in 1906.

Last year's hard, brown lawns now look like jungles and owners are cursing the grass they once coaxed as they groan behind their lawn mowers trying to cope with the effects of the rainiest summer since 1938.

The Weather Bureau reports that 11.63 inches of rain fell during June and July of this year. The norm for the two-month period is 7.01 inches.

Geographical location often determines the play given weather stories. Heavy snow in winter might get relatively little play in Montana. Two inches of snow in Baltimore, Maryland, could be big news.

In Florida, hurricanes are a grim fact of life. They get big play in Florida newspapers. Here is the start of a *Miami Herald* hurricane story:

Tropical storm Frances became Hurricane Frances late Sunday night as winds reached 75 miles an hour, while Hurricane Emmy stalled in the Atlantic, far from any land area.

Frances, which grew from a depression late Saturday, was located about 700 miles east northeast of Antigua and moving toward the northwest at 15 miles per hour.

At 10:30 P.M. Frances was centered near Latitude 19 North and Longitude 53 West.

She is expected to continue strengthening today.

The National Hurricane Center advised small craft in the northern Leeward Islands to remain in port until further notice.

Emmy, maintaining 100-mile-an-hour winds, continued to meander in the Atlantic at Latitude 35 North and Longitude 53 West, drifting toward the east at between 10 and 15 m.p.h.

DISASTER STORIES

Floods, earthquakes, avalanches, hurricanes, and tornadoes claim lives and cause great destruction. If that happens they become disaster stories—not just weather stories.

Disaster stories tend to inspire anthropomorphic imagery in reporters. Hurricanes, especially, bring out the dramatists in reporters as they have hurricanes "roar," "punch," "howl," or "scream."

Here is a lead on a UPI hurricane story, written by Orval Jackson:

TAMPA, Fla. (UPI)—Hurricane Abby, grown weak and flabby during a night of milling around off the coast, headed for the Punta Gorda area south of here today with winds that reach hurricane force only in gusts.

It was expected to strike inland by noon, struggle across Florida and spill into the Atlantic near Cape Kennedy early tonight.

Some of the things to look for in weather-related accident stories are these:

- The dead
- The injured
- Hardship (people doing without food, heat, light, supplies)
- Rescue operations
- Disaster aspects (the homeless and marooned)
- Damage (property, crop losses)

Damages sometimes cannot be anything more than estimates. Always go with the lower or more conservative figure when estimating damages.

Damage in the Detroit riot of 1967 was initially estimated to have been $250 to $500 million. Later the actual damage figure was set at $50 million.

Wire services often come up with disparate figures for deaths and damages in disaster stories. Always go with the lower figure. You can always raise figures in follow-up stories. It is embarrassing to have to lower them in follow-ups.

Here is a Reuters disaster story:

MANILA—More than 4,000 people have died in the worst earthquake ever to hit the Philippines, the National Disaster Center announced early yesterday.

Hundreds of bodies were being washed up on the shores of the southern Philippines, where villages were swamped by tidal waves that followed the quake early Tuesday morning.

Thousands of others still are missing, victims of havoc and destruction caused by the giant tidal waves.

Whole villages were sucked out to sea by the receding waves, which crashed up to 500 yards inland along the southern coast of Mindanao Island, where the worst destruction occurred.

Authorities began immunization programs as a precaution against disease.

Bodies found along the shores were being laid out on the main square of Pagadian City for identification.

Many of those unidentified were buried in mass graves before they could become a menace to health, officials said.

Hundreds of people were in hospitals or treatment centers.

Nearly 90,000 were homeless, according to the National Disaster Center.

Many thousands were camping out, afraid to go back to their homes for fear that one of the many continuing aftershocks—at least 22 by late afternoon—might prove to be another killer.

Air Force General Antonio Villanueva, just back from surveying the worst stricken areas, told a television interviewer:

"I have seen a lot of disasters, but this devastation is very saddening."

Relief efforts were hampered by heavy rain, which forced at least one plane carrying supplies to return to Manila.

Several other planes unable to land were diverted to other airports in the region.

Survivors told the general that they heard the rumble of waves but the water came so fast that many had no time to flee from their flimsy coastal homes.

After rushing inland, the waves swept back in a vast torrent carrying houses and people, many of them young children.

The casualty rate is already 10 times more than that from any previous earthquake in the country and damage is running into millions of dollars.

Reporters constantly refer to the past in writing weather stories: record snowfalls, record death tolls, record flood levels. Do the clips—morgue files—for records and accounts of previous disasters, storms, and floods, for recalling "the blizzard of '88."

SOURCES

The most obvious source for weather stories is the National Weather Service. But many other sources are available depending on the story. Possible weather-story sources are:

- Police and fire fighters
- Hospitals
- Airports, bus terminals, train stations
- Survivors
- Eyewitnesses
- Public officials (governors for disaster declarations, emergency actions such as calling out the National Guard)
- Red Cross and other emergency-aid groups

WEATHER BRIGHTS

The weather provides good feature copy. The official arrival of the seasons is often the basis for "shorts" such as this from the *Detroit News*:

Autumn officially arrives in the Detroit area and Michigan at 5:48 P.M. tomorrow.

That is the moment the sun will be directly over the equator—over the middle of the Pacific Ocean near Christmas Island.

The moment is called the autumnal equinox.

With it, nights become longer and days shorter until Dec. 21, when there will be nine hours of daylight and 15 hours of darkness.

Dec. 21 marks the official beginning of winter.

Some weather stories are "brights" of the type filed from Punxsutawney, Pennsylvania, each Groundhog Day. Here is one:

GOBBLER'S KNOB OVERLOOKING PUNXSUTAWNEY, Pa.—(UPI)—Keep those earmuffs, mittens, snow boots and hot toddies handy—the nation will have at least six more weeks of winter.

This is the word from the weather seer without a peer—the famed Punxsutawney groundhog.

The rodent bounded out of his burrow at 7:25 A.M. Thursday, saw his shadow and bounded back into his retreat.

Tradition has it that if the Punxsutawney groundhog sees his shadow Feb. 2 be prepared for six more weeks of winter.

The old saw says that coming events cast their shadows before them.

And the Punxsutawney groundhog is a conformist.

The groundhog has been a weather harbinger in this northwestern Pennsylvania community since 1898 and has been wrong only once—in 1936.

Other weather features can be based on a scientist's report about the width of the stripes on the woolly caterpillar. Stories from farmers' almanacs make good feature copy.

Here is one:

DUBLIN, N.H.–(AP)–Abe Weatherwise, the meterological sage of The Old Farmer's Almanac, predicts a cold and bitter winter east of the Mississippi and dust storms, droughts and ruined crops next year in other parts of the nation.

Abe has been predicting America's weather since 1792 in the almanac, which says it is the nation's oldest continuing publication. Abe claims he has been right 80 percent of the time.

The 1977 edition of The Old Farmer's Almanac, 192 pages long, came out last Thursday, predicting a cold winter for the East, a mild one for the West and droughts for the western and central Great Plains.

"February and March together should tax the heating systems and snow shovels of most residents in the Northeast," Abe says.

Caution

Don't overplay forecast stories. The weather can be as unpredictable as a sports contest. Playing up a bad weather forecast can be embarrassing if the prediction does not come true.

For example, a Baltimore newspaper once carried a page-one banner headline over a story on an eight-inch snow forecast. It not only did not snow, but department store advertisers pulled ads they had intended to run in the next day's paper.

Chapter 19

Libel

Who steals my purse steals trash. . . . But he that filches from me my good name
robs me of that which not enriches him and makes me poor indeed."

Shakespeare

Every time veteran reporters of the *New York Times* saw the paper's libel lawyer,
they would quip, "I was off that day." It was their lighthearted way of saying
that they had nothing to do with the story that prompted the latest libel
action.

Libel is a constant concern of newspapers. Although decisions on whether
to publish will be made by editors, reporters must be aware that libel can be
costly to the paper, damage people's reputations, and embarrass the paper. Reporters do not need to be lawyers, but they should have gut feelings about what
they cannot print.

Journalism students ought to take a law of the press course before
they graduate. In the meantime, they should acquire a redimentary idea of
libel.

LIBERTY VERSUS LICENSE

Laws are enacted by governments to keep a balance between freedom and anarchy. If people can kill you with impunity, that is freedom for them—but hardly for you.

What does that have to do with newspapering? Plenty. The First Amendment provides for freedom of speech and freedom of the press. But the First Amendment does not give the press *carte blanche* to print anything it wants to.

The limits of free speech and a free press were set forth by Oliver Wendell Holmes in a Supreme Court decision: "The most stringent protection of free speech would not protect a man in falsely shouting fire in a theatre and causing a panic."

Libel laws are a balancer between freedom (liberty) and anarchy (license).

DEFAMATION OF CHARACTER

Libel is written defamation of character. The law as to what is libelous varies greatly from state to state, from court trial to court trial. Increasingly the legal gambit is to sue for invasion of privacy rather than libel.

Students must realize that the press is a powerful weapon. As reporters they should strive to use that power responsibly. The press can do immense harm to people's reputations. Shakespeare presents the case perfectly in *Othello*:

"Reputation, reputation, reputation!" Cassio says. "O, I have lost my reputation! I have lost the immortal part of myself." Later Iago notes that "good name in man and woman . . . is the immediate jewel of their souls."

Two terms need to be defined: libel *per se* and libel *per quod*. Libel *per se* means libelous on its face. Plaintiffs do not have to prove that their reputations have been harmed. If you write falsely that a doctor is a quack, the statement is libelous *per se*. In American society, it is libelous *per se* to write falsely that someone is a Communist.

Hence, reporters do not cavalierly refer to people by such terms as "bigamists," "extortionists," "swindlers," and "homosexuals."

Most libel suits involve libel *per se*. Libel *per quod* suits are rare. In libel *per quod* what appears innocent on the surface may be defamatory because of extrinsic circumstances. In libel *per quod*, plaintiffs must show how their reputations or businesses have been harmed by publication.

For example, to report falsely that a woman gave birth to twins is not libelous. But, if the woman had been married only two months before giving birth, it could be libelous *per quod*. It could be libelous *per quod* if you advertised even inadvertently that a kosher butcher sold bacon.

The law of libel is constantly changing. Changing times, mores, and locales change libel laws. It once was libelous to print that someone was an anarchist. It could be libelous in some states to call a white person a black.

Students should jettison any notion that something you print is not libelous because you merely quoted someone else's words. "Tale bearer" information can be libelous. If "A" libels "B" and your newspaper quotes A, the newspaper can be sued for libel just as much as A can be.

Journalists must be absolutely scrupulous about protecting reputations until it is evident that some people have no reputations to protect.

Reporters can do some things to prevent libel suits. They can be accurate— checking and double-checking. They can avoid printing rumor, hearsay, and gossip. They can print no charges without attribution.

DEFENSES

Truth   Newspapers are not defenseless. Truth is powerful. With truth on their side, reporters have an absolute defense in most states. However, the burden of proof lies with the newspaper in most cases.

Herschel Fink, Detroit-area attorney who handles libel cases, says truth is a difficult defense. Since it is sometimes hard to convince juries of the truth, he argues that libel attorneys often seek "safer grounds" to defend libel actions.

"I prefer to rely on a legal defense rather than a fact defense," Fink says.

By that he means that since a jury is a trier of fact—and the judge decides the law—libel defense attorneys prefer to defend cases on constitutional grounds and avoid jury trials if possible.

As Fink says, quoting a law axiom, "Truth is what the jury believes."

Privilege   This is the right to print fair and accurate reports of public records and proceedings by public bodies. Reporters can cover Congress, state legislatures, courts, commissions, and public bodies without fear of libel. Even if what is said in a court document is not true and reporters unwittingly report the falsehood, their papers are not open to libel suits.

- Caution: Most state laws insist on a fair and true report of privileged records and proceedings.
- Another caution: Statements made outside a privileged sanctuary are actionable. A United States representative was once sued for libel because on a television program he called someone a "bag woman," a go-between for police graft. The woman collected. If the congressman had said the same thing *only* on the floor of the House of Representatives he could not have been sued.

Fair Comment   This permits criticism of public performers—athletes, actors, entertainers. You may comment on their artistic demerits but not on their personal lives. You can say a book is disgusting, but you cannot say the author is a homosexual unless you are sure you can prove it. You can say the dancer is lewd, but be wary of saying she is sleeping with the mayor.

Constitutional Defenses   The Supreme Court has greatly broadened the constitutional defenses for reporters. Beginning with *New York Times v. Sullivan* in 1964, the court has moved to free libel restraints on the press. The *Sullivan* decision said newspapers could print anything about public officials regarding the performance of their duties short of "actual malice."

Justice William Brennan in the majority opinion defined this as publication "with knowledge that it was false or with reckless disregard of whether it was false or not." Since it is difficult to prove malice, the ruling greatly curtailed libel suits by public officials against newspapers.

The court's rationale in the *Sullivan* case was that the widest possible comment about the performance of public officials is essential to a democracy. A muzzled press cannot alert the public to misconduct or harmful policies by officials.

As the late Supreme Court Justice Hugo Black said in a concurring opinion in the *Sullivan* case: "An unconditional right to say what one pleases about public affairs is what I consider to be the minimum guarantee of the First Amendment."

Subsequently the court extended the public-officials doctrine to public figures and public issues. The court seemed to be moving toward the absolutist position of Justice Black, who urged an end to libel laws.

Recent Supreme Court decisions, however, have swung the pendulum the other way. In the *Gertz* case, the court said private persons, even though they are involved in matters of public interest or concern, no longer have to meet the heavy burden of the *Sullivan* ruling to recover libel damages.

This is good since it is questionable whether libel laws should be abolished. Politicians can usually take care of themselves. But the little people, the obscure people, should have legal recourse if they feel a publication has libeled them.

RETRACTIONS

Newspapers can do other things to mitigate libel damages. They can print retractions or corrections. These may not free them from libel action, but they show courts a lack of malice. By showing that they made an honest mistake, newspapers usually prevent libel action.

By using "police said" as an attribution for a charge, reporters show that their hearts are in the right place. They may still be sued for libel if the police were wrong, but it is a mitigating circumstance in any possible court action.

One of the problems has been that the denial seldom catches up with the charge. Newspapers, after playing the accusation with prominent headline and position, too often bury the retraction.

Obviously editors can rarely give equal play to a retraction. But they can at least run retractions in a prominent position with a boldface box or some other typographical device that calls attention to them.

CODA

As important as it is for reporters to develop a strong respect for people's reputations and the libel laws, newspapers should not let that serve as an excuse for cowardly journalism. It is good to be legally defensive. But it is bad for newspapers to be so afraid of libel shadows that they become impotent.

One of the marks of a good newspaper is that it is often facing libel suits. This does not mean irresponsibility. Rather, it means the paper is bold, courageous, and vigorous about going after good stories—the libel suits be damned.

Kenneth Murray, *Detroit Free Press* libel lawyer, has called defending libel actions the most engrossing field in law. He suggests that the advantage is with the newspaper.

First of all, libel lawyers get the paper to offer to print a retraction. Then they show plaintiffs that greater harm can come to their reputation if the case goes to trial and all that dirty linen is hung out.

The major gambit of libel lawyers is to look for skeletons in the closet, to suggest that the suer has no reputation to uphold. It is not surprising, then, that most libel suits are settled out of court.

Murray tells of the time in 1939 when Father Coughlin, the radio priest, sued the *Free Press* for $4 million because one of its columnists wrote that Coughlin was "congenitally unable to tell the truth"—in blunter words, a born liar.

In support of the defense of truth, Murray and his staff drew up a list of more than 200 instances where Coughlin had lied, quoted books out of context, or falsified quotations by dropping "nots." They presented the list to Coughlin's lawyers. Not wanting such things spread on the public record, Coughlin's attorneys dropped the suit.

George Norris, late legal eagle for the *New York Times*, once put it this way: "After 35 years on the defending end of libel suits, my advice to prospective plaintiffs is—don't bring your linen suit to court unless it's completely spotless."

Newspapers are like cannon. They must not be shot carelessly and with abandon.*

—Louis Nizer

Caution

Everything in a newspaper could be libelous: news stories, letters to the editor, photographs and captions, comic strips, advertisements, and syndicated columns.

SUGGESTION TO INSTRUCTOR

- Draw up a basic libel quiz for students to do on an overnight basis and to discuss in class.

*Louis Nizer, *My Life in Court*, Pyramid Publications, Inc., New York, 1963.

Chapter 20

Photojournalism

The camera is the eye of history. . . . You must never take bad pictures.

Mathew B. Brady

Most reporters do not have to learn how to use a camera. But it is not a bad idea for reporters to learn the rudiments of taking and developing pictures. Photography knowledge and skill can abet newspaper careers.

Big papers have separate photo and news departments. While the twain do meet for assignments, photographers and reporters have separate roles. On the other hand, one of the conditions for a job on a small paper may be to take pictures and to report stories.

Trying to be a photographer and a writer simultaneously is not recommended. Reporting and photographing are two different skills, two different crafts. It is tough to do both jobs at once—and do either well. Juggling camera equipment while you are trying to wield pad and pen is no good. Trying to do both jobs, you can miss a good picture or miss a good quote.

Still, it is good if a reporter knows how to take pictures. If, for example, you get an assignment out of town or out of the country where it would be too expensive to send a photographer along, it is a bonus if you can come back with pictures.

Also, as journalists you should be interested in photographs as a major ingredient in newspapers. If you doubt that photography is an art, see the works of Karsh and Eisenstaedt, see what the old *Life* magazine did with pictures.

Anyone who is serious about being a photojournalist should study the *Best of Life* and hundreds of other photography books, subscribe to the photo magazines, and study good pictures the way a writer reads good literature.

Art is terribly important to putting out a newspaper, to laying out a page. In short, don't rush out to buy $3,000 worth of photo equipment. But don't spurn a chance to learn photography.

Perhaps you can take a photojournalism course. Maybe it will help you overcome a flaw of many newspaper editors: visual illiteracy. Most newspaper people are still word-oriented as opposed to the visual-oriented outlook of much of society. What is needed is more journalists with photo mentality. Many reporters some day will become managing editors and photo editors.

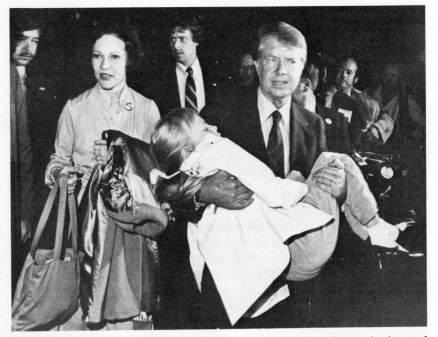

SLEEPING AMY—Jimmy Carter carries his daughter, Amy, in the early morning hours of the day of his election as thirty-ninth President of the United States. Amy, then nine, fell asleep en route to the Carter home in Plains, Georgia. Carter's wife, Rosalynn, is at left. *(Photo by United Press International, Inc.)*

SHOT-AT-SUNRISE PHOTOS

Good photojournalists—and just as important, their editors—should avoid cliché pictures. Cliché photos are pictures of people shaking hands or handing over checks; officials standing around a table; or five members of the garden club standing up straight, gap-spaced, and in a perfect shot-at-sunrise pose. They are photographs lacking drama and emotional impact.

The problem is that often editors say they need such photos to accompany a story. Suggestion: Throw the photos away. Admittedly that is easier for editors of metropolitan papers to do than it is for weekly editors.

If your paper must use cliché photos, imaginative photographers can make the best of a bad situation. Circus roustabouts once warmed up an Ohio crowd with a downtown parade. Because a photographer got a shot of the crowd under the belly of an elephant, it made a good, nonroutine photo.

However, the same photographer carried an old tennis shoe in the trunk of his car, using it to hoke up pictures of kids struck by cars. The art was good, but the ethics deplorable.

Candid, unposed pictures are best. One way to do this is by taking multiple shots. The more photos you shoot, the better your chances of getting good film.

Ed Bailey, Detroit free-lance photographer, covered the 1967 Detroit riot for *Time* magazine. He said he took about 11,000 pictures on that one story, trying to capture every possible mood and angle. Most newspapers cannot afford the luxury of taking so many multiple shots.

Indeed, film costs have risen so much that newspaper photo chiefs are cracking down on profligate film usage. Sandy Colton, AP director of photography, sent a memo to photo editors suggesting that it was ridiculous to use ten roles of film to cover one football game from which two or three pictures were used, or to use three rolls of film to shoot one headshot of a speaker. "All it really shows is insecurity on the part of the photographer," Colton wrote. He estimated that more judicious use of film could save AP $50,000 a year.

Tony Spina, chief photographer for the *Detroit Free Press*, considers each assignment, no matter how routine, a challenge. Covering the inauguration of President Johnson in 1965, Spina drew off from the horde of photographers. While they swarmed around the President and the Chief Justice for the oath-taking, Spina used a telephoto lens to catch a striking profile of Johnson and the Vice President.

Imagination is one of Spina's strengths as a photographer. A Detroit transportation boss once ordered all bus company employees to take buses to work. The city editor called Spina to request a mug shot, a standard head shot of someone in the news. "How does he get to work?" Spina wondered. The next morning he and a driver stationed themselves outside the man's house. Spina began taking a series of telephoto shots, beginning with the bus boss rolling up his garage door and climbing into a Cadillac, and ending with him parking 15 feet from his office. Spina's paper ran the photos in teasing sequence from page one to page six.

Sometimes, however, journalistic imagination can run wild—too wild. The late and unlamented New York *Daily Graphic* was so lurid it was dubbed the "daily pornographic."

And in 1928 the New York *Daily News* ran what was perhaps the most grisly picture ever run in a newspaper. It was a photo of the exact moment electricity coursed through the body of Ruth Snyder at her execution for murder. Photographs were forbidden, but a resourceful, if demoniac, photographer took the picture with a camera strapped to his ankle.

Photographer Bailey distinguishes between a photojournalist and a reporter with a camera:

The photojournalist seeks to create strong story-telling pictures that are not dependent on captions for their meaning or clarification. Reporters with a camera, on the other hand, usually take record shots that could never stand alone and are totally dependent on both captions and story content for their validity.

The *Free Press's* Spina says a good photojournalist looks for these criteria in pictures:

- Subject interest
- Composition
- Lighting
- Creativity
- Visual impact

FEATURE VERSUS HARD-NEWS PHOTOS

Too many photo editors are still addicted to the hard-news syndrome. They would rather see a third-rate piece of art about an automobile accident than a first-rate feature photo.

Sometimes the photo editor says of the feature art: "That's good. I'll run it tomorrow." The good photo gets shuffled to the bottom of the pile. Tomorrow other hard-news photos come in that the editors feel they must use.

Nothing is wrong with art for art's sake. Photos of sunsets, clouds, lovers, birds, old people on benches, belong in a newspaper even if there is no hard news connected with them.

The *New York Times* once ran a photo of a ghetto youngster pulling an orange crate, pretending it was a wagon. It was not "news," but the picture was a tribute to the indomitable human spirit.

Getting great shots is sometimes luck—and photographers being alert to

ART FOR ART'S SAKE—This feature photo is a perfect illustration of the fact that every newspaper picture doesn't have to be "hard news." It ran $9\frac{1}{2}$ inches deep and $6\frac{1}{2}$ inches wide when it appeared on page one of the *Detroit News*. Photo shows a winter scene at the Ann Arbor, Michigan, municipal golf course. Photographer George Waldman took the picture at $\frac{1}{250}$ of a second with an F11 stop. *(Photo by the* Detroit News.*)*

take advantage of luck. Two photos immediately come to mind. One was the photo of Lee Harvey Oswald, alleged slayer of President Kennedy, taken at the moment Oswald was shot by Jack Ruby. The other was a photo of a South Vietnamese police chief shooting a Viet Cong suspect, the picture showing the moment the bullet struck, jarring the man's head.

PHOTO ADVICE

Be aware of the following:

- Run photos large for maximum impact.
- Crop photos effectively, again for maximum impact. Detroit photographer Bailey crops with his eye when he shoots.
- Think. Photographers are paid for "thinking around" clichés.
- Good photos tell their story without cutlines or captions.
- Experience will sharpen the shooting of photographers, but that "good eye" is innate.
- Discipline. Some assignments must be taken, as routine and dull as they may appear. Photojournalists, like reporters, are great gripers, but disciplined newspaper photographers know that that unattractive-sounding assignment must be covered, even if it is just a mug shot 40 miles away.

A Question of Taste

Photo editors and managing editors often wrestle with questions of taste. When former Vice President Nelson Rockefeller was photographed "giving the finger" to hecklers during a campaign speech in 1976, many newspapers in the country ran the photograph. As Gil Smith, executive editor of the Utica (N.Y.) *Press* and *Observer-Dispatch*, put it: "It was news . . . the photograph showed a man frustrated and we used it."

Yet some editors disagreed. Scott Hayden, managing editor of the *Buffalo Courier-Express*, said: "I don't care whether it was Rocky or a kid in the street. It was a vulgar, obscene picture and we're a family newspaper."

The *New York Times*, which has high standards of what is proper for a "family newspaper" to print, did not run the picture. Diane Bath, picture editor of The *Times*, argued:

I would not normally run a picture of that kind of a vulgarism. The fact that it was the vice president doesn't really change that and the picture was not germane to the main story, which was the opening of the GOP campaign in New York State. The picture simply was not consistent with our criteria.

Brady's Aspiration

Mathew B. Brady, America's greatest photojournalist, worked with the crudest and clumsiest equipment before and during the Civil War. Yet in a lifetime of photography he strove diligently to avoid taking "a bad picture."

SUGGESTIONS FOR INSTRUCTOR

- Assign a free choice feature story.
- Have students do these kinds of stories under deadline: a drowning, a plunge from a bridge or a building, an announcement of construction plans by a big company.

Chapter 21

Radio and Television

Radio and television suffer from delusions of adequacy.

Richard Tobin
Saturday Review

Some of the best radio and television broadcasting in the United States originates in Canada. In some places in the United States you can get more music, talk, theater, and news from the Canadian Broadcasting Corporation than you can on any single United States radio and television station.

Most United States television and radio stations do not begin to tell you enough about public affairs to provide a solid basis for informed public opinion. This is particularly grievous because the majority of Americans use television as their primary news source.

Walter Cronkite has said that his nightly newscast would fill no more than six to eight columns of the daily *New York Times*. Mike Royko, syndicated *Chicago Daily News* columnist, has written: "The actual news presented on a typical news show can be obtained by skimming any newspaper in five minutes or less."

Sketchiness. It is the bane of journalists who monitor the electronic media. Radio gives you a one-sentence report on a crisis in Greece and adds a smug reminder, "And that's the latest from Athens."

David Brinkley has admitted the problem. He once made this point about the difference between television and newspapers:

We are fast. We are instantaneous. You can't get any faster than that. You can't compete with that, so don't even try. But when it comes to covering the news in any thorough way, we aren't even in the ball game. It's physically impossible to do so on television.

Background on events, so common and so necessary to newspapering, is often missing in radio and TV reports. This kind of thing: "The latest Cyprus crisis was touched off by a disturbance in the village of Theodoros in which 24 Turkish Cypriotes were killed."

The problem is that radio and TV are commercial enterprises first, news-gathering agencies last. Newspapers, too, need to be solvent or they don't publish. But for good newspapers, the prime concern is news.

The late Chet Huntley was once asked why he had given up a lucrative job in television broadcasting. This was his reply:

I got fed up! All we ever could do was skim the surface of the news. We were just reading headlines. I'd often get embarrassed by the public attention we would get when we would travel with members of the print media.

There would be some really hard working newspaper reporters and writers with us, but we would get the attention mainly because of the medium. Some of the newspaper guys would glare at us and they'd resent our big salaries. And I think they were right. We were overpaid.

Radio and television can never cover what newspapers do in such depth: sports box scores, stock market tables, and texts of important speeches. (Most newspapers do not even provide what the *New York Times*—a paper of record— does frequently: texts of presidential press conferences, excerpts from Supreme Court decisions, and full reports from United States and presidential commissions.)

POSITIVE SIDE OF RADIO-TV

If that seems like an overly harsh view, consider the source: a print journalist with a typical bias against the electronic media.

The fact is that radio and television have some outstanding reporters. Dick Femmel, who directs the radio-TV sequence for the Wayne State University journalism department, puts it this way: "Electronic journalists have the same devotion to accuracy and truth as print journalists. They have good writing skills. They have the inquisitiveness needed by any print reporter."

He cites people like Fred Graham of CBS and Carl Stern of NBC as outstanding electronic journalists.

Femmel argues that the "street reporters are the real guts of broadcast journalism—these people are the nuts and bolts of the business." He insists that "great things are possible in radio and television."

The advantages of radio and TV are obvious. It is instantaneous. You are seeing and hearing things now. Viewers are practically participants. Radio and TV offer an extra dimension to news that newspapers cannot provide.

For instance, after the death of labor leader John L. Lewis, newspapers expended countless words on his obituary. But no newspaper could produce the chilling effect of hearing Lewis's sonorous and theatrical voice as radio and TV did.

Money   It is better in television. A top reporter on a metropolitan newspaper might make about $25,000 a year. The TV anchor person in the same town will make three times that.

Lou Prato, formerly of NBC radio in Chicago, argues that money is not better in TV. "Maybe for the big shot anchorman it's true," Prato says, "but not for the working stiffs. In fact, newspaper salaries have surpassed most TV salaries."

Despite the commercial, show-business approach, TV is always looking for good reporters. TV news, developing its own talent, does not have to raid newspapers as much as it once did. But in the early days of TV most of the top broadcasters were former print journalists—people like Eric Sevareid and Howard K. Smith.

Edward R. Murrow, the greatest broadcast journalist, put together an outstanding CBS news staff, most of them former print journalists. CBS headquarters in New York often complained that his men sounded terrible on the air. Murrow would counter: "I'm hiring reporters, not announcers."

Unfortunately, the commercial powers that be in TV are more interested in appearances and selling. Charles Kuralt, CBS on-the-road correspondent, gave a devastating talk at a convention of the Radio Television News Directors Association. After asserting without fear of contradiction that he had seen nearly every local telecast in America, Kuralt said his overwhelming impression was of hair—anchormen's hair.

"Hair carefully styled and sprayed, hair neatly parted, hair abundant and every hair in place," Kuralt said. He then said:

I don't care what the station managers say, I don't care what the outside professional news advisers say, I don't care what the ratings say, I say this is the continuing disgrace of this profession.

The plain truth is that in a society which depends for its life on an informed citizenry, and in which most citizens receive most of their information from television, millions are getting that life-giving information from a man whose colleagues wouldn't trust to report accurately on his afternoon round of golf. . . .

I *would* like to be proud of this profession we are in.

Unfortunately, I know it to be riddled with glib, highly paid poseurs who wouldn't last two weeks as $125-a-week cub reporters on the local newspaper.

I am ashamed, I think we all ought to be ashamed, that 25 years into the television age, so many of our anchormen haven't any basis on which to make a news judgment, can't edit, can't write and can't cover a story.

Radio man Prato, former television news director in Detroit, agrees with Kuralt. But he says the fault is the TV consultants who "have taken over the minds of the station owners." That annoys him. He says the Kuralt view overlooks "the hard-working, well-qualified TV reporter who keeps in there battling the windmills. There are a lot of fine ones. They're trying. But station managers have not yet allowed the inmates to take over."

DEATH OF THE SCOOP MENTALITY

Television killed the extra, the special edition newspapers put out after normal press times because a big story broke. It also forced newspapers to abandon most of their scoop mentality. The blessing of this has been that newspapers have been producing more analytical and interpretive stories about world and national events.

Television and radio stations are also doing much less rip-and-reading than they used to. Yet medium-sized and small stations, woefully understaffed, still do far too much rip-and-reading ever to attain quality broadcasting.

You can probably offer as many criticisms of television as you can of newspapers. But TV will probably never shake its worst feature—blatant commercialism.

Like newspapers, TV often lacks guts. It frequently refuses to come to grips with hard problems or approaches them in an oblique, noncontroversial way.

The ills of commerical broadcasting could be lessened if Congress were to create a fourth network equal in time, resources, and money to the three commercial networks. This public network needs to be a true alternative untainted by the labels of educational television and Public Broadcasting Corporation. Only then can the United States move toward the superior programming of Canada and Britain.

In the meantime, broadcast journalism can do something about one of its worst shortcomings—editorializing by newscasters. Print journalists are offended by such editorial tricks as these in news broadcasts: grimaces, smirks, voice inflections, rolling eyeballs, raised eyebrows.

There are leading questions, too. But probably most offensive are the corn-ball antics of telecasters who think they are more important than the news. Pain-ful jokes, small talk, and bantering among the "action news teams" are as in-furiating as they are embarrassing. The hope is that by the time you read this, TV "happy talk" will be out of vogue. Worse, newscasts that stress violence to boost ratings will probably be "in."

One other indictment: Local television stations often display monumental bad taste in covering disaster stories. "Street reporters" will thrust a microphone in front of disaster survivors and ask question like this: "How did it feel to see your whole family wiped out in the fire?" Callousness seems to be *de rigueur* in reporting for local TV newscasts.

PARALLELS TO NEWSPAPERS

In writing copy for broadcast, the major difference is that between the spoken and written word. The spoken word goes by swiftly and irretrievably for the listener. The reader can always check back.

Hence, radio-TV copy is written much simpler even than newspaper copy. It aims for the conversational approach. It uses simpler sentences and simpler words, avoiding entangling clauses that the eye may unravel but the ear cannot.

Figures are written out in broadcast copy to avoid stumbling by announcers. Names are spelled phonetically for the same reason. If Strauss is pronounced "Straws," it is written that way.

It is always painful to hear announcers mutilate pronunciations. This happens most often in the boondocks. Things like this: "Mikado" coming out "Mick-a-doo" and Johnny Unitas coming out "Uni-tas." Read broadcast copy over at least once, if not twice, before going on the air with it. You will have fewer surprises—and so will the listeners.

Many journalists who switch from newspapers to broadcasting have trouble at first. The copy they were used to writing for newspapers is unread-able over the airwaves.

- The twin skills of the print reporter—getting the facts and presenting them well—are needed by radio and television journalists.

Quote and Unquote

I'm not a newsman. I'm an entertainer.

—Walter Cronkite

Our true internal enemy is not bias, but haste—and the compression of the material required.

—Eric Sevareid

A television newsman, arriving at the base of his first overseas assignment, asked the bureau manager: "What kind of stories should I be looking for?"

Without hesitation his superior replied: "I'd say, about a minute-10, a minute-20."

The anecdote may be apocryphal, but television's foreign correspondents relish it because it goes to the heart of their frustrations with the news priorities in their medium.

—Les Brown of the *New York Times*

Chapter 22

Public Relations and Advertising

Some journalists think that going into public relations (PR) is selling out. It isn't. Public relations is an honest job if you believe in the firm or institution, if you believe in a company's products and/or services, if you believe in an institution's causes.

There is nothing unethical about it. The fact is that many newspaper people go into PR. The biggest reason is that the money is better.

But until you switch camps, journalists need a warning. As reporters you represent the newspaper and the public. The PR counselor represents the company or institution. The difference in viewpoint is tremendous.

The people who bring you Dodge once put out a PR handbook entitled, "Public Relations and Your Dodge Dealership." Among the points it made were these:

- Make friends with newspaper editor or reporter.
- If journalists come in for a car, make it a point to give them "a really good deal," to give them preferential treatment.
- Whenever you schedule an event involving food, provide places for the press. "Treat them as guests. It will pay dividends in your story."

Caveat emptor.

Public relations departments have two functions: cultivating a good public image for the company, institution, or government and serving as an information center.

A PR firm's information function is important to journalists. It provides copy and photographs. It arranges press conferences. Reporters need PR departments to get information when something newsworthy happens.

One former UPI reporter, whenever he came to Detroit to do a story on the auto industry, had a regular source in the Ford Motor Company public relations department. A fifteen-minute talk with him—off-the-record but on the level—helped him immensely.

In an article in *Editor & Publisher*, entitled "Let's Not Denigrate Publicists,"* the president of a New York public relations firm made the point:

In my more than six years as head of a PR counseling firm, there have been countless times when editors called us for information, for opinions and for last-minute requests for copy or photos . . . .

Thus, the relationship between publicist and editor is really a two-way street. . . . Each needs the other in order to do his job as well as possible . . . .

Public relations practitioners know that their material must be well conceived, crisply written and appropriately directed if it is going to be published. If they don't know this, they simply won't be able to earn their living in the public relations field very long.

NEWSPAPER TRAINING VALUABLE

Newspaper training is a valuable springboard for PR work. One former reporter, now working in PR, said she was grateful for her newspaper background. She said it gave her an edge on colleagues who never worked for newspapers.

More and more, too, electronic journalists are going into public relations.

As Allen Phillips, former Michigan Gas Company publicist, puts it: "Employers are conscious of the impact of radio and TV—which newspaper-oriented people lack depth in—and so larger outfits are hiring people who know how to cut a radio tape or set up a presentation for the benefit of the cameras."

The reporting and writing skills of reporters are essential in PR. No wonder PR firms are heavily stocked at the top with ex-journalists.

"Where handouts are concerned, the news-oriented PR person tries to put it in the same language as he would hope to see the story written," Phillips says. "Consequently, he will cast the handout in those terms."

But then he says something that should alert journalists. "When it's bad news, but you are under some obligation to put it out, you get terse, leave

*Nov. 16, 1968, p. 94.

things out or obfuscate," Phillips says. "Again, a news-trained PR person knows well how to do this, to get around the inquiring reporter."

That is precisely what can be so disillusioning about public relations, particularly in politics.

One Wayne State University student expressed incredulity, chagrin, and a determination to stay away from public relations after an internship with county government public relations: "I saw how double-talk, hiding facts and other quasi-ethical practices are designed to give constituents a misrepresentation of what their elected officials are accomplishing."

Reporters switching to public relations work can also be annoyed by the seemingly endless clearances that releases must go through. Releases are sometimes edited by so many people in the chain of command that they often are unrecognizable to the writer by the time they are okayed.

REFUSAL TO COOPERATE

One of the most frustrating problems journalists face in dealing with public relations people is refusal by a company to cooperate. Companies have tons of handouts about good news, but they fall silent when reporters want details about bad news.

Sometimes reporters get a no-comment from officials. Other officials are afraid to talk. Sometimes the company takes three days to put out a carefully worded statement that has to go through eight vice presidents for approval, each of whom will insist on making changes.

The best policy for PR people is to be candid with journalists. It is best to level with the press. PR people should cooperate with reporters as much as possible short of giving them the combination to the safe.

Pulsebeat, a McGraw-Hill internal publication, stressed this point in an article by Charles Obertance:

If the subject is sensitive (and if the reporter *came to you*, it may well be), *don't* try to suppress the story by refusing to cooperate. As a matter of pride, most reporters will then work day and night to get the story—if necessary over your dead body.

The published story is sure to upset you, for the reporter's sources will not have had all the information available to you and there are bound to be inaccuracies . . . .

Some years ago an explosion at a southeastern chemical plant killed nearly a dozen employees and injured more than 100 others. Company officials closed the plant, instructing employees not to speak with reporters pending an official investigation.

One enterprising newsman, however, bypassed police guards at the city hospital and talked with injured employees, putting together a detailed story which was prominently displayed on his paper's front page.

For three consecutive days, the reporter managed to round up enough information to keep his story on page one.

Each story pointedly said the company was withholding comment pending outcome of an investigation. About the time public interest in the story had waned, the company's version was released, pretty much confirming what the reporter had dug out of employees. It duly appeared—on page 48 of the classified section.

LEAVING NEWSPAPERS

Aside from the fact that money is better in public relations, reporters have other reasons for leaving newspapers. Often it is disgust with newspapers for lack of courage in printing news, for sacred cows and policy stories, for protecting advertisers at the expense of honesty. Sometimes reporters get sick of shortsighted editors, a general narrowness in attitude-of-mind.

Whatever the reason for leaving newspapers, reporters entering PR have a problem in point of view brought about by reversing roles. It cannot be overstressed. Richard Tobin sketched the problem in an article in *Saturday Review*:

As a public relations man he will do the courting and the news sources that have been inviting him to parties and to lunch will dry up completely and instantly. Instead of writing about events he will be creating them and then issuing press releases trying to gloss them over.

He will become a doer as contrasted to an observer, a man on the playing field rather than the press box. He will have to pretend that certain things are news and he knows in his heart they are only ersatz.

His former associates will question his motives and ridicule his pose and his prose. The projects he is involved with and highly paid to promote will usually be un-exciting by comparison to the news stories he has covered.

The dull conventions he has to sit through and try to make sound important will bore him to the fingertips but he must never show his boredom in any way. Worst of all, he will have to live with himself.

The basic torment, however, may be the simple act of changing a habit of fairness and objectivity into a life of partisan persuasion.

SOME DOS AND DON'TS FOR PR PEOPLE

If you are aware of the following, you will spare yourself a number of headaches:

- Never go over a reporter's head, hoping to balk publication by persuading the reporter's superiors to cancel or alter a story.
- Know what's going on. Reporters have contempt for PR people ignorant of company affairs and policies.

- Don't sell journalists bilge. Most publicists respect most the reporters who don't swallow the company line.
- PR people have contempt for journalists begging for the use of the car, tickets, and other freebies—so don't "beg" to get a news story printed. (One PR man insists his standards are as high or higher than those of the sources he deals with.)
- You must believe in your product. So you cannot undermine your effectiveness by saying with a wink, "This is the company line, but in truth. . . ."
- Mail releases with plenty of lead time. The mails are often slow. Sometimes papers get releases as late as the day of the event—far too late for publication.

HOUSE ORGANS

Allied to public relations is the vast field of industrial editing, putting out company and trade publications. No one has an exact number, but the *Wall Street Journal* a few years ago counted "45 insurance journals, 50 grocery publications, 57 covering metalworking, 62 in the brewing industry and a staggering 228 medical journals."

The quality ranges from slick, four-color magazines to mimeographed sheets. It ranges from IBM's *Think*—a high-grade magazine of general interest more than a publication to boost the company—to the unprofessional internal organs publishing notices of weddings, bowling scores, promotions, and new employees.

The point is that all these myriad publications need editors. For such jobs, it is good if a student develops competence in reporting and editing, knowing particularly the principles of good art and good layout.

MADISON AVENUE

"It is essential in the first instance to make good merchandise," Calvin Coolidge once wrote. "But that is not enough. It is just as essential to create a desire for it. That is advertising."

Intellectually, that is the problem with advertising. It creates a desire for something that may not be needed. Advertising is mass swaying of public opinion, preying on public gullibility. It is often a commercial obscenity—"anything to make a buck."

Be that as it may, advertising is supplying art and copy to newspapers and magazines, or film and scripts to radio and TV stations. The purpose is to get the product message to the consumer. In the battle for markets, advertising is an essential weapon to increase sales and profits.

Advertising requires imagination with art and copy. The cleverness is obvious, Volkswagen ads being one of many outstanding examples.

Adroitness with gimmicks helps, too. The emphasis in commercials today, fortunately, is on humor and soft sell rather than the old hard-sell hucksterism.

In short, advertising is an art as well as a business. It puts a premium on creativity and imagination. Salaries are high—but so are exacerbated ulcers.

Once again, the reporter's skill should stand you in good stead if you switch to advertising.

Eleven Commandments for Business PR People

- Send your press contacts all annual and interim reports to keep them informed.
- Alert the press to new products and developments.
- Don't blame the reporter if your story is chopped or garbled. Things like that happen in newspapering.
- Observe your contact's deadlines.
- Don't ask for get-acquainted interviews. Interviews must have a news-story point.
- Never stand up a press contact.
- Don't keep reporters waiting. They are just as busy as your bosses.
- If you don't get the play you hoped for, remember tomorrow is another day—with another story.
- Don't front for your executives. Your purpose is not to shield them but to help the press get information.
- Don't patronize reporters. Most of them can't be bought or flattered.
- If a publication wants to write a story about your company, it will—with or without your cooperation.

—Adapted from *Marketing* magazine

"So Much Money"

And because advertisers can spend so much—so much talent, so much money, so much time—on every detail of every second, they can create a market by literally buying their way into our minds.

—Jeff Greenfield writing about TV commercials
in the *Columbia Journalism Review.*

"Secrets of Success"

The secrets of success as an editor were easily learned; the highest was that of getting advertisements. Ten pages of advertising made an editor a success; five marked him as a failure.

—*The Education of Henry Adams*

Chapter 23

Ethics and Taste

I wished my wife to be not so much as suspected.

Julius Caesar from Plutarch's *Lives*

Journalism deals with questions of ethics daily. Many precepts all journalists agree on. Others are matters of opinion, fueling much debate at journalists' conventions.

Few would argue with tenets of good newspapering: accuracy, fairness, and objective intent.

Reporters should be absolutely scrupulous about getting facts no matter whose ox is gored. Fairness: If Ralph Nader issues a blast against General Motors, get the GM reply. Objective intent: an unswerving effort to be fair and unbiased.

Responsible journalism is another important tenet, although journalists will argue about what is responsible and what is irresponsible. Responsible journalism, for one thing, is not printing rumor, hearsay, and gossip. It is not printing stories on the basis of one phone call. Check things out. Go to the source. Seek confirmation.

If objective intent is lacking, your journalism will be slanted. A story can be slanted by what is left in—and what is left out. Sometimes the slanting is subtle, but it is there. Sometimes it is unintentional, but it is still slanted.

Here is a lead from a campus newspaper: "The Inter-Fraternity Council and Pan-Hel face eviction from their offices for being irrelevant student organizations." Irrelevant to whom? That is editorializing as it stands. Attribution will save the lead angle. It would be better to write the above this way: "The Inter-Fraternity Council and Pan-Hel face eviction from their offices for being what the Student Council president called irrelevant student organizations."

A metropolitan newspaper printed this lead: "Despite Detroit's bleak financial outlook, Mayor Gribbs has hired a newcomer to his personal staff to act as special assistant to the mayor." The introductory phrase is loaded. If the editorial writers want to criticize the appointment, let them. It is not the reporter's job.

Reporters cannot write that "Jones is well qualified for his new job as school superintendent." That is editorializing. But you can make the same point by citing Jones's record, credentials, and background. You can quote school board members.

Sometimes phrasing is incautious, leading to subtle editorializing: "The Smith car crashed into the Jones car." That puts the onus on Smith. Write it neutrally with attribution: "The Smith car crashed into the Jones car, police said." Or you can phrase it so as not to blame anyone, such as this way: "The Smith car and the Jones car collided."

"Police saids" are invaluable when laying blame. You should not try a case in the newspaper. "Police saids," while no protection against a libel suit, show that you had no malicious intent. You got the information from the police.

Here is one more example of subtle editorializing that even metropolitan newspapers are often guilty of: "The chairman of the Democratic Party criticized the governor for playing politics in the racial situation in Flint." Maybe the governor did play politics—and maybe he didn't. Let the editorial writers decide. As a reporter, you should write that the chairman "*accused* the governor of playing politics."

Students often make the same kind of mistake. They write: "She warned the drug industry it risked harsher federal laws if it continued its irresponsible practices." It should be "*what she called*" irresponsible practices.

LOADED WORDS

Watch your adjectives. They can be slanted. "Brilliant." "Stupid." "Beautiful." Reporters use such words with care. Many a reporter has written that some woman was beautiful only to have an accompanying picture belie that adjective.

Do not write that insurance companies "stridently oppose the bill." A fairer word is "vehemently."

Time magazine in the heyday of Henry Luce refined slanted journalism into a reprehensible art. The Republican Eisenhower was a hero to *Time*, so he strode briskly through its pages. The Democratic Truman was a bum so he slouched pitifully through its pages.

Be careful with words and phrases that are pejorative. In the late 1960s it was fashionable to sneer in print at hippies as "long-haired demonstrators."

The *New York Times* once wrote: "The man on trial is a flabby, hard-eyed member of the Ku Klux Klan." As *Winners & Sinners*, the *Times* in-house critique sheet, noted, "It is easy to imagine a Klan publication describing him as heavy-set and keen-eyed."

Look at how you can use words to slant your story:

Fair	Unfair
Labor organizer	Labor agitator
Government subsidy	Government handout
Labor leader	Labor czar

Choose words with care. When in doubt, look them up. Make sure the word you want is the precise one. Make sure the word you use is not slanted in its connotation.

FOUR-LETTER WORDS

Newspapers have gotten much more sensible about swear words in recent years. Years ago the family newspaper concept frustrated reporters. A reporter would write "stink bomb" and it would come out "stench bomb." On some papers you could not write "rape." (On some papers you still cannot.) You had to use the euphemism "criminal assault."

H. L. Mencken once ridiculed the evasion, citing a newspaper report that a man struck a woman, "dragged her down the cellar-steps, beat her with an iron pipe and then assaulted her."

The latest newspaper trick is using the bleep technique just as TV bleeps obscenities: " 'It's a bleeping rule,' Houk said." That is silly, too. Since Houk did not say it that way, the quotation is absurd and inaccurate. Recast such quotes or paraphrase the idea.

If obscenities are necessary to the full meaning of the story, use them.

The suggestion is not that newspapers become free and loose. Nor is the suggestion that newspapers shock or titillate readers as some sophomoric writers of the underground press once thought they had to do to "shock the bourgeoisie." Rather, newspapers should use obscenities that are essential for the full meaning and impact of a story.

When the word "shit" turned up in the Nixon tapes, some papers rightly printed it. The *Detroit Free Press* boldly put it on page one. Yet only 30 percent of the newspapers checked by AP printed the undeleted expletive.

"FAMILY NEWSPAPERS"—This Larry Wright cartoon drawn for the *Detroit News* deals with "the family newspaper concept" in newspapers, although Wright doesn't use the phrase. Reprinted by permission of Newspaper Enterprise Association. *(Cartoon by Larry Wright for Newspaper Enterprise Association and the* Detroit News.*)*

Significantly, an AP survey indicated no public outcry over printing the words in full—showing once again that the public is far ahead of newspaper editorial judgments on so many matters.

During the 1972 Presidential campaign, candidate George McGovern was quoted as saying, "kiss my ass." A spot check by UPI of 33 papers, mostly in metropolitan areas, showed that 16 papers used the full quote and 17 used dashes.

The point once again: The Victorian era is long past. If words such as "shit" and "ass" are essential to the story and said by important people in newsworthy contexts, they should be used.

Still, it is a matter that will be out of your hands as reporters. You may argue the case, but decisions will be made by higher-ups.

Such a decision caused an editor of the *Dayton* (Ohio) *Journal Herald* to resign. His publishers refused to support his judgment in printing the word "fucking" in a story about the slaying of a Treasury agent. The editor, Charles Alexander, explained his decision:

We reported the story of a savage argument in which the obscene word was directly crucial to the outcome, a fatal fight. My first impulse was to take it out and that was a healthy impulse. But if I pulled it there would have been nothing left, because they were the last words of a man drawing his gun to kill a fellow agent and a long-time friend.

Alexander was right and should have been supported—a judgment that many newspaper editors will disagree with. Anyway, your paper will have a policy on four-letter words. Whatever your personal feelings, you will have to follow that policy.

Most American newspapers drew a line indicating their outer limits in the Earl Butz episode of 1976. Butz, former Secretary of Agriculture, uttered a racist joke. He said of blacks: "I'll tell you what coloreds want. It's three things. First, a tight pussy; second, loose shoes; and third, a warm place to shit."

The quote obviously troubled even newspapers that have jettisoned the label "family newspaper."

Some papers resorted to euphemisms. The *New York Times* first paraphrased the remark this way: ".. The things were listed, in order, in obscene, derogatory and scatological terms." By the third day of the story the *Times* described the quote as "... satisfying sex, loose shoes and a warm place for bodily functions."

The *San Francisco Examiner* used a fill-in-the-blanks technique: "first, a tight p_____, second, loose shoes, and third, a warm place to s___."

Only two newspapers in America published the quote verbatim: the *Madison* (Wisconsin) *Capital Times* and the *Toledo* (Ohio) *Blade*.

Bill Day, assistant managing editor of the *Blade*, said his paper originally withheld the quote, but finally published it because "the remark led to Mr. Butz's resignation" and may have affected the "outcome of the election and therefore the future of the country."

The surprising thing was, Day said, that the paper got only eight phone calls after printing the quote, six protesting and two approving.

Day made the right decision. Certainly printing the exact quote was no worse than those newspapers that completely baffled readers on the first day of the story by not even hinting at Butz's racist remarks.

JUNKETS, GIFTS, AND FREEBIES

Once upon a time reporters who came to Detroit to do a story on the auto industry were provided with a Cadillac—or some other auto company car—gratis during their stay. The fairy tale came to an end with most newspapers adopting tougher ethical codes.

The free use of the car probably had no influence on the reporter's story. Most journalists kept their integrity whatever freebies were available.

But it is good that the newspaper freebie business—a traditional newspaper way of life—is ending. Reporters used to argue that they were not paid enough so free tickets to a ball game or the movies helped to equalize their salaries. But that rationale does not hold up to the Caesar's wife principle: Journalists should be above suspicion. Their standard is one set by Supreme Court Justice Louis Brandeis who once turned down an honorary degree because that college might come before him in litigation.

That is a high standard—some will say too high. But no standard is too high for newspapers aspiring to professionalism.

Carol Sutton, assistant to the publisher and editor of the *Louisville Courier-Journal* and *Louisville Times*, has said that her staffers must even buy tickets to movies and plays which the paper reviews.

That is carrying the Caesar's wife principle too far. No critics worth their

NOT FIT TO PRINT?—When former Vice President Nelson Rockefeller was photographed giving a campaign-trail heckler "the finger," it caused tremors in news rooms. To print or not to print? Many editors, feeling the photo was newsworthy, printed it. But the stuffy *New York Times* deemed it unfit to print. Cartoonist Larry Wright of the *Detroit News* used the incident as an outlet for his wit. *(Cartoon by Larry Wright of the Detroit News.)*

pay have ever written a favorable review or muted their critical guns because they got free passes to a performance.

Newspapers should keep a proper perspective even on ethical questions. It is perfectly proper for newspaper critics to accept free admissions.

Jay Carr, George Jean Nathan award-winning drama critic for the *Detroit News*, has never refrained from panning a play just because he saw it for nothing. (Indeed, newspaper critics are such long-suffering souls they should be *paid extra* to cover some performances.)

Many newspapers have adopted an outright ban on accepting gifts, junkets, and any form of a freebie.

The *Detroit News's* policy statement on ethics forbids staffers to accept passes and free tickets to sports events, movies, and theaters. *News* staffers may accept only gifts of "insignificant value—calendars, pencils and key chains." They may not accept discounts at stores or from auto dealers.

As for travel, the *News* "will pay all costs involved in travel for news coverage or background information for staff members on assignment.... Junkets, free trips and reduced rate or subsidized travel may not be accepted."

Finally, the *News* policy directs staff members to "avoid involvement in public affairs and outside activities that could create a conflict of interest, or the appearance of one."

The last point provokes a lot of trade publication questions about what is a conflict of interest. But the principle is sound.

SUSPICION OF AWARDS

Newspapers ought to be suspicious of awards to its reporters. If a reporter gets an award from an insurance association, shouldn't you wonder whether his copy represented the public point of view—or the insurance industry's?

A *Newsday* reporter rightly turned down a $500 prize from the New York Medical Society for stories "making a significant contribution to public health and medicine."

In short, editors should be suspicious when any interest group wants to hand out an award.

MORAL DILEMMA

One of the toughest moral dilemmas reporters face is lying to get news.

The era when reporters burglarized apartments to get photographs belongs to shady journalism history. But plenty of tough police reporters have gotten information from cops by posing as one of their superiors.

Many reporters have used deceit, misrepresenting themselves, to get news. The *Atlanta Journal* once fired a reporter after he lied to get a news story.

"Each reporter must decide for himself whether the importance of the facts he is after justifies the compromises he must make to get at them," *Newsweek* once wrote. "But there are moral as well as practical limits. In the long run, journalism cannot be based on habitual deceit—if only because a reporter who practices it would lose both his credibility and his sources."

The best advice is not to lie. But that is not always the best prescription for good reporting.

INFILTRATION REPORTING

Infiltration reporting is a form of deceit but easier to defend than lying. Infiltration reporters join a group or organization to get an inside view of the operation—say, the Ku Klux Klan or a commune. Reporters have feigned insanity to get an inside view of an insane asylum.

Such stories usually produce legitimate exposé stories that often bring about public reform. Some reporters believe in going to any length to get a story, including swiping documents from officials' desks. When George Romney was governor of Michigan, he used to turn over all papers on his desk when reporters approached. He was protecting his papers from the thieving eyes of reporters.

RELEASE DATES

Release dates should be observed. Most papers feel, however, that they are free to break a release date if they get the information from another source.

If release dates—or embargoes—are broken, papers no longer feel bound by the decision.

Clifton Daniels, former head of the *New York Times* Washington Bureau, put it this way: "We feel that a release date is a contract between the giver of news and the receiver. We are grateful for having news in advance, particularly when long documents and major issues are involved, and we don't want to jeopardize such arrangements by premature disclosure."

That is responsible journalism.

NEWS UNFIT TO PRINT

Newspapers do not print all the news and photos they get. Editors use taste and discrimination, although this poses a question of whose taste and judgment.

Some photos are too gory to print. The names of rape victims are withheld. The names of juvenile offenders are usually not used.

Editors always ask if the public needs to know about something. Perhaps information would titillate the public. But does it really have to be published?

During a campaign for a United States Senate seat in Michigan, the *Detroit News* printed a story about an office affair one of the candidates had while a Congressman. The affair had taken place seven years earlier. The woman was an unpaid volunteer on the Congressman's staff. She was not on the public payroll. The Congressman had permitted tape recordings of their "love talk."

Was the story relevant? Should *The News* have printed it?

Martin Haydon, editor of the *Detroit News* at the time, argued that the public ought to be informed about every facet of the candidate's life so it could judge his qualifications for the Senate.

- Question: If you were editor of the newspaper, would you have printed the story?

Stanley Walker's Commandments for Reporters

Stanley Walker, city editor of the New York *Herald-Tribune*, wrote *City Editor* * in 1934. Some of his injunctions are still worth pondering:

- Observe the laws of good taste, something which is impossible of exact definition, but which most gentlemen and ladies know by instinct.
- Be fair. . . . Every effort should be made to get the other side of the story, to avoid distortion and injustice.
- The lead . . . should be clear, provocative and so simple that anyone can understand it.
- Most news accounts are improved by quotes. Speech should be quoted exactly as spoken.
- Because a story is important, it doesn't follow that it must be long.
- Sentences and paragraphs should be short.

*Frederick A. Stokes Company, New York, 1934.

• Pick adjectives as you would a diamond or a mistress. Too many are dangerous. Because one adjective is as revealing as a lightning flash, don't think that 10 will make the story 10 times as good.

• Go to the source on every assignment. . . . Use your legs, or go to the telephone. . . . Most so-called big men are as approachable as any peasant.

• Don't be afraid to write facts on the mistaken assumption that "everybody knows that."

Part Two

Advanced Reporting

Chapter 24

Press Conferences

Covering press conferences is much like covering speeches. The press-conference format is different, but the technique of reporting and writing it is about the same.

News-story leads should stress the main item or items that come out of the press conference. Those points can be developed before reporting other important aspects of the press conference.

For most papers, one reporter will handle the complete press conference. Big papers like the *New York Times* may cover a presidential press conference with five or six reporters. The *Times* may publish five or six stories, each reporter assigned to one aspect of the news coming out of the conference. One reporter may cover tax aspects, another writes about the economy, a third handles Congressional matters, and other reporters pick up the remaining major aspects.

Sometimes if you are working for a wire service or for a newspaper that only wants one story on the press conference, you can use the bullet technique to summarize key points.

The bullet technique is used on many kinds of stories, but it is particularly effective in press-conference stories. It is this kind of thing:

Ford also said:
- He opposed young people's smoking of marijuana.
- He had "great sympathy for the people of New York," but probably would not sign a bill to rescue the city from financial troubles.
- He favored military and economic aid to the anti-Soviet faction in the Angolan civil war.

Indent bullet paragraphs as you would any other paragraph. Put periods at the end of the paragraphs, not semicolons. Do not hold back or indent second or third lines of bullet matter. Treat bullet matter like any other paragraph.

Make sure bullet-precede paragraphs agree in tense and number with the bullet item. Make sure you have parallel construction. Don't switch tenses, writing in one bullet paragraph that "Carter says" and in the next "Carter declared."

You cannot drop names and references to situations and events into a story without giving the fill-in and background. If you refer to Cyrus Vance you must identify him as Secretary of State. If you mention a Mideast crisis, you must tell what you are referring to.

- Advice on note-taking. In covering speeches, press conferences, and meetings, it is a good idea to use side-slashes or stars on your notes to indicate major items.

Some reporters use some system such as this: one star for an important item, two stars for a very important item, and three stars for a possible lead angle. Such a system makes it much easier to pick out important points and quotes from your welter of notes.

PROBLEMS OF PRESS CONFERENCES

You can probably make a good case for abolishing press conferences by public officials. Edwin Newman in *Strictly Speaking* says: "The presidential news conference is vastly overrated, anyway. This may be heresy . . . but it would hardly matter if it weren't held at all."*

It is an arguable case. In press conferences by federal, state, and city officials, the press spars with chief executives—but rarely wins.

Press conferences are stacked in favor of executives. Executives answer only the questions they want to. They can resort to circumlocution. They can

*Edwin Newman, *Strictly Speaking*, The Bobbs-Merrill Company, Inc., Indianapolis, 1974.

filibuster. They can shut off questioning with a no-comment. The witty ones can answer with a quip—a case of style but no substance.

Presidential press conferences suffer from unwieldiness. With more than 350 reporters clamoring for attention, they are anarchic and undignified. They also suffer from topic-hopping, although that situation has improved in presidential press conferences now that reporters can ask a follow-up question. Even so, what often happens is that a question about foreign policy is followed by something like this, "Mr. President, will you attend the football game tomorrow?"

George McGovern, as a Presidential candidate in 1972, promised to hold one-topic press conferences to allow deeper questioning on and exploration of subjects of national interest. He never got a chance to fulfill that promise.

Presidential press conferences pose other problems. Soft questions are one. Excessive deference to the executive, a politeness almost to the point of awe for "his majesty," is another. Grandstanding and showboating are problems of the TV age. Some reporters love to bask in the klieg-light glory, enabling their editors back home to see them.

Reporters at press conferences are guilty sometimes of asking a question in the form of an opinion. The late Bill Lawrence of ABC news said he wouldn't blame a President if he asked "a long-winded questioner whether he wanted an answer to his *opinion* or his *question.*"

A moderator of a panel session in New York, exasperated by a five-minute question, asked wearily, "Would you please creep up on your question mark?"

It is sometimes necessary to preface a question, but reporters should ask questions pointedly and tersely.

PRESS SECRETARY'S ROLE

The press secretary is essentially a transmission belt. The executive makes policy, the press secretary announces it. As George Reedy, former press secretary to President Johnson, has said, the President has no press problems—just political ones.

At city and state levels, press secretaries can have more influence, writing speeches and perhaps even suggesting policies that the boss implements.

Still, presidential press secretaries can be useful. Patrick Anderson in *The Presidents' Men* tells of the time President Truman raged because two railroad unions had rejected his demands to call off a nationwide strike. Truman dashed off a speech denouncing the labor leaders as "liars and Communists" and ending with a plea "to hang a few traitors."

Truman handed the speech to press secretary Charlie Ross to have typed. But a horrified Ross bluntly told Truman the speech wouldn't do—it was too shrill. Another aide rewrote the speech, the tone and content winning wide approval, Anderson relates.

Word-Spinning Versus Facts

Notice the difference between a writer who merely spins words and one who is not too lazy to look up facts to make his case more compelling:

"Bob Gibson may end up with the best earned-run average in the history of the game. It's a big occasion when anyone scores against Gibson. And Bob is a tremendous competitor who gets tougher in the important games."

—Toledo (Ohio) Blade sports columnist

"Bob Gibson has won 21 ball games this year compared with 25 victories for Juan Marichal and 29 for Denny McLain, yet anybody who wanted to argue that the glowering overlord of the Cardinals' corps was the best pitcher in the business could find plenty of support in his record.

"Gibson's 1-0 victory over the Reds in 10 innings Labor Day was his 12th shutout of the season and his 24th complete game in 29 starts. More significantly, the 10 scoreless innings shaved his earned-run average to 0.99 per nine innings."

—New York Times sports columnist Red Smith

SUGGESTION FOR INSTRUCTOR

• Hold a mock presidential, gubernatorial, or mayoral press conference. Have students question you as if you were President, governor, or mayor. Perhaps you can open with a prepared statement. Allow about twenty-five minutes for statement and student questioning. Then have them write the story under a deadline of twenty-five mintues.

Chapter 25

New Leads, Inserts, and Add-alls

New-leading is a reporter's way of updating a story without rewriting the whole. It is a way of reporting the latest angle on a space shot, court trial, or earthquake without rewriting everything.

New leads are used regularly by multiedition dailies. One-edition dailies rarely use them and weeklies almost never.

While the first paragraph of a news story is called a "lead," journalists also call the whole story a "lead." For example, the reporter will file a lead on a space shot. Then throughout the day he or she will file new leads—fresh tops on an old story.

Here is a typical edition sequence:

1st edition—apollo (lead)
2d edition—1st lead apollo
3d edition—2d lead apollo
4th edition—3d lead apollo

Sometimes reporters write as many as six or seven new leads a day. In some newspaper offices, editors use the term "new lead" for each story rather than saying first lead, second lead, etc.

New-leading is like writing a second-day lead except you do it all on the same day, often several times. You are updating a story with the latest angle without the necessity of rewriting everything.

Suppose you file this lead for a wire service:

FLEMINGTON, N.J.–(AP)–More than 100 state troopers moved cautiously through dense woods today in search of an armed fugitive who is wanted for murder and kidnaping.

Their quarry is Warren Lee Irwin, 26, of Muskegon, Mich., a former convict who is accused of abducting a 17-year-old girl in Washington, D.C., after fleeing from police who sought to question him about the murder of a service station operator in Muskegon.

The story goes on for six or seven more paragraphs. Then you get a new development and want to update the story. So you write a new lead:

1st lead/search

FLEMINGTON, N.J.–(AP)–Fifty FBI agents joined 100 state troopers as they moved through dense woods today in search of an armed fugitive who is wanted for murder and kidnaping.

(Pik up 2d graf: Their quarry xxx).

Thus, the story can be updated all day without rewriting everything.

Sometimes reporters write a new lead that is a "write-through." This is a new lead that subs entirely for a previous story. Reporters end such a story with this: "No Pickup." Editors kill the earlier story. UPI signs off write-throughs this way: "includes previous."

Write-throughs mean so much new information is available that the earlier story is useless. For example, on big trials, metropolitan afternoon papers often go to press with a "holding story" or a "dummy lead" for the first edition. Once the trial opens, the holding story is subbed with a new lead.

BRIDGE PARAGRAPHS

Pickups from the new lead to the earlier story must be smooth. You need an easy transition. Often it is no problem, the pickup going smoothly without the need for a bridge paragraph.

However, sometimes you need a *bridge graph* to incorporate earlier information yet have the story read as smoothly as if it had been originally written as one story.

A wire service filed this lead:

DETROIT—(UPI)—Harold J. Schachern, religion editor of the Detroit News for 13 years, died today a few hours after he returned from covering the elevation of Archbishop John Dearden to cardinal in Rome.

The story continued for five or six paragraphs. Later the wire service might have moved a two-paragraph new lead. The second paragraph is a bridge graph, incorporating information of the lead in the first story:

DETROIT—(UPI)—Services for Harold J. Schachern, religion editor for the Detroit News for 13 years, will be at 11 A.M. tomorrow in St. Paul's Cathedral.
Schachern died yesterday after returning from Rome where he covered the elevation of John Dearden from archbishop to cardinal.

If you are dictating the story and do not know where you want the pickup, just end the new lead with "PICKUP" and let the copy desk handle it. If you have a carbon of an earlier story, you can indicate where you want the pickup. Thus: (Pik up 5th graf: Carter said xxx).

AFTERTHOUGHT COPY

An *insert* is a paragraph or paragraphs inserted into a story to expand it or update it. An insert is a way to make changes in a story without rewriting it.

Sometimes inserts are based on information received after the deadline but not worth a new lead. Sometimes an insert contains a rebuttal to a charge not available for the previous edition.

Often inserts are afterthought copy, a way of getting more important aspects—that you initially overlooked or forgot—higher in a story.

Inserts are slugged in sequence: insert A/slay, insert B/slay, insert C/slay.

With video display terminals, inserts can simply be inserted into a story where desired before it is released to the computer. If the story has already been sent to the computer, reporters write the insert and mark it for insert in the original story.

If you are still using paper for copy, remember these things about inserts: each insert goes on a separate take or book. Each insert must be a complete paragraph. You cannot insert a fragment.

With paper copy, slug it like this: insert A/fire. Then end it—not with the double-dagger (#)—but with this: End insert A.

Inserts are usually one or two paragraphs. Sometimes you have a lengthy insert of six to eight paragraphs. If you have a long insert, slug it: Insert A/fire, write "MORE" at the end of the first take, and start the next take with: 1st add/insert A/fire.

MARKING INSERTS

If you still have the copy, mark inserts on the margin this way:

The vote was 8-1

Insert A

The opinion cited pervasive coverage by the media.

If you are dictating a story or if you have no carbon and you do not know where you want the insert, let the desk handle it. If you have carbons or dupes and know where you want it, slug it this way:

Insert A/fire
(To folo 3d graf: Chief Jones saidxxx).

This means that the insert goes after the third paragraph, beginning, "Chief Jones said." Some papers key on the word ending a paragraph, like this:

Insert A/drug
(To folo 4th graf: xxx he said).

In this case the insert goes after the fourth paragraph, ending in "he said."

Sometimes you have an insert on material that came from another city. That material should be inserted with parentheses. For instance, suppose your story, datelined Washington, is about a speech given to the Pharmaceutical Manufacturers Association. However, your insert material comes from New York. Handle it this way:

Insert A/drug
(Stanley R. Carruthers, executive secretary of the PMA, denounced Ley's remarks as an "unwarranted attack on the drug industry."

"Drug firms do care about human lives," Carruthers said in a telephone interview from his New York office. "Drug firms are responsible.")

Technology in many newspapers is rendering insert methods obsolete. But you should learn the old way. You may need to know it someplace, sometime.

SUBSTITUTE PARAGRAPHS

Suppose you write a speech story before the speech is delivered, throwing in a disclaimer phrase: "Kennedy, in a speech prepared for delivery."

After you hear the speech, you decide it is not worth a new lead. But you want to update that disclaimer paragraph. So you write it this way:

Insert A/kennedy
(Sub for 3d graf: Kennedy, in a speech xxx).

Make sure inserts read smoothly fore and aft. This is easy if you have the carbon in front of you. It can be tougher when dictating. Then you may not know where you want the insert.

ADD-ALL OR END-ALL

An *add-all* is a way to tack paragraphs on to the end of the story. It is additional information, often written after the deadline for an edition just passed but something you want for the next edition.

The add-all—perhaps more quote—is not important enough to insert higher up in the story. Add-alls go on separate takes. Slug them this way: Add all/fire. End it with the double-dagger (#).

If you have a long add-all, write MORE at the end of the first take and write "1st add/add-all/firo" on the next take.

Orphan Quotes

Fragmentary or *orphan quotes* are unnecessary partial quotes. Here are some: Smith said he was "greatly concerned" about the CIA. Any special reason for the quotes? Any need for them? Don't use them.

Ditto for this: Police said Jones was "despondent."

Partial quotes are needed in some special senses: The "dead" came back to life. They are also needed for attribution in such senses as this: Hanoi said the "puppet" government of the United States in Saigon was to blame.

Partial quotes are also perfectly proper in sentences such as this: The gunman said "heads will be chopped off and thrown out the window" if his demands were not met.

SUGGESTIONS FOR INSTRUCTOR

- Give students the text of a speech. Have them write a story. Then, after they have written the story, have them write two or three inserts and an add-all.
- Give students an assignment requiring them to write a story needing a new lead. Have them write the first story and then write a new lead, handing in both versions.

Chapter 26

Dictation: Shooting from the Lip

Dictation is a special knack of the trade developed by reporters who must shoot from the lip, so to speak, to put fast-breaking stories on their way immediately.

Relman Morin, AP Pulitzer-prize winner

General assignment and beat reporters often dictate stories to make edition dead-lines. They cannot take time to go back to the office to write the story. It is a waste of time, effort, and high-priced talent to give notes to a rewrite person.

By dictating, reporters can wait at the story site until just before deadline. This enables them to get the latest developments. And, unlike leg people who may have just part of the story, beat and general assignment reporters have the whole story.

Dictating is composing a story in your head while "writing it" over the phone. Reporters leaf through their notes, dictating off the top of their heads. It is just like a boss dictating a letter to a secretary.

Here is a suggestion for dictating: Formulate a lead in your head as you leave the story scene and head for a phone. Sometimes while waiting to get through to the desk and the dictationist you have time to scribble a lead in your notebook. Sometimes you may have enough time to jot down key points you want to include in your story.

Other suggestions: Keep phrasing simple. Simple, declarative sentences help: subject, verb, object. Avoid convoluted, involved phrasing. Think simple sentences until you get the hang of it.

Psychological problems hit the beginner. It is easier to stare at blank copy paper or the blank video terminal screen than it is to stare into the void over the telephone.

Many reporters are more confident and more secure at the typewriter or video terminal keyboard. "Bleeders," writers who struggle over leads to say things just right, especially like to see what they are writing. It is much easier for them to self-edit copy when they see it.

Phrasing is looser when speaking off the top of the head. Few people speak as economically as they write.

Another Problem: Forgetting What You Said.   Dictation for the cub reporter can be an ordeal. Hemming and hawing has caused many a dictationist to grumble about "inexperienced people the paper is hiring these days."

Sometimes you dictate a dangling modifier or a repetition which you are not aware of. Your chagrin increases when the paper comes up. You wonder why the copy desk did not catch the error.

However, the more you dictate, the more confidence you will gain. With experience, the psychological block vanishes. Indeed, many "old pros" prefer to dictate rather than to punch out their copy. It is faster and easier—the lazy reporter's godsend.

John Hightower, AP veteran, has neatly capsulized dictation:

Dictating . . . is the easiest way of writing once the technical and psychological problems of dictation are licked. The chief technical problem is organization of facts.

The psychological problem is a kind of stage fright, a fear of starting to dictate and then failing to think of the next thing to say . . . .

I found I could dictate over the phone to the office without pressure and thus learned to save much time, even on long explanatory or analytical pieces. . . . [Sometimes] I've had to revert to typing and . . . that took special effort, mainly because typing seemed so much slower.

The growing use of portable video display terminals—units the size of typewriters—allows sports reporters to carry them to games. Some reporters are using VDTs to file copy from a courthouse press room. Some reporters on out-of-town assignments are using them.

Use of the portable VDTs allows reporters to type their stories directly in the TV-like box for transmittal to the home-office computer, in some cases doing away with the need to dictate stories.

DICTATING INSTRUCTIONS

Reporters must give instructions to dictationists. They will say while dictating: "quote," "close quote," "period," "comma," "colon," "paragraph." They signal unfamiliar organizations that must be capitalized by saying, "Uppercase, the Association of Black Students."

Unfamiliar names should be letter-spelled. S's and f's are easily confused over the phone. Make up your own phone code.

Figures cause trouble. Say it and spell it out: "$5,000, dollar mark five zero, zero, zero."

Reporters dictating can ask the dictationist to read back a sentence or a paragraph. But rarely does anyone have time for the whole story to be read back.

Dictationists can be helpful. The helpful ones point out that "you already said that." Or they ask, "Don't you want to get in where the meeting took place?"

The dictationist is responsible for editing the copy before it is turned in. Slugs are similar to those in the leg person-rewrite setup: "UAW/smith to jones." This tells desk people who dictated the story and who took it.

TRAINING YOUR MEMORY

As reporters, you need to sharpen your memory. Practice taking mental notes. Occasions will arise when you do not want sources to know you are taking notes.

For example, if you are doing infiltrating reporting—posing as a member of the Ku Klux Klan or a member of a commune, say—you don't want members of the group to see you taking notes. If they see you writing notes, they will throw you out—or do worse.

Train your memory to take mental notes. Then jot down notes "under the covers" or some other place where no one will see you.

Above-ground situations also require mental note-taking. Many of the stories in Washington, the state capital, or city hall come from talking with sources at a bar.

This is not cloak-and-dagger stuff. The sources know you are a reporter. You just do not want to be obvious about taking notes. Sources will either freeze up or at least be inhibited if you take notes openly.

In formal interviews, some journalists do not take notes. They find notebooks inhibitors to relaxed conversation, to development of rapport.

A reporter for the *Baltimore Evening Sun* once interviewed a retired United States senator for an hour. The reporter never wrote a note. But the feature story he wrote was so accurate that the ex-senator called to express his amazement.

Some reporters do not take notes but listen carefully during interviews, concentrating on quotes and phrases. As soon as they leave the interview they scribble down everything they can remember.

It is a good idea to cultivate your memory. The trick is fierce concentration. Truman Capote, interviewing for his book *In Cold Blood*, got long, verbatim quotes without using a notepad or a tape recorder. He trained by memorizing long passages from literary classics.

Few of us have such strong memory powers. But concentration helps. Good bridge players know every card that has been played. Poor players are wool-gathering or are chatting. They fail to concentrate.

If you walk into a party and are introduced to seven or eight people, you seldom pay attention to the names—except in the case of a striking brunette or a good-looking male. However, if you walk into the room and make a deliberate effort to remember names, you will be surprised at how many names you retain.

Did you ever play Concentration, the card game in which you spread out a pack face down and try to turn up matching cards? Concentrating will improve your Concentration game.

The same principle applies to the game Boy Scouts used to play—Kim's game. You spread out about twenty-five objects, studied them for one minute, and put them away. Then you tried to write down the name of each object from memory. Playing that game, too, will improve your memory.

Self-Puffs

Too many newspapers still indulge in self-puffery. This sort of thing: "The mayor told the Daily Blab today." It is as if the mayor does not talk to reporters from other papers.

This sort of thing: "According to figures compiled by the *Washington Post* from city reports." It is a newspaper's business to learn, to be told, to get the facts. It is no cause for self-congratulation.

It is this sort of thing: Under the headline, "Bikers cleared of murder," this drop head appeared: "*Detroit News* efforts free 4 innocent men." A newspaper is supposed to comfort the afflicted, afflict the comfortable. It should campaign to get innocent people free—without bragging about it à la Hearst.

Helpful Analogies

Suppose you are writing a story about the governor proposing an increase in the state income tax from 2.6 percent to 3.6 percent. A simple paragraph makes that strike home vividly for the reader: "A person paying $200 a year in state income tax would pay about $275 under the proposal."

Try to keep human beings in mind when you are writing. What does this story mean to people? A *Quill* article made the point by printing different leads on the same story. The first was technically correct but meaningless to all but the half-dozen city planners among the paper's subscribers. "The City Planning Commission yesterday recommended addition of an RM 1600 zoning classification to the Seattle Zoning Ordinance."

A much better lead on a story like that might be: "Low-income people would be able to buy a large apartment if the city adopts a recommendation of the Planning Commission."

"Write around It"

Sometimes reporters battling a deadline do not have all the facts for a story. "Write around it," editors say. So reporters do fancy word-painting to fudge the fact that they do not have all the information.

Students should not make a habit of "writing around" anything. Newspapering is a fact business. Be specific whenever possible.

You can write that "Richard Nixon defeated George McGovern handily in Michigan in 1972." That is the easy way. But if you are not racing a deadline, a quick check of the almanac will show you the exact figure. Using that figure, or at least rounding the figure off, is more meaningful to the reader.

It might be a good idea to keep references handy in your reporter's desk. Sure, the morgue will have all of them. But if you want to look up something quickly, you only need to dive into a drawer at your side. It takes time for the copy clerk to get what you want. It takes time for you to go to the morgue yourself. In either case you may be tempted to say "the hell with it."

Suggested Desk References

The following materials can be very helpful:

- Dictionary—Use it for spelling. Right word? Precise word?
- Latest almanac—Quick check on populations, records, vote totals, information on foreign countries, the United States Constitution, dates of the Johnstown flood, the sinking of the Titanic.
- Desk encyclopedia—Who was Mark Hanna? What does "thermidor" mean?
- *Bartlett's Familiar Quotations*—Who said that? Is that the exact quote? Don't trust your memory. Look it up.
- *The Reader's Encyclopedia*—Literary allusions. Who was Uriah Heep? Mme. Defarge? Lochinvar?

SUGGESTIONS FOR INSTRUCTOR

- Divide your class into dictator-dictationist teams. Send dictionists out of the room. Have the reporters pull a story out of you. Then call in dictationists. Have dictators pretend they are using a phone—no kibitzing, no looking at the typewriter or video terminal. Then reverse roles so all students get a chance at dictating.
- Give students a memory assignment. Have them do a story, pulling notes from you with notebooks closed. As soon as they finish questioning you, give them five or ten minutes to jot down everything they can remember.

Chapter 27

Interpretive Reporting

Interpretive reporting is explanatory or analytical reporting. It entails that over-worked and abused term "in-depth reporting." It is reporting that gives the background, the deeper meaning of the news. It is giving the why of news, the most important of the "five W's."

It is telling readers what the news means, not just what happened. James Reston of the *New York Times* has said that journalism today must "think about the causes of violence, rebellion and war, rather than merely reporting the struggle in the streets."

Like the journalists who disdain the label "feature," some newspaper people reject the term "interpretive reporting." Vermont C. Royster, former editor of the *Wall Street Journal*, once said: "I don't use the term. All good reporting is interpretive reporting."

Perhaps. It is true that interpretive reporting does not have to be a long story on some public affairs problem. It can be a paragraph or two in a hard-news story.

The *New York Times*, in a story about a House committee considering a proposal to increase third-class bulk mail rates, carried this interpretive paragraph: "Of all the classes of mail, third class has always been the most controversial. Critics have used the term 'junk mail' to describe it, while its backers have contended that it performs an essential marketing and advertising service."

Interpretive reporting is telling the reader what the news means, putting it in context. It is sorting out and explaining complex events. It is going deeper than the government handout or statement. It is motivational reporting, explaining reasons for actions of groups and individuals.

Interpretive reporting requires: getting the facts; giving the background and explanation of a situation; telling what the facts mean against that background; and analysis backed by support—observations, quotes, anecdotes, and examples. Only in that way can reporters give the fuller meaning to public affairs issues and controversies.

The *Wall Street Journal* produces some of the best interpretive journalism in America. It specializes in trend-spotters. It provides background stories that clarify murky situations. Students can profit by reading its page-one "takeouts."

Other papers, too, do an excellent job with such stories. The *Los Angeles Times* runs outstanding "leader pieces" on page one every day. The *New York Times* and the *Detroit Free Press* excel in interpretive reporting.

EDITORIALIZING

Interpretive reporting carries an ever-present danger: editorializing, stepping over the line of objectivity into subjectivity.

Some papers use a makeup "bug"—"a news analysis"—to get away with editorializing in the news columns. This sort of thing: "Chinese ping-pong players are hardly the kind of customers to bring out the full craftsmanship of Chou's ability to hoodwink Americans." That is opinion. It belongs in a personal column, not in news columns.

Any newspaper that uses interpretive journalism to push its editorial line is a bad newspaper. Most readers see through such subterfuge. Interpretive reporting is no excuse for editorializing.

The *New York Times*, reporting on a gubernatorial race in Arkansas between Orval Faubus and David Pryor, suggested that Faubus was cutting into "Pryor's strength with a harsh personal attack that questions his opponent's patriotism, independence and competence."

The *Times* reporter did not call Faubus a liar. Yet he fairly showed how Faubus was distorting Pryor's record, giving examples to make his point. It was interpretive reporting, not editorializing.

Here is an example of obvious editorializing: "A short-sighted city council has cost the lives of five people by refusing to install a traffic light at Vine and Pugh."

You can make the same point without editorializing. You can cite the facts: five lives lost in accidents and no traffic light. You can quote a traffic official saying that a light should be at the intersection. You can quote a highway official saying his department asked for a light but the council refused. In fairness, you should find out why the council refused to install a light. Perhaps it had no money.

Lester Markel, retired Sunday editor of the *New York Times*, argued that the line between interpretation and opinion was not difficult to draw. Markel used an example something like this: Smith resigns from a city job—fact; why he resigned—interpretation; whether he should have resigned long ago—opinion.

"Interpretation is an objective process, based on full background, and in part is appraisal," Markel said. "Opinion is a subjective process, involving argument and emotional impact. Interpretation is an essential part of the news. Opinion should be confined almost religiously to the editorial page."

Agreed. But it is not so simple. Interpretive reporting requires the honesty and integrity of reporters. If interpretation is biased, the reporter probably should be in public relations. In interpretive reporting it is essential that editors know and trust their reporters.

Integrity? It can be illustrated by a negative example. A campus newspaper won several awards in a state contest. Why, a reader wondered? The paper was not that good. It turned out that the state's best campus daily did not participate. When the reporter fairly tried to include that fact—to put the award in perspective—the editor killed the reference, saying it would detract from the honor.

All interpretive reporting—like all good newspapering—requires honesty and integrity.

ESSENTIALS FOR INTERPRETIVE REPORTING

To avoid problems, keep the following in mind at all times:

- Absolute integrity. Honest, fair, and accurate reporting is a must—not the kind of reporting often done in newspapers in which reporters come up with a story suiting their editors' preconceived notions.
- Facts. The damned facts keep getting in the way of our opinions. "The only effective reporting and writing is that which convinces the readers by the recitation and logical presentation of facts," the *AP Log* has written. "This requires that the reporter know his subject thoroughly."
- Knowledge of the beat and the subject. You cannot write good interpretive stories without it. Experience and time in developing sources and contacts will make you a still stronger interpretive reporter.

Good interpretive reporting blankets an issue so well that disinterested readers can make up their minds after reading your pros and cons.

Time and Money

Interpretive reporting requires time and money that too few publishers are willing to spend. To the publisher's cash-register eyes, it is difficult to justify paying a reporter $400 a week when he or she does not file copy for a couple of weeks.

The *Los Angeles Times* once sent a reporter into San Francisco's Haight-Ashbury for a month without getting a piece of copy. When the reporter got back to his paper, he wrote a "sixty-book-page," five-part series. It was worth the time and money. Yet too few publishers will pay that price for putting out a quality newspaper.

REQUIREMENTS FOR LONG INTERPRETIVE PIECE

Always be aware of the following details:

- Nature of plan, problem, or proposal. The background.
- Pros and cons. Who is for it? Against it? Arguments of both sides.
- Prospect of passage or solution. This must be substantiated.
- What is at stake? Consequence of success or failure?
- Research. Check morgue, libraries. *The Reader's Guide to Periodical Literature*, those wonderful green books in libraries, will guide you to references for backgrounding and understanding issues. Perhaps your library has some editorial research reports, impartial and reliable facts on problems.
- Interviewing dozens of people connected with the story.

TAKE TIME TO BE BRIEF

"Excuse the length of my letter," Pascal wrote in *Provincial Letters*. "I don't have time to be brief."

Usually reporters do not have time to write drafts. But interpretive pieces can always be improved by writing at least one draft. It takes time to be brief, but it is worth it.

Writing a second draft enables you to boil out top-of-the-head writing in the first draft. Rewriting enables you to cut wordiness, to smooth the prose, to tighten copy. You can "slay your darlings." That means taking out show-off writing, beautiful words, phrases, and quotes that sound great but do not fit the piece.

INTERPRETIVE MASKS

A cartoon in *Colliers* years ago showed a reporter standing by the city editor who was reading the reporter's copy. The city editor asks: "When you say 'unimpeachable authority,' Mulligan, I presume you mean that bunch that hangs out at Sloppy Mike's?"

Sources are a problem, unimpeachable or otherwise. Whenever possible, name sources. If you do not, you are not leveling with readers. Moreover, sources that do not want to be named can be using you for their own devious purposes.

There are times, however, when sources simply cannot be named. To name employees in a mental institution who are your sources can cost them a job. If Earl Caldwell of the *New York Times* had to reveal his sources in the Black Panthers, he would lose those sources. If you named a Teamster official as a source, the official might be dead the next day.

The need for anonymous sources is obvious. The Watergate investigation by Woodward and Bernstein could never have prospered without anonymous sources.

Reporters often use interpretive masks: "political observers feel," "sources close to the governor say," "White House insiders." "Viewed" is a necessary interpretive verb.

For example, suppose through your knowledge and experience of the beat you know something is true. You cannot say it flat out because that would be editorializing. You do not want to embarrass sources by naming them. So you make the point by using the word "viewed": "She is viewed as a good administrator and 'a nice lady' by many members of the school board, but not as a strong leader."

"Political observers feel" is often no more than the reporter's personal feeling. Since reporters cannot use "I," they resort to the interpretive mask. This leads to that potential danger of editorializing. It is imperative to have an editor and reporter with integrity and reliability.

Neal Shine, managing editor of the *Detroit Free Press*, tells of a series on drugs his paper ran. The informants were members of the U.S. Bureau of Narcotics. Using their names would jeopardize their jobs and *Free Press* sources. But they were reliable and trusted sources so the *Free Press* went with the story.

Humor can be found in all the grim sources business. Russell Baker, humor columnist for the *New York Times*, once wrote that he was "threatened with banishment from the Press Club bar when, covering the State Department beat," he discovered and printed that " 'diplomatic circles' was any man higher than a GS-6 encountered in a State Department bathroom."

One of the more amusing sources is "usually reliable." The reader can't help asking, "Is this one of those unusual times?"

WRITING INTERPRETIVE STORIES

Interpretive pieces must be well written. You have done all that research and interviewing. You cannot fritter it away with dull writing. You do not write a Ph.D. thesis for newspapers.

Interpretive pieces are written in the feature formula. In effect, you are writing a magazine article for your newspaper—without editorializing. You have plenty of information to give to the readers. You must present it attractively or you will lose them.

Reporters writing interpretive pieces can use all the devices of a fiction writer: dialogue, scene-setting, narrative, descriptions, and flashbacks. *Newsweek* once began a piece on LSD with a description of someone on an LSD trip. A *National Observer* article about Protestant theological unrest began with this dramatic narrative lead:

The kettledrums shuddered, then rumbled ever louder in a powerful crescendo.

"Why is there no dawn?" asked the reader in the requiem at North Carolina Wesleyan College. "Why do our dead only die? Why do our living only live?"

"Your God is dead!" cried the chorus as tears began to form in the eyes of some of the 600 students. "He died in the darkness of your image. . . . He died because you held his hand too tightly."

Then, just before the final crash of the kettledrums, the chorus screamed the litany's stunning, apocalyptic words.

"GOD IS DEAD!"

That was a powerful opening on a long, throughly researched interpretive article. Like a good feature story, interpretive pieces need good endings. Here is the opening of an interpretive story in the *Miami Herald*, written by Carl Hiaasen:

Callie Miller carefully sheared the legs off a pair of pantyhose and slipped six bottles of pills into each one. She wrapped the stockings around her waist and put on a blue pants suit.

Her husband Danny stashed more tablets inside the tail lights of the rented Ford Pinto. With Callie at his side, he nervously drove the blue compact out of Tijuana through the dusty summer heat toward the U.S. border near San Ysidro, Calif.

Moments later, the young Fort Lauderdale couple passed the customs checkpoint and became drug smugglers.

Callie Miller is 31, deeply religious, a devoted mother of two. Danny is 35, a congenial $200-a-week maintenance worker. They are the unlikeliest of outlaws.

But one day last June, Danny took leave from his job and packed the family into their camper. On borrowed money and donations from their church, they began a month-long, 2,000-mile odyssey to search for Callie's future.

She is fighting a losing battle against cancer. After three operations and 11 painful months of chemotherapy, Callie has desperately turned elsewhere for hope.

She brought it back from Mexico, hidden under her clothes, a six-month supply of a contraband substance known as Laetrile—banned by the Food and Drug Administration since 1963. . . .

Here is the ending of that same *Miami Herald* story:

If caught, her supply of Laetrile will be seized and destroyed, but Callie Miller probably will not be fined or prosecuted.

The government is after bigger game: commercial producers, distributors, big-time smugglers.

"We have a lot of sympathy for the problem a cancer victim faces," one FDA official said. "We do not seek to add to them."

It is the principle—not the economics, not the politics and not the medical evidence—of this Mexican standoff that bothers members of the Laetrile underground. They simply don't like the idea of breaking a law to save their lives.

"If I have to, I will," Callie Miller vows quietly. "I'm only doing what I think is best for me and my family. It's hard for me to sit here and say what's right and wrong."

Multipart Series

Interpretive articles sometimes run in series of three, five, or more stories. Be sure to write each part as a unified whole. Each part needs a good lead and a good close. You cannot arbitrarily chop a long article into three parts.

Each part needs fill-in and background. You cannot assume the reader has read or remembers an earlier article. You cannot refer to characters in previous chapters without identifying them.

Each article in the series needs a precede and a postscript. Precede: (First of a three-part series on drugs). Postscript: (Tomorrow: A look at the marijuana controversy).

Editors want all parts of a series in hand before they run part I. They don't want to be embarrassed by running two parts and then have something happen to you with three more parts promised—but unwritten.

Interpretive Reporting Tips

• Like a good feature story, interpretive articles need a unified theme. The story must be kept flowing. . . . Reintroduce unfamiliar figures who turn up again in your story after several takes. For instance, on your first reference you write, "Eugene Bush, deputy treasurer." Three takes later the reader needs a reminder: "deputy treasurer Bush."

Wall Street Journal Takeout

This start of a *Wall Street Journal* takeout on atomic fuel possibilities is typical of interpretive journalism the *Journal* does so well every day of the week:

MILLSTONE, Conn.—Despite its deceptively pastoral setting, this seacoast town near Long Island Sound is very much part of the atomic age. Far down one of its back roads sits a hulking nuclear power plant capable of churning out enough electricity to supply a city of 600,000 at a cost far below that of most conventional plants.

The Millstone Point power station is very much part of the atomic age in another way, too: It doesn't always work. From last September to March of this year, in fact, the $103 million facility owned by Northeast Utilities didn't run at all.

First, seawater mysteriously seeped into Millstone's reactor, corroded hundreds of parts and forced a closedown. While fixing that, people at Northeast discovered some unrelated mistakes made when certain key parts were first installed.

And while these were being remedied, the dismayed utility people learned they had been shipped some defective replacement gear by a supplier, General Electric.

By the time it was finished, Northeast had a repair bill exceeding $10 million. And the electric power industry had yet another sign that nuclear power plants so far aren't all they were cracked up to be.

Indeed, their unreliability is becoming one of their most dependable features. The incredibly complex facilities are plagued by breakdowns that experts blame on faulty engineering, defective equipment and operating errors.

Failures range from hour-long annoyances to months-long closedowns. Repair costs run into millions of dollars and some utilities stoically shell out up to $200,000 a day for replacement electricity to distribute to their customers in the meantime.

Boxed Sidebars

Interpretive pieces are often helped by *boxed sidebars* that give readers the background on an issue. If you are running a takeout on Angola, this kind of sidebar is helpful: "Angola at a Glance" with paragraphs such as: "The Land, Its History, Its People, Its Government, and Its Economy."

SUGGESTION FOR INSTRUCTOR

- Assign an interpretive article of six to eight takes. It can be about any current public affairs issue or topic of controversy. Stress local or state aspect of problem. Keep in mind possible publication in campus or community newspaper.

Chapter 28

Court Reporting

What percent of newspaper stories deal with crime? Most students would probably guess about 25 percent. The answer is less than 5 percent. For most papers the truer estimate is 1 percent.

Even the New York *Daily News*, which probably devotes more space to crime news than any other daily paper in the country, runs under 4 percent. In one year 11,724 felonies were committed in New York City. The *Daily News* reported only 41 of them.

Most people would probably guess higher because of the psychological factor. Big cases—Hearst and Manson—get big play. Also, people tend to read one local crime story and cluck, "Isn't it terrible, all that crime?"

Yet on one day chosen at random the *Detroit Free Press* did not have a single local crime story in a thirty-six-page paper. Its rival, the *Detroit News*, has a much bigger news hole. Yet in an eighty-page paper the same day it had only five local crime stories, four of them shorts and one of them a second-day slaying story.

The fact is that crime news, a newspaper staple often sensationalized since Penny Press days in the 1830s, has finally been placed in perspective. Newspapers today are devoting more attention to pollution, poverty, and ecology than to ax murders and mayhem. Papers are reporting more stories that help people to live their lives better.

A corollary question: What percent of court cases make the newspapers? The answer: about one-half of 1 percent. Despite the multitude of courts—from justices of the peace at the local level to the Supreme Court at the top of the federal system—only a fraction of cases are ever reported.

Those that are covered meet the criteria of what is news. Some factors are:

- Importance—Assassinations or attempted assassinations of Kennedys, Kings, and Wallaces. Political-social trials such as those of the Black Panthers, the Chicago Seven, and Daniel Ellsberg. Trials of public officials and public figures.
- Murder—Such cases carry the inherent drama of a person being on trial for his or her life. Multiple slayings increase the national news value.
- Constitutional rulings—Cases that deal with civil liberties. Appellate court rulings on abortion, busing, the Pentagon Papers.
- Oddities—Unusual court decisions. Cases such as someone willing $1 million to a cat—and the family contesting the will.

LEGAL KNOWLEDGE HELPFUL

You do not have to have a law degree to cover the courts. But legal knowledge is helpful. The better you understand the law, the better you will be able to cover the courts. Good court reporters are constantly doing their homework, reading about legal history and law controversies.

Linda Deutsch, the AP's West Coast court reporter, has written in the *AP Log* that a trial is often "peppered with references to specific decisions in case law. . . . It's wise to check up on any such cases because a trial ruling could lead to a new precedent. If there's time, look up the case in a law library or ask an attorney to show you his copy."

One of the secrets of court coverage is to translate the complexities of the law into lay people's language without distorting meanings.

If you do not understand clearly the issues, problems, and technicalities of the law, your reporting will suffer. For instance, students often make the mistake of having the Supreme Court convict someone. It never does. The court upholds or overturns a lower-court conviction.

If you are working on a complicated legal story, or get an opinion in a complicated case, don't hesitate to call a lawyer source to make sure you have interpreted the matter correctly for readers.

COURT BEAT SOURCES

Clerks of the court, prosecutors, lawyers, and judges are good sources for court reporters.

You can get dockets, trial dates, legal briefs, and opinions from clerks of the court. You can get information on indictments and investigations and grand jury reporters from prosecutors.

Lawyers must be "courted and cultivated." They are excellent sources for tips, background, and legal fill-ins. They are particularly helpful on civil cases, noncriminal cases such as divorce, child custody, disputed wills, and zoning cases.

Judges are good sources for background information. Interviews with judges are often necessary when dealing with court problems and controversies—stories about case backlogs, for instance.

Reporters do not discuss with judges the guilt or innocence of defendants in cases before the court. They should be wary of doing anything that could be construed as contempt of court—interfering with the administration of justice.

However, reporters should not be overawed by the majesty of the law. Louis Heldman, former court reporter for the *Detroit Free Press*, observes that journalists tend to be afraid to ask judges tough questions.

Lawyers have to be deferential for obvious reasons. Reporters do not need to be.

Heldman offers this advice to court reporters:

Lawsuits filed, divorces, motions, decisions—in fact, all public papers filed with the court clerk—should be checked every day. They often provide the leads on stories months or even years before the matter comes before a judge.

I was always terribly frightened that I might miss something big if I didn't get to the county clerk's office before it closed. Eventually, through the cleaning ladies, I was able to work my way in even after it closed.

COVERING TRIALS

Trials make good copy. Lives—or long jail terms—are at stake. They have built-in excitement and drama. That is why courtroom scenes can be so gripping in plays or movies. The adversary situation—the conflict between prosecutor and defense—packs inherent drama.

"Court conflicts are often very human, providing elements of high tension, anxiety, melodrama, hatred and even laughter," Louis Heldman says. "Pity the readers of a newspaper whose editors think court stories should be dry."

Colorful attorneys enliven court cases. Flamboyant lawyers play on the emotions of jurors with tears and tricks like advising clients to wear conservative clothes and wedding bands. A roll of famed courtroom lawyers would include William Fallon, Clarence Darrow, Louis Nizer, Melvin Belli, Edward Bennett Williams, and F. Lee Bailey.

All that flamboyance carries a flaw: trial by trick. The use of courtroom gimmicks often wins cases at the expense of justice.

Dostoevsky in *Diary of a Writer** wryly notes a lawyer's eloquence in playing on jurors' emotions: "Gentlemen of the jury! What kind of woman would she have been if she had not stabbed her rival? Gentlemen of the jury! Who among you would not have thrown the child out of the window?"

Mark Twain called the jury system "the most ingenious and infallible agency for defeating justice that human wisdom could contrive." True. But neither Twain nor anyone else has come up with a better system.

ASSIGNED TO COVER TRIALS

Reporters assigned to cover a court case do the clips first. They get the basic facts of the case. Arthur Everett, AP court reporter, has advised:

Courtroom backgrounding is vital. You can't raise your hand to interrupt a district attorney who has brought up a certain name or location or date in his questioning of a witness. So it's invaluable in trial reporting to have a small notebook filled in advance with every name, age, date, incident and quote that can be found on the case.

Caution: Don't convict defendants in advance stories written from the clips. This kind of thing: "Then he pulled the trigger." If that comes out in trial testimony, naturally you can use it—but not before.

Another caution. Be sure to update ages and other facts you get from morgue clips. There is always a time lag between the crime and the trial.

Reporters should make pretrial checks with attorneys to verify facts from the clips. Prosecutors should be asked the verdict sought, the number of witnesses to be called, and an estimate of the length of the trial. Defense attorneys may tell you their line of defense.

Much pretrial questioning has been foreclosed because of curbs on pretrial publicity that could be deemed prejudicial. Lawyers are much more reluctant to speak about cases than they used to be.

The First Amendment guarantees a free press and hence the public's right to know. The Sixth Amendment guarantees a fair trial. Most newspapers today are wary of trial by newspaper. In the Sheppard case in 1966, the Supreme Court overturned a murder conviction because of prejudicial publicity in pretrial and trial stages. Since then newspapers have been much more responsible about protecting defendants' rights.

Many newspapers have applied voluntary restraints to balance the public's right to know with the accused's right to a fair trial. Bar associations have recommended pretrial coverage that bans publication of the following:

*Charles Scribner's Sons, New York, 1949.

- Previous criminal records
- Confessions or statements
- Extrajudicial statements touching on guilt or innocence

Guidelines must be voluntary. No government or court should ever get away with telling the press what it can publish. Editing of newspapers should be left to editors no matter how irresponsible the press sometimes is.

A wire service once filed a story about a University of Texas student charged with murdering a female student. The story quoted a roommate as calling him "a little bit mixed up." Then the report said, without attribution, that the suspect "never did get along with anybody."

Such statements are prejudicial and should be kept out of pretrial stories. If they turn up in trial testimony, then they can be reported. Court reporters avoid editorializing. This kind of thing: "The most damaging evidence yet against Richard G. Herr, a Lansing car salesman accused of murder of a Grand Ledge housewife, was revealed in municipal court here today."

Let the evidence speak for itself. Let courts convict defendants.

CANON 35

The American Bar Association's Canon 35 prohibits cameras in courtrooms. Since technology today would permit use of cameras in courtrooms without upsetting judicial decorum, the ban may be unnecessary.

Three states—Alabama, Colorado, and Washington—permit tape recorders and cameras in the courtroom. Although no courtrooms have collapsed because trials have been photographed by TV and still cameras, Canon 35 is observed in all federal courts and by most state courts.

Newspapers rely mainly on courtroom sketches by artists. In one way this is good: Sketches have more impact than most photographs would have.

WRITING TRIALS

As reporters covering court trials, you are the eyes and ears of the public. You should take your readers into the courtroom, enabling them to see, hear, and feel the drama.

You need color and descriptive touches. Don't overdo it. But give readers "you-were-there" emotion. This sort of thing: "The sallow-faced and thin defendant appeared in court today with a fresh haircut"; "The 22-year-old farm youth sat impassively across from the counsel's table."

Or this from the *Detroit Free Press* describing a witness:

Whalen, 30, is swarthy and slightly built. He wears a thick black beard and mustache. He was neatly dressed in a blue suit, blue shirt and blue striped tie as he testified.

He spoke in a deep, husky voice with an occasional stutter.

Quotes help any copy. They are essential in trials. For example:

Brindle smiled for almost the only time in the trial when the prosecutor asked him if Westcoat was strong.
"Oh, yes," Brindle testified. "He lifted weights. He was a runner up in a Mr. Maryland contest."

Sometimes in reporting trials you can heighten the drama. Let's say you are quoting someone on the stand who was recounting an attack. Interrupt the testimony with an interjection by the prosecutor, "Then what did he do?"
For example, during the Patricia Hearst bank robbery trial, attorney F. Lee Bailey questioned Hearst on the witness stand. This was the exchange:

"Was your blindfold removed?" Bailey asked.
"Yes."
"Did he make you lie down on the floor?"
"Yes."
"Then what did you do?"
"We had sexual intercourse."

The AP's Deutsch has said that much of trial reporting is boring, filled with legal technicalities. But she stresses the need to set up sources—prosecutors, defense attorneys, and even bailiffs.
Reporters for wire services or multiedition dailies often have to slip out of the courtroom during a recess or while the trial is on to dictate new leads. If they miss testimony while they are gone, they can get a fill-in from another reporter.
Court reporters for morning papers are luckier than their afternoon counterparts. The A.M. reporter usually does not have a deadline until after court adjourns for the day. Reporters for P.M. papers often have to dictate two or three new leads.

BIG TRIALS

Two reporters from the same paper often cover big trials. One can dictate and the other can continue taking notes to avoid missing key testimony.
The AP's Everett says another secret of trial reporting is good note-taking. "The ear gradually becomes attuned and you'll abandon one unfinished quote to get on to the more important one on its heels," Everett has written. "The knack

is getting the part that's most essential—it may be only a paragraph, a sentence, a phrase or a word."

A-MATTER

Sometimes court testimony is dictated as *A-matter*. This means dictating copy for a story before the lead is written. That way reporters can call in takes to get copy into type before the lead is written. This saves time and avoids a copy jam-up at deadline. Reporters simply slug each take as "A-matter/pope," "B-matter/pope," etc.

On big stories many papers print question-and-answer (Q. and A.) testimony. The Q. and A. testimony is set up with a precede paragraph and goes like this:

The chief counsel, George W. Latimer, questioned Calley as follows:
QUESTION. What was your feeling when you say this?
ANSWER. I don't know if I can describe the feeling.
Q. Well, at least try.
A. Anger, hate, fear, generally sick to the stomach, hurt.

No quote marks are needed in question-and-answer testimony. Begin a new paragraph for each change of speaker as you would in writing any dialogue.

Trials of national interest have produced complications for the press. Security is tight. Reporters may be limited in movement in and out of the courtroom. They may be frisked, making them feel like defendants.

APPELLATE COURTS

Covering appeals courts requires reading opinions. The AP's Deutsch has written: "The rule of thumb favored by many under time pressure is to flip to the last page of the decision to get the judge's ruling and the story's lead. But it's essential to read the entire document to get explanations on how the decision was reached."

When you get the text of a decision—and time is not a factor—read it carefully. Mark key quotes and points you want to use in your story. Sometimes you will need to make phone calls, see lawyers, and do some research to get background on a story.

The usual lead is a summary of what the court ruled, capsulizing the decision in a nutshell. Here is one from the *New York Times*:

WASHINGTON—The Supreme Court freed the New York Times and the Washington Post today to resume publication of articles based on the secret Pentagon Papers on the origins of the Vietnam War.

The lead, aside from summarizing the court's ruling, can take an interpretive approach, such as this from the *Detroit Free Press* does:

WASHINGTON—The Supreme Court, continuing its shift to the right, ruled Tuesday that police may question a suspect in some cases even after he or she has insisted on the right to remain silent.

Appellate court decisions should include the vote and a breakdown of who formed the majority and who the minority. If the vote was 8-0 and the court has nine members, be sure to tell who did not participate and why.

The rationale of the decision should be high up, perhaps no later than the second paragraph. Get the rationale of the dissent high in the story, too.

Pay close attention to dissents. Dissenting views are often more interesting than majority views. More important, dissents are often the law of the future, becoming the majority view the next time the case is decided.

The classic example of this is Justice John Marshall Harlan's dissent in the *Plessy v. Ferguson* separate-but-equal segregation case decided 8-1 by the Supreme Court in 1896. Harlan's view that the Constitution was color-blind, while it took an ungodly long time, became the law of the land in the 1954 *Brown* case.

Stories should contain background on the origins of the case and a recap of the appeals route to the higher court.

Warning: Don't get trapped by the legal terminology the court uses in opinions, such things as "my brethren" or "Mr. Justice Brennan."

Go to the heart of the matter. Use nontechnical words in reporting the case. Write that "Marshall said," not "wrote."

ADVICE FOR STUDENTS

- Be sure to tell in what court the trial is taking place and what judge is presiding.
- Note reactions of defendants and family when reporting verdicts brought in during big trials. The *New York Times*, dramatically reporting the first-degree murder conviction of a woman, told that the woman shrieked, collapsed at the counsel table, and screamed, "Oh, my God, how could they do it?"

Court Reporting Tips

Louis Heldman, former court reporter for the *Detroit Free Press*, offers these court-reporting suggestions:

- Attribution is as essential in trial coverage as it is in any other type of reporting. "Too many students tend to take the word of the prosecutor or police as gospel and never bother to attribute the source of information."

- Fairness demands that you try to get both sides' viewpoints into each day's coverage. "If the prosecutor says in his opening statement that he will prove the defendant chopped up his wife and flushed the remains down the toilet, the reporter should ask the defense attorney if he has any response. It may well be that the response will be that 'the defense will present its case later.' But if the defense wants to respond immediately in print, I think you have an obligation to include the response."
- Students should be warned that anything a judge orders reporters to do—leaving the courtroom, for example—"is the law for the moment." "Let them get the company lawyers involved if they think an order is unconstitutonal."
- In writing about written decisions, a good reporter will tell readers what they mean, particularly if it is likely to have wide impact. "White children from 36 Detroit suburbs will be bused into the city under court order . . ." probably means a lot more to the reader than, "A U.S. District Court Judge Tuesday ordered the implementation of a cross-district busing plan aimed at alleviating segregated school systems in 36 communities surrounding Detroit." Too much court reporting takes the balky, technical approach.
- Students should know the difference between *civil* and *criminal* cases. "Sometimes you see students writing about the defendant being 'convicted' in a civil case."

Court Stories

Here are a couple of beginnings of typical court stories:

Gus T. Zanos, the last of four defendants in the embezzlement of $418,000 from the Allegheny Valley Bank of Pittsburgh, yesterday was sentenced to six years in prison and fined $5,000.

U.S. District Judge Daniel J. Snyder Jr., who accepted guilty pleas from all four defendants in the case, imposed the sentence on Zanos, 51, of 1304 Carlisle, St., Natrona Heights, owner of the Coffee Shop Restaurant, Southside.

Asst. U.S. Atty. Daniel H. Shapira said Zanos was the apparent mastermind of a scheme that involved two bankers and another restaurateur in a check-kiting and cover-up scheme at the bank.

—Pittsburgh Post-Gazette

By WILLIAM NOTTINGHAM
St. Petersburg Times Staff Writer

TAMPA—Anthony Antone, a self-employed air-conditioning repairman, was found guilty Friday of participating in the gangland execution of ex-Tampa Policeman Richard L. Cloud.

His sentence: death in the electric chair.

When Antone heard the sentence, he showed no reaction.

The verdict came after a five-man, seven-women jury deliberated one hour and 40 minutes.

Now, exactly 10 months from the day Cloud was buried, three men—

Antone, Ellis Marlow Haskew and the late Benjamin Foy Gilford—have either confessed to or been convicted of the slaying.

Until gunned down in the doorway of his home April 23, the 33-year-old Cloud had waged a one-man war against organized crime in Tampa.

"He (Antone) deserved it, didn't he," said Cloud's widow, Wanda, after the verdict was announced by jury foreman Tom B. Smith.

Since Cloud's contract assassination, area law enforcement agencies have stepped up efforts to battle organized crime.

Asked if that meant her husband had not died in vain, Mrs. Cloud said, "It's not worth it . . . it's not."

Antone's verdict was heard by a courtroom filled with leading state and federal law enforcement officers.

"He must have been some kind of cop, they wanted him out so bad," special state prosecutor Aaron K. Bowden told the jury as it prepared to decide if Antone should receive the death penalty or life imprisonment.

After the verdict to convict, Antone's co-counsel, James Alfonso, said he would appeal.

Here is the "top" of a court story that appeared in the *Arizona Republic*, written by Charles Kelly:

Arizona Republic reporter Don Bolles was able to indicate before he died of a June 2 bomb attack that he had met with his accused killer before the bombing but had not been threatened, a detective testified Tuesday.

Phoenix Police Detective Jon Sellers delivered that testimony in a hearing before Maricopa County Superior Court Judge David J. Perry.

The hearing, which has been continued pending the appearance of another witness, dealt with a defense motion to dismiss the murder charge against John Harvey Adamson, 32.

Adamson's attorneys contend that Sellers, who signed the murder complaint issued by Marion Reno, Northwest Phoenix justice of the peace, did not supply Reno with enough information to justify issuance of the complaint.

In eliciting from Sellers details of his investigation of the Bolles killing, defense attorney Gregory Martin asked the detective about a hospital interview police had with Bolles after the bombing.

Sellers said Bolles was able to answer Sellers' questions by nodding his head. In that manner, the detective said, the reporter identified Adamson from a photo, and indicated he had received a phone call from Adamson and had met with him.

"I attempted to determine where he (Bolles) had met him," Sellers testified. "I was unable to decipher what he was trying to tell me."

Terminology

Court reporters should learn frequently used legal terms. Whether they use them in their stories depends on reader familiarity. If the term is unfamiliar, paraphrase it or use the term and define it.

Although there is no legal plea of innocence, newspapers usually report that someone pleaded innocent because in the actual plea, not guilty, "nots" sometimes get dropped in the printing process. Occasionally reporters need to untangle police terminology. The official charge may be "robbery not armed," but reporters write it "unarmed robbery."

Here are some terms you should know:

Amicus curiae—Friend of the court. Brief of individual or group not involved in case but with an interest in outcome. Your state attorney general might file an amicus curiae brief with the Supreme Court because its ruling could affect law in your state.

Brief—Written legal argument lawyers present to courts.

Change of venue—Moving a trial to another locale because of excess publicity and the possibility of a prejudicial jury.

Continuance—Delay of trial allowing attorneys more time to prepare case.

Felony—Offenses such as burglary, robbery and murder—serious crimes—for which punishment can be at least one year in prison. In contrast, misdemeanors are less serious offenses such as disorderly conduct and loitering.

Hearsay—Second-hand testimony; testimony by a witness about what he (or she) has heard from another person rather than what he knows or experienced himself.

In camera—In the judge's chambers; out of earshot of jury, press, and public.

Injunction—Judicial order to do something—or refrain from doing something.

Leading the witness—Putting words into the mouth of a witness; suggesting desired answers.

Mandamus—Judicial order to do something.

Moot—No longer at legal issue. This would be moot case: You file a suit contending that you were denied admission to law school because of discrimination; by the time the court hears your case you have been admitted to the law school.

Mute—Refusing to enter a plea, in which case judges enter innocent plea.

Nolle prosequi—Nol pros; dropping case; placing indictment on inactive list.

Nolo contendere—No contest plea; a legal gambit that says, in effect, that you are guilty in this criminal case but pleas cannot be used against you in a civil suit.

Plea bargaining—"Copping a plea." Pleading guilty to a lesser charge in order to avoid a longer sentence if convicted of a more serious charge.

Sequestered jury—Keeping jurors in a motel or hotel without access to print or electronic information about the case they are hearing.

Star witness—Most important witness for prosecution.

Stare decisis—Precedent; ruling based on earlier court decision.

Stipulate—Agreeing to facts; a way to save court time by obviating the need for testimony to make a point.

Veniremen—Body of prospective jurors.

Voir dire—Questioning of prospective jurors.

Recommended Books

Students particulary interested in court coverage should read two books, *Gideon's Trumpet* by Anthony Lewis and *One Man's Freedom* by Edward Bennett Williams.

Gideon's Trumpet is an excellent primer on the workings of the U.S. Supreme Court. It also deals with a precedent-setting legal issue, the pauper's right to counsel in felony cases.

"It has become axiomatic that the great rights which are secured for all of us by the Bill of Rights are constantly tested and retested in the courts by the people who live in the bottom of society's barrel," Lewis writes.[*]

One Man's Freedom makes the point that too few Americans appreciate: one person's freedom is every person's freedom. The so-called despicable people, the outcasts, are as entitled to legal counsel as the pure heart.

In the introduction to the book, Eugene Rostow writes of Williams: "Once asked why he represented a man of unsavory reputation, he is reported to have said that 'no one would think of reproaching a doctor for removing Earl Browder's appendix. Why is there any difference when a lawyer stands up to defend his legal rights?' "[†] (Browder was head of the U.S. Communist party.)

One other book is recommended: *Anatomy of a Murder* by Robert Traver, pseudonym for John D. Voelker.[‡] The book is a novel, but it was written by a man who had been prosecutor, trial lawyer, and a Michigan Supreme Court justice. It contains some of the most accurate descriptions ever written about how the judicial process operates in America's medium-sized and smaller jurisdictions.

SUGGESTIONS FOR INSTRUCTOR

• Give students handouts on crime terminology and the structure of state and federal court systems. Also, give them a roster of court personnel and an explanation of the function of each office.

• Assign students to cover a court case, preferably in a court of record. Facts and figures of the case can be gotten from the clerk of the court or attorneys.

• Give students the text of an appellate court decision—perhaps by the state supreme court or the United States Supreme Court. Give them the background and have them write a story datelined from the city of origin.

[*]Anthony Lewis, *Gideon's Trumpet,* Random House, Inc., New York, 1964.

[†]Edward Bennett Williams, *One Man's Freedom,* Atheneum Publishers, New York, 1962.

[‡]Robert Traver (John Voelker), *Anatomy of a Murder,* St. Martin's Press, New York, 1958.

Chapter 29

Government Reporting

The first (assumption) is that every government is run by liars and nothing they say should be believed. That's a prima facie *assumption, unless proven to the contrary.*

I.F. Stone

The scope of government reporting varies greatly from paper to paper, from jurisdiction to jurisdiction. Big papers might staff your state capital with three to four people. They might cover city hall with two or three reporters. Other papers might have one reporter responsible for all government news of one county. Small papers may have one reporter to cover everything—council, school board, courts, and even police.

The vastness of state and federal government makes a cozy maze for the bureaucracy. There are agencies and bureaus of federal and state governments that their own presidents and governors never heard of.

Covering government requires a knowledge of the machinery: how it works. Taking as many political science courses as possible is a helpful preparation.

Students who want to be government reporters must cultivate an interest in—if not a love of—politics. Governing is political. The whole fabric of government is political. Politics by definition means who gets what, how, and when.

Appointments of governors and presidents can turn regulatory agencies into extensions of executive policies. Presidents and governors make appointments to courts with political predilections and background in mind. Legislatures are constantly passing laws—or not passing laws—with their minds on the upcoming election.

On the local level, reporters need to understand zoning, bonding, millage, and taxing. Such things need analysis, explanation, and interpretation. The readers, befuddled by such matters, need light, not heat. Reporters must tell them what public affairs mean.

Government reporting requires study, research, and constant reading of newspapers, magazines, journals, and books. Reporters must know the history and background of issues. Reporters need this background for interpretive reporting. They must be able to give readers "the hows and whys."

Sometimes in covering government, reporters have lively, controversial issues such as abortion. But they also have dull hearings of water boards and zoning boards. Yet those issues too must be covered and understood.

Budget hearings may be the dullest of all. But they are the most important stories reporters write because they determine who gets what. Budget stories do not have to be written dully. A spritely lead such as this from the *Detroit Free Press* is an invitation to read forbidding news:

LANSING—A precarious and thinly stretched state budget, offering Detroit an appetizer but hardly a meal, was proposed to the Legislature Thursday by Governor Milliken.

SOURCE CULTIVATION

Source cultivation, necessary in all reporting, is vital in government reporting. It is essential to cultivate elected and appointed officials.

Even if sources are not regular newsmakers—say, lieutenant governors—they may be valuable sources for tips, background, and understanding of a political situation. A regular chat with them and their aides could pay off in good stories.

In addition to cultivating lawyers and politicians, as reporters you should cultivate secretaries, staffers, and aides. They too provide valuable tips.

Sources should be checked regularly in person or by phone. If reporters build up trust and confidence, sources will call them. Excellent sources can fill them in on what went on at those secret meetings government officials are ceaselessly fond of.

David Broder, *Washington Post* political reporter, has written: "What is important to me is being able to have access to people who are knowledgeable about a situation at a time when that situation is in the public eye."

As reporters make their beat rounds they may come up with five or six stories a day. Some they file as "overnights." The "hot stories" they work on a daily basis.

LOST MOMENTS IN AMERICAN HISTORY

'In calling for the declassification of this sensitive document, Mr. Jefferson forgets that it touches on the decision-making process leading to a major war.'

"CLASSIFIED"—Editorial cartoon illustrates the propensity of the United States government to stamp documents, no matter how insignificant, "classified." It was drawn by Draper Hill, editorial cartoonist for the *Detroit News*, while he worked for the *Commercial Appeal* in Memphis, Tennessee.

If you are sent on an out-of-town assignment, the best place to begin is usually with the local newspaper editor. The editor can be instructive about the politics, history, culture, mores, and attitudes of an area.

Reporters covering statehouses often do half of their reporting in bars. Lawmakers and other sources unwind there. The information reporters get is particularly useful in interpretive reporting.

Cultivating sources courts a danger: buddy-buddyism. It poses the classic reporter's dilemma. Journalists need to cultivate sources. They need to get close to sources of power. But if they get too close, they can lose their objectivity.

While being a pal to the powerful flatters the ego and gives reporters news breaks, it can turn reporters into public relations staffers.

Outsiders such as former Washington gadfly I. F. Stone do not get the inside scoops. But they have a priceless possession: independence.

The *Post's* Broder says, "We . . . are naïve when we complain . . . about politicians managing the news, because there's no way in the real world that I've observed in which we could ever expect politicians to leave the news unmanaged, not to shape it to their purposes."

Patrick J. Sloyan, Washington correspondent for *Newsday*, once offered this advice: "Keep up your hostility. The angrier I am, the better the story. I haven't become a member of the Nasty Wing of the profession. But I can do better work if I'm on the offensive. It is too easy in this business to take everything in stride, particularly after it seems as if you've written the same story several times before."

In short, an adversary relationship should exist between press and government.

Where do you draw the line? If reporters are too rough on public figures, they dry up as sources. If reporters are too gentle, they are working for public figures, not the newspaper and public.

William Rivers, former magazine reporter in Washington, has said such a relationship requires a "delicate balance of tact and antagonism, cooperation and conflict." Remember this: Ultimately public officials need the press more than the press needs them.

VETERANS VERSUS NEWCOMERS

Which is better: a long time on the beat, or a short time? It is probably best to keep a balance of oldtimers and newcomers on government beats. The veteran knows where the bodies are buried.

Newsday's Sloyan wrote that it took him two years as a U.S. Senate reporter for UPI before he really felt he got "an authoritative grip on the run." He added: "There is no substitute for experience on this job. Any reporter can come in cold and do a passable job. But to get behind the facade and the obvious to report what is really happening takes a lot of just plain hard work and connections."

Being on the beat too long, however, carries the peril of cronyism. It carries the peril of nonchalance: "We've done that story before." It carries the same peril as that for an athlete who is not hungry, who does not hustle.

Newcomers to government reporting often bring a fresh outlook, unjaded eyes and ears to their reporting. They hustle. They are enterprising.

HANDOUTS

Be wary of handouts in government reporting. City hall and state capitol press rooms are hit by twenty pounds of press releases daily. Reporters flip through all of them. Intriguing items are checked out. Good reporters *never, never* let themselves be victimized by writing handouts verbatim.

Bob Kotzbauer, who used to cover the Ohio statehouse for the Akron *Beacon-Journal*, once put it this way:

I always rewrite a handout. I don't mean just changing the lead. I try to put the story into perspective—to tell the reader what it means, to interpret it to a degree.

One day the Ohio Welfare Department decided to change the method of paying aid to the aged. We got a handout saying that the department was merely changing the formula of the program. It sounded innocuous. But we dug into it. We found it would have cost a lot of money. It would have made some people suffer.

SECRET MEETINGS

Secret meetings are as persistent as black flies on a Lake Erie beach in summertime. Despite "sunshine" or open-meeting laws, public bodies find ways to hold executive sessions. Their feeling is that it is their business. It is not. It is the public's business.

A reporter's recourse? Fight, fight, fight. If public bodies insist on executive sessions—gathering informally before the public meeting, thrashing out controversies and rubber-stamping their actions at official sessions—reporters use the newspaper's clout. They hound "the SOBs" with stories, photos, and editorials about the secret meetings. Filing suit sometimes forces a halt to secret sessions. Cultivating a dissident on the board or council may help break through the "secret curtain."

School boards make a good case when they say they need executive sessions for two matters—purchase of property and personnel matters. Yes, property values will go up if the newspaper reports that the board is interested. Yes, newspapers should not print—and usually do not—stories about morals cases.

But these things should be held out at the discretion of the editor. Reporters should be able to cover meetings where such matters are brought up. Editors, exercising good taste and judgment, seldom print them.

SUGGESTIONS FOR STUDENTS

• Break up long council or school board stories rather than running one 26-inch wrap-up. Shorter stories prevent items from getting buried. The individual stories get separate headlines. If your editors insist on single long stories, at least get highlights high up in the story by using "bullets."

• While you are covering government beats, store up notes, quotes, and anecdotes that do not make your daily or overnight file. The things you have squirreled away are good for "thumbsucker copy"—Sunday stories, interpretive and analytical takeouts.

• Get the latest editions of the *Congressional Directory*, state manual, county and municipal manuals. These books are fruitful sources of facts, figures, laws, constitutions, election results, functions of government agencies, and biographies of officials and politicians.

• Write profile pieces—personality stories—about the powerful and important on the government scene.

• Be alert for brights, oddities, and humorous shorts to enliven your government reporting file.

• Think of running weekly boxscores or charts showing the status of bills from committee to enactment or veto. If the legislature votes on an important bill, provide a breakdown of how individual lawmakers voted.

• The *AP Log* has stressed the need to get consumer and people angles into stories rather than parliamentary wrangles that interest legislators but not most readers.

• Be sure to use the conditional when talking about measures introduced: "The bill *would* provide a chicken in every pot."

Capital Reporting

So many stories come out of state capitals, especially when the legislature is in session, that capital correspondents usually handle only the major stories. Their papers rely on the wire services for routine stories. Here are the beginnings of two state capital stories by correspondents:

By LARRY STAMMER
Times Staff Writer

SACRAMENTO—Opposition to enactment of permanent state controls of coastal development all but dissolved Monday as the state Senate approved a key appropriation to fund landmark coastal protection legislation awaiting Gov. Brown's signature.

Assembly Speaker Leo T. McCarthy (D-San Francisco) said the 30-10 Senate vote on his appropriation bill meant that conservationists had overcome the last serious challenge to implementing the coastal protection bill.

The coastal bill by Sen. Jerome Smith (D-San Jose) was sent to the governor after winning final legislative passage Aug. 23.

However, the Smith bill contained no money to fund it.

—The Los Angeles Times

By JOHN ELMER
Chicago Tribune Press Service

SPRINGFIELD—A bill cutting back on major workman's compensation benefits won by organized labor last year was signed Monday by Gov. Walker.

The measure, supported by business groups even though it was not all they wanted, is expected to help reduce soaring workman's compensation insurance costs which in some cases have doubled since the 1975 law took effect.

A main provision of the new bill, which becomes law Oct. 1, sets a maximum of about $12,000 on annual workman's compensation payments.

That maximum is based on the statewide average weekly manufacturing wage, now $231.42 a week.

Under the current law, there was no limit on the amount an employee or a survivor could collect. The employee could get up to 50 percent of his salary regardless of its size.

—The Chicago Tribune

Budget Story

Here is the top of a budget story from the *Houston Post:*

By FRANK DAVIS
Post Reporter

The city council, sharply divided on whether city employees can be given a 6 percent pay increase, Wednesday approved the long-delayed record $385 million budget for next year.

The vote on the budget submitted by Mayor Fred Hofheinz was 5-4.

No increase will be required in the present tax rate of $1.58 for each $100 of assessed valuation or in the 53 percent assessment ratio.

Individual tax bills will go up in many cases, however, because of the city's property revaluation program.

Mayor Hofheinz drew the votes needed to approve the budget from council members Judson Robinson, Jr., Homer Ford, Jim Westmoreland and Johnny Goyen.

Council members Larry McKaskle, Louis Macey, Frank Mancuso and Frank Mann voted against the motion to adopt the budget.

Except for deletion of $75,000 earmarked to pay for now-cancelled public performances by the striking Houston Symphony Orchestra, the budget was adopted without changing any of the expenditures Hofheinz initially proposed when he submitted the budget June 28.

The new budget is up 17.4 percent over last year's expenditures.

Westmoreland initially proposed adopting the budget with a provision that city employees receive a 6 percent pay increase in December using money which the departments were budgeted, but which were unspent.

End Papers

*Sidebar—*Story that runs alongside another. If the lead is Watergate, the sidebar is slugged: "with Watergate."

Obscure places—Locate obscure places for readers. This way: "50 miles west of St. Louis," "25 miles north of Miami."

Syntax—As Will Rogers once said, it has to be bad with sin and tax in it. A common error in newspapering is switching from third person to first person. This way: "Fortas said he would take the secret 'with me to my grave.' " Recast the sentence so it reads, "Fortas said he would take the secret with *him* to *his* grave."

Tense agreement—Grammatical purists insist that it should be: "Carter *said* he *believed* abortion was wrong" (all three verbs in the past tense). However, it is all right to write: "Carter said he believed abortion is wrong." Those who say the second version is all right argue that Carter believed it when he said it and he still believes it.

Correct—Reporters use "CQ" to indicate that unusual spelling is correct: "Smyth (cq)." With video terminals, reporters sometimes use white backgrounding to show that the word is correctly spelled.

Addresses—Get exact addresses. Whether your paper will print them is a matter of judgment. Editors long ago omitted addresses of beauty queens to spare them lecherous phone calls.

SUGGESTIONS FOR INSTRUCTORS

- Assign coverage of a council meeting. Make sure students get an agenda, learning what are the major issues to be discussed. They can get background on the key issues and controversies from council members, clerks, journalists, and the audience. Caution for students: Filter facts from opinion. All but the journalists may be biased. Students should remember to report how individual council members vote on major issues.

- Assign coverage of a school board meeting.

- Give students handouts showing the organization of city, county, and state government.

Chapter 30

Elections and Politics

Politics is a story that never ends. It goes on 365 days a year—366 in leap year. The day after an election reporters write speculative pieces about contenders four years hence.

These are some of the kinds of recurring political stories: voter registration deadlines, candidates' filing deadlines, stories on candidates as they file, campaign coverage, candidates' profile pieces, election analysis stories, poll stories, preelection and postelection stories, and endless speculation stories.

Political reporters steep themselves in politics. They seldom have a day off because when they are not at the office they are "eating and drinking" politics. They attend party rallies and political meetings. They cultivate sources at all levels, from the highest party officials to humble precinct captains. Political writers without sources would soon be assigned to cover spelling bees.

Political writers know the election laws. They know the workings of political parties. They follow the parties' factional fights and power struggles. They study political science, history, and theory. They look for parallels in history that apply to politics today.

James Reston of the *New York Times* wrote a column about Presidents being abandoned by their own parties at nominating conventions. In four paragraphs he concisely cited the losing record of substitutes for sitting Presidents.

In short, good political reporters are constantly doing their homework. They study precincts and voting records. One of their "bibles" is *The Almanac of American Politics** by Michael Barone, which contains a description of every congressman or congresswoman. It carries a description of the political, social, and economic aspects of each district.

Political reporters also learn what buncombe is. (A North Carolina congressman from Buncombe County, asked why he had given such a flowery and insincere speech, replied: "I was not speaking to the House, but to Buncombe.")

During campaigns, political reporters yawn through "the speech" five or ten times a day. It is the same talk repeated constantly. The only difference is that each delivery is sprinkled with local reference to politicians, the sugar beet crop, the pottery industry, and "the need for protectionist trade laws" (or "free trade laws"; cross out one).

"The speech" can provide humor when candidates don't remember what town they are in or they mispronounce names of local politicians. In the 1976 Presidential campaign, Gerald Ford once even forgot what state he was in.

PREELECTION STORIES

Preelection stories need these ingredients:

- Office at stake, candidates, and parties.
- Brief biographies of opponents, age, address, job, and background.
- Favorite? Interpretive aspect needs support. Why favored? Polls? Rock-ribbed Republican district? What was the party vote in the last election? Which party does voter registration favor?
- District location with rough boundaries.
- SES elements. Social-economic-status of district: working class, middle class, or silkstocking; religious, racial, ethnic composition: Catholic, Polish, Jewish, black.
- Issues. Major differences. Incumbent's record. How do opponents stand on controversies?
- Liberal, moderate, conservative, radical, reactionary?
- Strategy. Tactics and campaign methods: door-to-door, plant gates, newspaper ads, saturation of radio and TV with commercials?
- Endorsements. Major support and backing.
- Polls open. Voters need a reminder each election.
- Weather. Possible influence on outcome.
- Turnout forecast. Election official's prediction of turnout. Higher or lower than usual? Why? Who will be helped, who hindered?
- Implication. What is at stake: leadership post, key committee seat, party balance in House or Senate?

*Gambit, Inc., Boston, 1973.

All these factors will not be present in every preelection story. But they are the kinds of things to look for.

Here is a preelection story from the *Detroit Free Press*:

By THOMAS C. FOX and KIRK CHEYFITZ
Free Press Staff Writers

Some controversial statewide proposals and a number of hotly contested federal, state, county and local races are expected to draw Michigan voters to the polls in record numbers Tuesday.

Bernard Apol, state election director, predicted 3,750,000 voters—72 percent of those registered—will cast ballots.

This compares with 3,490,000 who voted in 1972 when the turnout also was 72 percent.

The rate of voting in Michigan, Apol said, will be higher than the national average.

In Detroit, the City Clerk's office is predicting a lower turnout—about 65 percent of the 762,575 who are eligible.

Tuesday's turnout rate, however, is expected to be higher than in 1972 when 61 percent of eligible Detroit voters cast ballots.

Polls open at 7 A.M. and close at 8 P M with people in line at that time allowed to vote.

Weather forecasts call for Tuesday to be cloudy with a chance of rain.

The forecast for Detroit was for clouds and a chance of showers with the high temperatures near 50.

Besides voting to elect a president, Michigan voters will decide who will succeed Democrat Philip A. Hart in the U.S. Senate and which, if any, of four state proposals will become law.

Voters also will elect three Michigan Supreme Court justices, 19 U.S. congressmen and 110 state legislators.

In Detroit, voters will face proposal E, which calls for a five-mill property tax increase over the next five years to provide additional funds to operate the Detroit public schools.

Detroiters will be able to say whether they want a change in state law that would permit gambling in up to six casinos to be located in Detroit.

The vote on Proposal G, however, is an advisory vote and not legally binding.

Registration Figures

Sometimes a preelection story deals with registration figures. Here is one:

By FRANK M. MATTHEWS
Post-Gazette Political Writer

Allegheny County set a record in the number of voters registered between the April primary and the Oct. 4 deadline but still came up 119,196 short of the total number eligible to vote in the presidential election of 1972.

The decline in total voters reflected an apathy that does not necessarily apply to the coming Ford-Carter election but does demonstrate the disgust with politics that was generated in the Watergate, sex scandal years after 1972.

In those in-between years thousands upon thousands of voters simply failed to go to the polls and were automatically purged from the registration lists after two years of failure to vote.

The big gain in new and renewed registrations also has been abetted by the new ease of mail registration.

In any event, Elections Director Kenneth Dixon reported that 73,159 names were added to the registration lists for a county-wide total of 531,393 Democrats to 244,500 Republicans.

The county-wide eligibility to vote totals 801,679, including independents and small party members, compared with 920,875 in 1972.

The resurgence favored the Democratic party. In the City of Pittsburgh there are now 184,096 Democrats and 41,378 Republicans, an all-time low minority.

—Pittsburgh Post-Gazette

Sketching Contenders

Sometimes a preelection story sketches the contenders—and hints at a possible outcome. Here is one:

By BERNIE SHELLUM

Six months ago most people in Ramsey County couldn't remember when Joe Karth wasn't their congressman.

Those who could had to think back 18 years.

But now, a little more than four months after Karth unexpectedly announced his retirement, his constituents are sorting through a crowded field to choose his successor.

They're out of practice and the task isn't easy.

In all likelihood, the party's nominee will be State Rep. Bruce Vento, 35, who has the advantages of labor endorsement and an Italian Catholic name.

But then again it might be State Auditor Robert Mattson, who, at 28, is well known and has dozens of newspaper headlines testifying to his guardianship of taxpayers' dollars.

Or it might be John Connolly, 44, an Irish Catholic who holds no public office but has a long record in state and local politics.

All three are considered potential winners of the Sept. 14 primary in which victory is equivalent to election because of the Fourth Congressional District's heavily Democratic Farm Labor Party orientation.

Whatever the outcome, it is expected to be close. Campaign polling for Vento showed that in late July a majority of those likely to vote still had not made up their minds.

In trying to gain voters' attention, the three campaigners are providing the only primary contest in Minnesota that can compete for public interest with the pollen count.

—The Minneapolis Tribune

POSTELECTION STORIES

Here are checkpoints in postelection copy:

- Results. Winners and losers. Upsets? Surprise showings?
- Vote margins. Total vote and percentage of vote.
- Analysis. Whys of winning and losing. Interpretive aspect. Needs support: Turnout a factor? Bloc votes? Winning issues?
- Concession and victory statements.
- Implications and consequences.
- Trends and portents: swing left, swing right, law-and-order vote; economic discontent.

Here are excerpts from a *New York Times* story on the election of Thomas Bradley as mayor in Los Angeles:

Bradley, a 55-year-old City Councilman and former police officer, scored a surprisingly solid victory over Mayor Sam Yorty.

The triumph was even more remarkable for two reasons:

It came in the face of what were viewed as the mayor's appeals to racial fears and divisions and it came in the city where the Watts riot of 1965 sparked a wave of racial turmoil across the country.

For Yorty, who is now 63 years old, the defeat probably marked the end of a long career. . . .

Analysis of the returns shows that Bradley won almost half the white vote and ran particularly strong in liberal, Jewish districts on the west side.

He gained a small margin among Mexican-Americans, who backed Mayor Yorty four years ago, and won more than 9 of every 10 black votes cast.

Bradley's victory marked the first time that a black candidate has been elected mayor of a major city with the help of so many white votes.

When Richard G. Hatcher won in Gary, Ind., and Kenneth A. Gibson was elected in Newark, both cities were more than 50 percent black.

The story also carried this:

With all but one precinct reporting, the totals were:

Bradley	431,222
Yorty	334,297

This practice enables newspapers to update a story easily for the next edition by inserting the latest figures.

BIAS OF REPORTERS?

Do reporters' biases intrude on their political reporting? Not with good papers and good journalists. Most big-city reporters are probably liberal or left-leaning. Yet they will report Republican or conservative candidates as fairly as they do liberal Democrats.

The fact is that the press, whatever the preferences of individual reporters, is the enemy to many politicians. The relationship has been well summarized by the *New York Times'* Reston:

The candidates and the press are fussing at each other again and this is the way it should be. They have different jobs and in many ways they are natural enemies, like cats and dogs.

The first job of the candidate is to win, and he usually says what he thinks will help him win. The job of the reporter is to report what happens and decontaminate as much of the political poison as he can.

During the 1968 Presidential primary campaign, Michigan's George Romney displayed symptoms of foot-in-the-mouth disease. The quip became: "The press is killing Romney—it is quoting what he says."

The *UPI Reporter*, wire service newsletter, once commented:

A loser's complaint that he has been hurt by slanted copy often means no more than that the reporters have failed to redress the losing candidate's own mistakes. . . .

The reporter must be more than a recording spectator balancing claim and counterclaim to a cadence of bleak phrases. . . . The good political reporter is more like a professional witness. His stories enable us to taste the event and to understand what it means. He has no thought of helping or harming a candidate but only of reporting the news.

Partly because of bias fears, some papers rotate reporters covering candidates. More important, by switching candidates reporters get a perspective on the overall campaign—learning styles, issues, personalities, and campaign techniques first-hand.

OPINION POLLS

How accurate are opinion polls? Highly. The Gallup poll has been off an average of just 1.2 percent in national elections since 1952. Scientific and more sophisticated sampling have made polls much more accurate since the *Literary Digest's* incredibly wrong pick of Landon over Roosevelt in 1936. (It polled by telephone in a day when most phones were owned by prosperous citizens and hence Republican voters.)

The polling sample today is random, which in polling means just the opposite of haphazard. Random sampling means that every voter of the social-economic-status scale has a chance to be included. The margin of error in polling has been reduced to 3 or 4 percent.

What about the bandwagon effect? Do people vote for the leader in the polls? About 1 percent do. But this is balanced by the 1 percent who vote for the poll underdog.

However, if a candidate is trailing badly in the polls, campaign contributions dry up and the morale of campaign workers erodes.

More and more polls are being used by candidates to find out voter attitudes rather than just who is leading. It tells them what issues to stress and which ones to play down.

The problem here is politics by polling. Candidates tell voters what they want to hear rather than what they ought to hear. The contrary argument is that before you can be a political leader you must be elected. The theory is that by downplaying a potentially damaging issue on the hustings, a successful candidate can educate voters on vital issues once in office.

A larger menace, however, is electronic packaging. Joe McGinniss's book *The Selling of the President** is a frightening look at how Richard Nixon manipulated the media to win office in 1968.

"They shielded him, controlled him and controlled the atmosphere around him," McGinniss writes. "It was as if they were building not a President but an Astrodome, where the wind would never blow, the temperature never rise or fall and the ball would never bounce erratically on the artificial grass."

McGinniss's sad conclusion: "The TV candidate, then, is measured not against his predecessors—not against a standard of performance established by two centuries of democracy—but against Mike Douglas. How well does he handle himself? Does he mumble, does he twitch, does he make me laugh? Do I feel warm inside?

"Style becomes substance. The medium is the massage and the masseur gets the votes."

"Pols" Bearing Polls

Another gimmick in polling is for primary candidates to set low-expectation levels for themselves—say, 15 percent of the vote. They know they will easily surpass that figure. So when they get 25 percent of the votes, candidates claim a victory while masking the fact that they ran third or fourth.

*Trident Press, New York, 1969.

As pollster Burns W. Roper has warned the press: "Beware of 'pols' bearing polls."

Tape Recorders

"Use of tape recorders for campaign coverage is absolutely essential," the *AP Log* has advised.

"In every campaign, no matter how carefully reported, challenges arise and tape recordings of campaign speeches, press conferences and other comments are the best way to put down the challenges."

"PRECISION JOURNALISM"

The Knight-Ridder Newspapers chain is doing much more polling and opinion surveying, not just in politics, but in all its reporting. It tries to be much more scientific about voter and public attitudes in contrast to the old informal, "man-on-the-street-interview" approach.

Philip Meyer, of the Knight chain, who has written a book called *Precision Journalism*, has been the leading exponent of the more scientific and sociological approach to reporting.

Here is the top part of a Meyer "news analysis" story:

WASHINGTON—Somewhere between April and September, Jimmy Carter became more "presidential" in the eyes of the voters than the man who is president.

Now President Ford enters Thursday night's debate with a desperate need to outshine the formidable personality of his opponent, a new survey by Knight-Ridder Newspapers reveals.

In April, Ford was viewed as more honest, more able and more appealing than Carter. The former Georgia governor has turned all that around.

Ford is still rated as able and as honest as before, but Carter is now given even higher ratings on those key presidential qualities.

And on personal appeal—the factor which explains voter decisions more than any other—Ford has fallen while Carter has climbed.

The current flaps over Carter's tax plans and his views on sex and sin expressed in Playboy magazine hadn't happened when this latest survey was taken between Sept. 7 and Sept. 12.

But if those issues are like the others in this campaign, they won't last very long or have much measurable effect on the voters.

Earlier, controversial Carter statements about neighborhood integration and abortion have drawn flurries of interest from news media, but the survey shows few signs of lasting concern by the voters.

Ford therefore has much ground to regain in the debates. But the debates could help Carter even more.

The survey shows that much of the Democrat's support comes from people who are unlikely to vote. Anything Carter can do to stir up interest in the campaign will solidify his support.

In fact, when those who are now least likely to vote in November are not counted, Carter's big lead shrinks substantially.

Sharp editors are wary of "pols" bearing polls. They don't let their newspaper be used by politicians. But newspapers can do a better job in their reporting of polls.

It may not be the worst recorded example of unfairness, but an Alaska daily contested for the dishonor by writing: "another poll, taken by a person who did not wish to be identified, said. . . ."

Some papers such as the *Miami Herald* and the *Louisville Courier-Journal* have fairness guidelines for political editors and reporters. Some of the things poll stories should contain are: sponsor; sample size; timing of interview; method of contact; population definition; wording of question; error allowance; and base of results (men, women, age, occupation).

The timing of interviews is important. The poll may have been taken before an event caused the candidate's popularity to surge or to decline.

Nomination of a President

Here is the opening of a Washington correspondent's account of a presidential nomination for *Newsday* (Long Island, N.Y.):

By PATRICK J. SLOYAN
Newsday Washington Bureau

KANSAS CITY—President Ford won the Republican nomination early today after a party-wrenching struggle that sent him to Ronald Reagan's side for a joint plea for party unity in the November showdown with Jimmy Carter.

Despite hoots from Reagan diehards, the President and the former California governor beamed at a 3 A.M. (New York time) news conference like two weary but happy fighters.

"I don't think our fight has been a bitter one," Ford said after Reagan pledged his full support.

The ex-actor said, "It was a good fight, mom, and he won."

But it was a tattered GOP standard that Ford will accept tonight, won by a narrow 117 votes after nine months of primaries that left the Democratic ticket with a runaway lead in the polls and the Republicans little time to catch up.

At 1 P.M. today Ford selects a vice presidential candidate who could help him win the presidency in his own right only 10 weeks from now.

In the sweltering Kemper Arena last night, the Reagan delegates hooted and hollered and honked plastic horns so long that many Americans were asleep when Ford finally was nominated.

Victory for Ford came at 1:30 A.M. and within the hour his limousine was hurtling the three-mile route to Reagan hotel headquarters in this muggy cowtown. Boos greeted the President at Reagan's hotel and there were shouts of "no V.P."

But both men emerged after a private 15-minute meeting, their smiles hiding the drain of campaigning and the lateness of the hour.

Ford led off the joint news conference commending Reagan for his campaign.

"You really got us in shape," Ford said. "I thank you for your indication of full support."

Reagan replied: "As we both agreed from the beginning, when the fight was over we'd be on the same side."

Reagan said he planned to return to writing and his radio show.

Ford said that the battle "was good for the Republican Party—it was beneficial."

He predicted the nation would support the GOP philosophy and reject Carter.

Election Reporting Tips from UPI

Arnold Sawislak, UPI senior political writer, wrote an "Election Handbook" with some useful tips. Among Sawislak's points are:

- "Make contacts with political organizations, asking to be put on mailing lists for spot news releases, news conference announcements, and printed material distributed to party members.
- "Know where to contact campaign officials at night as well as during business hours. Visiting campaign offices helps build contacts that can be valuable when the campaign gets hectic—and on election night.
- "Keep current with political developments and party affairs. This can involve attending events or covering stories that might seem marginal. If there is time, a reporter can learn more in a half hour of circulating at a dinner or reception than in days of telephoning and interviewing. This also means a lot of reading: newspaper columnists, commentators, books and reports.
- "Maintain files. A political reporter's files can fill a room or a pocket. The important thing is to have background and source material at hand. Filing your own political stories is a start. Clipping newspapers, magazines and other material can build files that will give depth and authenticity to stories written under intense time pressure. The work that goes into files pays off.
- Calling winners is more than a mathematical trick. You must know which candidate should do well in what areas and why. Don't wait until election day to do your homework. Talk to political pros in both parties at every chance. Accept what they agree on and dismiss their puffery."

Definitions

Coattail effect—Pull of someone at the top of the ticket that sweeps others on the ballot into office.

Majority—One more than half the votes cast.

Plurality—In an election with three or more contestants and in which no candidate wins a majority, a plurality is getting at least one more vote than any other candidate in the race. A plurality is also the margin of the winner over the closest competitor in such an election. In the following election result, Young has a plurality: Young 237,000, Browne 167,000, and Mogk 110,000.

Precinct delegate—Grass root of political party. Person elected by neighbors to represent party in county or congressional district. District in turn elects officers and participants in party's state convention.

Safe district—One in which the incumbent invariably wins. A *marginal* or *swing district* is one that can go either way.

Silkstocking district—Upper-crust district.

Roorback—A false political report or a damaging story circulated just before an election with practically no rebuttal time available.

Why People Vote as They Do

Vote patterns are changing. Independent voters—as opposed to solid party voters—are increasing greatly. One political scientist estimates that one-third of the voters are independents. But some factors are still valid about voting. They are:

Peer group Voting as your associates do in your union, business, job, or occupation.

SES—Voting according to your position on the social-economic-status scale. Voting your "class."

Family tie—Once a powerful factor in how people voted, now fewer than 40 percent vote as their parents did.

Gut issues—Issues that hit voters where they live: peace and prosperity; the pocketbook—unemployment, inflation, and recession; and race—busing.

SUGGESTIONS FOR INSTRUCTOR

- Assign preelection story.
- Assign preelection analytical story, having students write a takeout on the race—candidates, issues, tactics, favorites.
- Assign postelection story.

Chapter 31

Cutlines: "No Pictures without Captions"

The sign in the photo lab of the *Detroit Free Press* is emphatic: "No Pictures without Captions." A photo without captions—*cutlines* or *indents*, as the photo information is variously known—is worthless to a newspaper.

Reporters and photo editors usually write cutlines. But the photographer is responsible for getting the information. Reporters often help photographers get caption information.

The basic rule of caption writing is to use the present tense for action taking place before the reader's eye: "President Carter signs housing bill"; "Mayor Beame speaks to council."

Do not mix present tense with past tense in the same sentence. It is illogical. This sort of thing: "Princess Cantacuzene, 90-year-old granddaughter of President Grant, watches the goings-on at the White House yesterday." Put the time element in the next sentence.

This is the way: "Jack Nicklaus flings his putter after missing three-foot birdie putt. Disappointment came on eighth hole of Memphis Open yesterday."

When photo and story "tie"—go together—the time element is often left out. The reader can tell the time element from the story.

Ideally, story and art should be together on a page. But because of ads or other layout problems, sometimes stories and accompanying photos must be separated. In such cases write a *refer line*—reference line—with the cutline: "(Story on page 7A)."

Leave out references to photos that are obvious to the reader: "Photo above shows. . ."; "Senator Hansen smiles as he greets supporters."

However, when you have combination art—several photos dealing with the same subject in a picture layout—sometimes you need to specify which photo you are writing about. You can do it this way: "(photo at left)," "(right)," or "(above)."

On the other hand, cutlines should explain action or situations not readily apparent to the reader. Are the men hugging or wrestling? If someone who baseball fans know is a catcher turns up in a photo wearing a first-baseman's glove, explain why he was playing first base.

If a photo shows Egyptians holding aloft their shoes, add this kind of sentence: "Cairo sources said the shoe-waving was an insulting gesture."

Translate foreign signs and slogans that appear in photos. Relatively few newspaper subscribers read French and even fewer know Russian or Chinese. Tell in your cutline that "À bas Nixon" means "Down with Nixon."

Be wary of editorializing. Let photos speak for themselves. A photo caption in a Detroit newspaper about a Grand Dragon of the Ku Klux Klan described him as tough-looking. But even if he had been, let readers reach that conclusion without prompting from the caption.

KEEP CUTLINES BRIEF

Captions should be brief, especially with art that ties in with a story. It is unnecessary to repeat facts in a cutline and a story. With a big story about an earthquake in Guatemala, the accompanying photo needs no more information than this: "A Guatemala City youngster cooks beans over an open fire amid the earthquake rubble."

A Detroit newspaper used to run 20-inch sports stories tied with art on the game. For some strange reason captions ran $1\frac{1}{2}$-inches deep under multiple-column photos with final score, attendance, and other facts given in the news story.

However, if you have "wild art"—photos standing alone without a story tie—your cutline information needs to be fuller. You should answer the "five Ws" and the "H" if possible.

ACCURACY

Before releasing caption information, take 60 seconds to double-check for accuracy. Check names, spellings, and proper order of identification from left to right.

Make sure story and cutline information jibe. Errors sometimes occur when one reporter writes the story and another handles the cutlines. This sort of thing: *Greene* in copy and *Green* in captions: *6,000* in rally story, *5,000* in cutlines.

Roy Copperud, in his *Editor & Publisher* column, recommended that cutlines should be written from the photo information of the same wire service whose story your paper is running to avoid factual inconsistencies.

"Keep such details as the toll in accidents out of the cutlines in a developing story," Copperud says. "Correction of the cutlines tends to be overlooked when the figure is updated in the story."*

Count the number of people in a photo. Have they all been identified? Are you sure those men are playing chess, as a *New York Times* caption once said when the photo clearly showed the men were playing checkers? Are you sure the woman is knitting, not crocheting, as a *Detroit News* caption wrongly said? Does your story say the politician appeared without his customary cigar but your photo shows him smoking a cigar?

Don't be afraid to get humorous touches in feature-photo captions. Hardnews cutlines have to be written straight. But tongue-in-cheek phrasing, if warranted, enhances feature photos.

If you run pure art feature photos, give some technical details such as F-stops and speed. Many of your readers are amateur shutterbugs and are interested in this kind of information.

CAPTION STYLES

Cutline styles vary greatly by paper. Some use catchlines, cutline headlines. Some put catchlines on the side of the caption, some above. Some papers use boldface cap lead-ins rather than catchlines.

Probably as good a cutline style as any is this:

—AP Photo

CAPITAL CRUSH—Democratic women surround President Carter during a reception on White House lawn.

The BFC (boldface cap) lead-in should be a short sum-up of the story. The BFC lead-in stands alone. It should not read right into the cutline (although that is the style on some papers). Keep BFC lead-ins short. No more than three long words should be used in BFC lead-ins.

The BFC lead-ins should be flush left (up against the left margin). They start without indentation. The credit line—the name of the photographer or the source—should go below the picture, above the cutline, flush right (up against the right margin).

*Jan. 2, 1965, p. 37.

If you have two people in the photo, you need to identify only one as "(left)." If you have a man and a woman, usually neither needs identification as "(left)" or "(right)." If you have a group photo, identify people as "(left to right)" or "(l. to r.)."

Cutlines should be slugged: "cutline/mideast/jones." Below that, write the column width and page number. Indicating the column width ensures that a cutline will be set the proper measure. Photo depth is written on the back of the art, but that is no concern of the reporter writing captions.

Some papers like the *New York Times* and the *Los Angeles Times* insist on captions that come out full (flush) at the end of the last line. Most papers do not think the unfinished appearance of an uneven cutline is worth the bother of making lines come out full.

Papers that do think it is worth the bother use caption blanks. This enables reporters to write cutlines that come out even. The cutline writer circles optional words, words that do not have to be set if the caption will come out flush right without them. For example, "he was stabbed with an army bayonet." "Army" can be circled, meaning it does not need to be set if the line comes out full without it.

SUGGESTION FOR INSTRUCTOR

• Get some news photographs with captions from a local newspaper. Have students write cutlines under deadline.

Chapter 32

Investigative Reporting

Investigative reporting is exposé journalism. It is exposing corruption and wrong-
doing in government and public institutions. At the turn of the century it was
called "muckraking."

Muckraking is an old, honorable newspaper tradition. It is not a "dirty
word," although in the public mind it often is. Somehow the public confuses
muckraking with cheap sensationalism, the sort of thing *Confidential* magazine
specialized in.

Modern muckrakers—Ralph Nader, to name a giant—are just as careful to
document their charges as Lincoln Steffens and Ida Tarbell were in the 1900s.
Nader and his staff of Nader's Raiders do prodigious research. They cannot afford to be slipshod. Their credibility rides with their work—not to mention libel
suits.

Even before the magazine muckrakers, many newspapers fought corruption. The most notable example was the drumfire of the *New York Times* in
the 1870s which helped topple the corrupt House of Tweed.

Crusade and *campaign* are used interchangeably by newspapers. But there
is a subtle distinction. A *campaign* is usually a newspaper drive *for* safe issues—
street lighting, parks, stadiums.

A *crusade* is a newspaper drive *against* something: exposing evils and corruption. The target is tougher: tougher issues and tougher people and institutions.

Typical crusade targets are corruption in public office—what Robert Woodward and Carl Berstein did with Watergate. Their relentless exposé earned the Pulitzer prize for the *Washington Post* in public service reporting.

Woodward and Bernstein tenaciously pursued that story in the face of denials from the Nixon administration and much apathy from the press. Students should read their book *All the President's Men.* It is a reporter's classic of digging, of wearying but unremitting pursuit of a story, of legwork, of diligence, of refusal to take "no" for an answer.

Other typical crusade targets are misuse of public funds and poor conditions in jails, hospitals, and nursing homes.

Ben Bagdikian, a leading press critic, once summed up the difference between campaigning and crusading:

The press needs to remember how to use spears, to do unfrightened investigative reporting. I don't mean those fearless exposés of overtime parkers or four-square opposition to typhoid fever. I mean reporting on the decisions of governments and corporations whose policies control our lives.

INVESTIGATIVE VERSUS INTERPRETIVE REPORTING

Investigative reporting is much harder than interpretive reporting. In interpretive reporting, facts and records are available. Sources are cooperative.

In investigative reporting, the records and files are often closed—if not shredded. Sources are uncooperative. It is difficult to get enough facts to break a story. Pressure is put on people to clam up, to refuse to talk to the press.

Historian Barbara Tuchman noted the problem in her book *The Proud Tower.** Investigators trying to reopen an inquiry into the notorious Dreyfus Affair in France at the turn of the last century faced "silence, obfuscation and closed doors," Tuchman wrote.

Sometimes newspaper publishers are pressured to call off the investigative "dogs." That pressure can come from Presidents of the United States. It can come from the wealthy, the powerful, the influential. The lives of reporters and their families may be threatened.

Indeed, investigative reporting can be hazardous duty, as the murder of an Arizona reporter showed all too painfully. Don Bolles of the *Arizona Republic* was killed while working on an article about the Mafia.

Bolles, a forty-seven-year-old reporter who had written exposés about land-fraud schemes and criminal elements with legitimate business "fronts," was

*The Macmillan Company, New York, 1966.

PRESS MARTYR—Don Bolles, investigative reporter for the *Arizona Republic*, was murdered while checking out a tip for his newspaper. *(Photo by the* Arizona Republic.*)*

fatally injured by a bomb that exploded when he turned on the ignition in his car.

Bolles was the victim of a setup. He had been lured to a Phoenix hotel by a call from an underworld contact who had promised information about a land deal. Before he died, Bolles told authorities: "They finally got me—the Mafia."

DETECTIVE'S INSTINCTS NEEDED

Investigative reporting requires dogged pursuit and tenacity. It requires a detective's instincts, a refusal to quit, a refusal to be put off.

Investigative reporting requires a willingness by the paper to spend large sums of time and money without seeing any stories.

The *Los Angeles Times* once sent a reporter on a six-month investigation of local corruption. When the case got hot, it sent in an investigative reporting team. The resultant exposé led to a Pulitzer.

That kind of journalism requires guts—from reporters, editors, and publishers. There can be no investigative reporting if editors and publishers do not back their reporters to the hilt.

Scott Christianson, investigative reporter for the Knickerbocker *News-Union Star* in Albany, New York, wrote in *Quill*:

Investigative reporting requires a newspaper to put itself on the line—to take a stand—to risk a libel action or a government subpoena—or worse yet, a loss in advertising.

It takes guts for a newspaper to call the mayor a thief and a gangster, even when it has the facts and can prove them in a court of law. . . .

My own newspaper suffered a devastating loss of legal advertising as a result of its criticisms of the local powers-that-be.

INVESTIGATIVE REPORTING ADVICE

To avoid pitfalls, observe the following:

- Never overlook a tip. Newspapers are deluged with crank calls. But check them out. Perhaps 999 out of 1,000 tips are worthless. But one could lead to an exposé and a Pulitzer.

William Lambert started the investigation for *Life* magazine that forced the resignation of Supreme Court Justice Abe Fortas following a chance remark from a low-level government official. Lambert stayed with the story despite blandishments and sweet talk from Fortas and the President of the United States.

- While interviewing, checking files and documents, keep asking: Who else is involved?

- Absolute care. Woodward and Bernstein tell of having had at least two sources verify every Watergate story. Bernstein wrote in *Quill*: "We had some rules that we used about not going with anything based on one source, simply because we knew some items of information were planted. We wanted to be able to check things out in two places."

- Documentation is essential. Photostating your records, deeds, and canceled checks is necessary in case the files mysteriously disappear.

- Stay within the law. Don't pry open safes or burglarize offices. Yet Jules Witcover, *Washington Post* investigative reporter, admitted in a panel discussion at a Sigma Delta Chi convention that investigative reporting requires lots of unsavory tactics. "Ordinarily I wouldn't break the law but if stakes are high enough—I do so," Witcover said.

After the late Drew Pearson broke a scandal about a Connecticut senator because the senator's aides gave him private files, the *New York Times'* Reston posed a difficult ethical question: Should Pearson have been arrested or been awarded the Pulitzer prize?

- Half-a-loaf technique. Sometimes papers are unable to button up an investigative story. They decide to go with "what they've got." The hope is that a partial story will spawn a flood of calls, visits, tips, and revelations that will complete the exposé.

- Things to check: land-buying deals, payroll padding, conflicts of interest, contracts for friends and officeholders, hiring of pals as payoffs.
- Verification. Investigative reporters are constantly asked by their editors—and libel lawyers—"How do we know this is true?"
- Tactics that sometimes work. Sources won't talk? Find out as much rumor and gossip about a situation as possible and then confront the source with what you know. Sometimes sources will talk. Brazenness. Sometimes you can pretend you know more than you do. By brashly confronting sources, reporters sometimes get sources to spill everything.

Robert Greene, *Newsday* editor who used to be a top investigative reporter, has rightly observed that investigative reporting cannot be taught in journalism schools. Experience is its only teacher. Greene, in a talk at an Association for Education in Journalism convention, made these points about investigative reporting:

- It is solitary work. Investigative reporters cut themselves off from friends and colleagues. They have little or no social life. They see little of their wives. They should be aware of the following:
- They need an instinct for the jugular.
- They should be the best reporter on the staff.
- They must immerse themselves in the story.
- They must be prepared for the worst cooperation of their reporting lives: lost documents, lost keys to record rooms, and delay after delay in filling information requests.

WRITING INVESTIGATIVE STORIES

Don't mar your solid reporting with lurid, sensational language. Tell it straight. Stick to cold, hard facts. They are more potent than polemics.

Don't brag about your exposé: "as revealed by the Daily Blah."

Crusading journalism shows a newspaper has character, courage, backbone. Do it for the public good, not Pulitzer prizes and circulation boosts—although those lagniappes are heartily welcome.

Finally, successful investigative reporting carries a great satisfaction for journalists. The wearying hours are forgotten in the glow of satisfaction. It feels great to have the power of the press used for a good end.

"Talk to Everyone"

Don Bolles once offered this primer for newspaper sleuths:

- "Talk to everyone. Don't reject a possible lead just because the person has been in stir, has a bad reputation or looks seedy.

"Once a con man told me about an $82 million fraud laced with impossible claims about blackmailing a U.S. senator and gold bars stashed in a Latin American hotel room. Every word was true—the man had been cut out of the deal.

- "Spend a lot of time making social conversation with important officials. . . . Listen. Earn their confidence.

"One time an official tested me with some secondary information. I protected him as the source. Then one day he asked, "Would you like to know who's bribing ____?" He proceeded to give me a list of the Who's Who of Arizona.

- "Learn where to look in public records. But don't neglect your own newspaper files. Check county recorder indexes, if you have one, to find out what suits have been filed against and by the person. Track the title on his house.

- "Check your state agency on any firms he may be involved in. Find out if he's ever filed for bankruptcy, or if there are any tax liens against him.

- "It's often a boring and tedious job, but pays handsome dividends. We cleaned up two free-spending state agencies, the Highway Patrol and Fair Commission, mainly from state auditor claims in the statehouse basement.

- "Above all, do not discuss what one source said with another and especially with anyone outside the newspaper."

The Professional Viewpoint

Two reporters for the *Detroit Free Press* have written a good book called *Investigative Reporting*.* The reporters, David Anderson and Peter Benjaminson, write from the professionals' viewpoint. They deal with some real situations. Media access and laws differ widely from state to state so some situations the reporters describe may not be pertinent in your state. They also pose some troubling ethical questions. Still, the book is instructive about investigative journalism.

*Indiana University Press, Bloomington and London, 1976.

Chapter 33

Profile Pieces

Profile pieces are like personality obituaries in that they try to catch the essence and character of individuals. What is the person really like? What makes him or her tick?

Research and interviewing are necessary for profile pieces. But your research should extract quotes and anecdotes that reveal character and personality rather than the lengthy quotes you might glean for other kinds of stories.

The quotes should be suggestive of what makes the person so fascinating or controversial. Find out what other people think and have said about the individual.

Don't forget a news peg, the reason you are writing about the person. Occasionally you will have no direct link to a news story. You will write a profile piece because it is there—a good feature story. But usually profile pieces are sidebars to hard-news stories.

For example, when the late Michigan Senator Philip Hart announced that he would not run for reelection, the *New York Times* ran a "Man in the News" profile which contained this news-peg paragraph: "Today, defying one of the basic instincts of his profession, Senator Hart announced that he would not run for a fourth term next year."

The news peg should be worked in by about the sixth paragraph. Often it can be handled in a simple appositional clause in your story: "Brennan, who was named yesterday to head the Department of Labor, ..."

ANECDOTES

One of the best ways for writers to portray character is by using anecdotes. The late Alva Johnston, profile writer for the *New Yorker*, specialized in revealing character by a series of anecdotes.

If you had been writing a profile piece about conductor Arturo Toscanini when he was alive, it would have been perfectly proper to write that he had an incredible memory. But that point must be illustrated in a profile piece.

You might have told the story of the time he judged a contest for young composers. Twenty-five years later a contestant met Toscanini and reminded him about the contest, remarking that "of course you don't remember my piece." Toscanini promplty sat down at a piano, played the first few bars of a composition he had not heard in twenty-five years, shook his head and murmured, "No, no—it's still bad."

That kind of anecdote tells more about Toscanini's fantastic memory than hundreds of adjectives could. Besides, readers remember anecdotes and love to relate them.

A *New York Times* profile piece about Mitchell Sharp, former Canadian foreign minister, told of his intensive efforts to learn French. Then it included this anecdote:

In the House of Commons, where ministers are expected to respond to questions in the language in which they are asked, Sharp follows tradition—up to a point.

One day an opposition member rose to ask in French about the impact of a bill on bank deposit insurance just introduced in the Quebec Legislature.

"Mr. Speaker," Sharp said, bravely embarking in French, "we have discussed this bill with the government of Quebec and the answer is too complicated to speak in French."

He joined in the laughter that filled both sides of the House.

The *New Yorker* specializes in profile pieces, but unfortunately its articles go on, and on, and on. Sometimes the *New Yorker* tells you more about a "chicken king" than you will care to know. But *New Yorker* profiles are well written.

The *New York Times* is the best regular producer of newspaper profile pieces. Journalism students should read them, not just for content but as examples of good writing.

It is easier to get anecdotes about famous people than nonfamous people. Still, you can pick up anecdotes about noncelebrities by talking to their friends and acquaintances. Never ask the person you are writing a profile on: "Do you know any good anecdotes about yourself?"

You must have support—quotes and anecdotes—for judgments you make about people. *Winners & Sinners*, the in-house critique sheet of the *New York Times*, once stressed the point in a piece about former New York Mets outfielder Ron Swoboda:

The story said that Ron Swoboda displayed maturity in words; that he "spoke openly and seriously about his attitude toward himself, his career, the techniques of baseball, the lessons of his experience, publicity, responsibility, eagerness and humility" and that Bing Devine (club owner) "couldn't help being impressed by the proper approach so many of Swoboda's remarks revealed." Want to know what some of those remarks were—or even one? Better buy another newspaper.

A reporter for the *Lorain Journal* in Ohio, Rick Zimmerman, opened a profile of Ohio Supreme Court justices with an anecdote:

COLUMBUS—The most important court in Ohio is made up of seven elected officials who operate in a publicity vacuum.

While the major decisions of Ohio's Supreme Court are often headlined, the men who make them are to most Ohioans sterile legal computers in black robes.

One veteran member of the highest court in Ohio—whenever the impressive marble halls and fawning of court functionaries begin to swell his head—strolls about the Statehouse asking average citizens if they know him.

Judge Charles Zimmerman has yet to find a person who knows him or his name. He has been on the court for 30 years.

Profile pieces should work in some description of mannerisms, physical appearance, and dress. They need some biographical data: age, career high-life-style, family.

The *New York Times* profile on Canada's Sharp described him as "a tall, lean man with a craggy face (and) a broad grin that cartoonists delight in caricaturing."

Profile pieces should never bog down into dull accounts of people. They should "sing"—like any good newspaper story.

Newspaper profile writers have the same choice of approaches as a biographer. Biographers can take the Parson Weems glorification approach, the debunking approach, or the black-and-white approach.

Russell Baker of the *New York Times* has satirized the tendency of newspapers and magazines to glamorize people in profiles:

WASHINGTON—The answer to the question—why is the world such a mess?— lies right before our eyes in the personality sketches of the world's shakers and movers that the newspapers and magazines are so fond of drawing.

If the sketches can be believed, all these men are unpleasantly alike. They are invariably "brilliant."

They all work sixteen hours a day and have magnificent senses of humor (according to their secretaries). Though they drive their staffs mercilessly, they demand twice as much of themselves.

They throw off ideas with an ease that astounds their colleagues.

Though they rarely go out socially—and on those rare occasions never take more than *one* drink—their backbreaking work schedules do not prevent them from helping their children with their algebra, rereading Immanuel Kant and keeping in trim with regular bouts of squash of golf.

English biographer Lytton Strachey once observed that it is "as difficult to write a good life as to live one." He sometimes overdid the debunking in order to avoid a "tedious panegyric."

The best profile piece is the balanced one that shows warts and halos. What is needed is a fair appraisal: neither a hatchet job nor a puff piece.

One problem, however, is that newspapers seldom dare to be too honest about local people. Honest profiles might cost the newspaper friends, sources— and subscribers. Another problem is that many papers lack space for profile pieces and lack sufficient staff to write them.

In writing profile features for newspapers you cannot make flat-out derogatory judgments about people as you might make in an opinion article for magazines. But newspaper reporters can be fair by giving opposing viewpoints. For example: "The judge's foes say he is lenient toward criminals. The judge says he is simply upholding the Constitution."

Profile pieces are really special kinds of feature stories.

Here is a lead on a *Detroit Free Press* profile:

When Mayor Young wants answers, he can pick up the phone and assign any of 10 well-paid aides, 32 department heads or 51 city lawyers to find them.

When the City Council wants information it relies mainly on Jay Brant, the largely anonymous director of the council's Department of Research and Analysis.

Lots of people in the City-County Building say that despite the numerical superiority of the mayor's forces, it has been an even match.

Not because the mayor's staff is anything less than competent, but because of the remarkable talent and personality of Brant.

In a time when the public image of public servants is laced with real or imagined dishonesty, incompetence and laziness, there remain many civil servants like Brant who are honest, competent and hard-working.

What the City Council has in Brant is more than that. He is a brilliant, well-organized, objective and respected man to whom they regularly hand the most complex problems and from whom they get rational, careful answers in a short time.

These judgments are supported by quotes from council members, incidents, and anecdotes.

"Man in the News"

Here are excerpts from a *New York Times* profile piece that exemplifies how a profile can be good, tough, and fair:

LOS ANGELES—Thomas Bradley stood in front of his cheering supporters last night at a moment charged with drama and emotion.

The returns showed that he would be the next mayor of Los Angeles—the first black mayor in the city's history.

"Tonight was the fulfillment of a dream, the impossible dream, because the people of this city have given me the highest honor that can be given to any citizen of our city," he said.

Sophisticates cringe at such talk. They think it belongs in B movies or bad novels. But in the case of Bradley, it happens to be true.

The "impossible dream" that came true for him is the dream that if a man works hard and lives right he can make it to the top, no matter where he started.

Over and over again, Bradley recalled his origins and one is not sure whether he is reminding other people, or himself.

He was born Dec. 29, 1917, the son of Lee and Crenner Bradley, on a cotton plantation in Calvert, Tex. . . .

His supporters believe that Bradley re-assures people, while a more flamboyant man, particularly a black, could frighten them.

Others are more critical and even his admirers have never accused him of excessive imagination.

"He's a very limited man," one prominent Democrat said. . . .

Some liberals are even dissatisfied with Bradley's failure to live up to their stereotype of the outgoing, fast-talking black.

One suburban woman even said last week in disgust, "He's just too white."

But there is little doubt of his toughness or his tenacity. He seldom takes days off and protests when his staff outlines a light schedule.

He makes one feel, at times, that small talk is a luxury he cannot afford.

He does not seem to have any visible means of relaxation and his idea of light reading is a government report on rapid transit.

SUGGESTION FOR INSTRUCTOR

• Assign students a profile piece on the most interesting local person they know or have access to: teacher, preacher, coach, athlete, public official, artist. Look for publication possibilities in campus or local newspapers.

Chapter 34

Wire Services:
Constant Deadlines

"They bring you in, use you up and let you go." That's an old lament of Associated Press (AP) journalists.

The remark is unfair and probably untrue. But it is indicative of a truth about wire service journalism: It can be exhausting work. The job is so demanding that it is easy to see why agencies can give reporters a sense of being used up early.

Joe Alex Morris wrote a book about United Press, forerunner of United Press International, called *Deadline Every Minute*. The title is literally true. Newspaper reporters might have three or four deadlines a day. Reporters for AP and UPI are always on deadline.

That is why wire services have the greatest constant pressure in journalism. They are not for the ulcer-prone.

Yet some journalists thrive on wire service conditions. One reporter wrote after ending a ten-year career with UPI: "Despite my grumbling over the years, it was difficult to leave the wire service. I really loved the work, the competition, the speed and the pressure. I don't think I will ever really outgrow it."

Rivalry between the wire services is intense. The eagerness for a beat—even by thirty seconds—is nearly as keen today as it was for James Gordon Bennett in the nineteenth century.

Rich Oppel, former AP bureau chief in Detroit, argues that this is no longer true: "AP practice now is not to mention beat time—except in transcendent news situations—unless it's a beat of hours or more."

Perhaps. But house organs of both agencies still boast of having scooped the rival on a major news story, even if it is only by one minute and thirty-seven seconds.

Working for wire services, reporters learn to handle pressure. They learn the reporting business—getting the facts, writing compactly, and working at top speed.

AGENCY DRAWBACKS

Wire service journalism has drawbacks. To begin with, there is an element of impersonalness. Your byline rarely appears in the city you work in. Your byline may appear out of town, but you seldom see it unless you check the out-of-town papers.

It's a minor point. Reporters can't live on bylines. But bylines do nourish egos of journalists. Furthermore the lack of identity with a newspaper may cause discontent.

A more serious problem, particularly at smaller bureaus, is small staffs. During the civil rights march in Selma, Alabama, during the 1960s, the UPI bureau manager in Atlanta had to write two stories at once. One story dealt with the march, the other was a sidebar on the violence. Almost incredibly, the bureau chief wrote a take of one story, then a take of the other, so he could move both stories over the wire simultaneously.

Short staffs often mean wire service reporters seldom have time for digging and probing. They often cannot do takeouts on important social and political problems. That often leads to skimming the surface of news.

But AP has moved mightily on this problem in recent years. It is posting special assignment teams to do series on major social and governmental problems. It is prodding its bureaus to come up with enterprise stories and takeouts with strong impact.

Wes Gallagher, former AP general manager, has put it this way: "The man in the street had become more cynical and what he wanted was more interpretive reporting. He wanted to know what to do about problems. He needed them in a cooler perspective."

Moreover, since some editors do not want interpretative stories—"just the facts, Ma'am"—agency journalists tend to write shallower copy. They do not dare to file interpretive reports that might offend some editors.

There is one other problem: the constant shifting of reporters and editors from bureau to bureau. Usually a shift is a move to a more desirable bureau in a larger city.

On the other hand, agency reporters do not have to cover so much of the dull, routine stories. Reporters can think more in terms of regional, state, or national news.

Agency reporters have a different perspective on what is worth reporting and how much detail is necessary. For example, in your hometown paper you might write that "two cars collided at Route 127 and Jefferson Road 10 miles south of Jackson at 3:22 P.M." Wire services would simply say "two cars collided 10 miles south of Jackson."

An obit or a fire story that your local newspaper thinks important will be of no interest to a wire service unless it has an angle of statewide interest.

CLICHÉS

Clichés are a problem for all reporters. But they are a particular problem for wire service reporters who must do so much top-of-the-head writing under severe deadline.

Edwin Newman in *Strictly Speaking* poked fun at the wire services' penchant for clichés. Marxist President Walter Ulbricht of East Germany was either "spade-bearded" or "aging" in wire service stories. Ulbricht would sometimes meet "other prominent politicians whose first names were Balding or Left-leaning," Newman wrote.

BUREAU SETUPS

The Associated Press is a cooperative, membership agency. Newspapers that are AP members turn over their carbons to the local AP bureau.

The *AP Log* has noted: "Membership cooperation with the Associated Press' own staff in the prompt reporting of news has been a basic tenet of AP from its beginning."

The log once told of how "membership assistance from newspapers and broadcasters was important in news and picture coverage of three major stories in the San Francisco area."

In contrast, UPI is not a cooperative agency. Subscribers purchase the wire service. Yet UPI has a network of stringers, usually UPI clients, who get paid for stories they submit.

Both UPI and AP have a web of bureaus around the nation with headquarters in New York. The typical wire setup runs something like this: A wire—national news; B wire—regional or state; F wire—financial and business; sports wire; race wire; and broadcast wire.

AP and UPI run an A.M. and P.M. cycle, the circuits open twenty-four hours daily.

ROUNDUP STORIES

UPI and AP often file undated or roundup stories. This means that a story has no central point of origin. Here is the start of a typical wire service roundup story:

A tornado smashed into Galesburg, Ill., last night, causing an estimated $50,000 damage to airplanes at its airport.

Only one injury was reported: a woman hit by flying glass.

Several buildings were damaged when a tornado struck northwest of Salisbury, Mo., injuring one person slightly.

At Virginia Beach, Va., a teen-aged surfer was swept five miles out to sea by raging winds.

He spent Sunday afternoon gripping the surfboard in the cold Atlantic before he was rescued by a Navy helicopter.

COMMUNICATION LINKS

Communication links are essential for reporters, as any war correspondent will testify. A story is worthless if you cannot phone, telegraph, or cable it to the home office.

Communication links are especially important for wire service journalists. AP and UPI are totally computerized today. Gone is the incessant clatter of teletypes in wire service bureaus. Reporters write with noiseless, dustless, and smokeless video display terminals.

The new technology enables AP and UPI to move 15 percent more copy on the wires daily.

SUPPLEMENTARY AGENCIES

The use of supplementary wire services has been growing. The major ones are the Los Angeles Times-Washington Post News Service and the New York Times News Service.

The supplementals do not try to compete with UPI and AP in hard-news coverage. Rather, they specialize in exclusive stories and interpretive reports that AP and UPI do not have.

As *Newsweek* has noted:

The reasons for the success of the supplementals seems clear. Subscribers can buy not only the prestige of the papers that sell them, but also relief from the "lowest common denominator" copy of the AP and UPI daily reports.

AP and UPI have to provide everything from a superalarm system that tips major papers to a developing story—so they can send their own men in and play their own stories—to a finished news story that "rip and read" announcers can deliver over the air with little more than a glance.

Newspapers should use UPI and AP if they can afford it. That way they get two versions of one event and hence a choice of stories. Or desks can combine AP and UPI versions, taking the best parts from each.

Moreover, having two services provides backup protection. For instance, once AP's Nashville bureau moved a story saying that James Meredith was "shot dead" during a Mississippi civil rights march. UPI's version was correct: Meredith was shot in the head, but not dead.

Sometimes, too, one wire service may file a story on an event that for some reason the other does not handle or moves a skimpy account of.

POOL COVERAGE

Pooling is sharing facilities, services, or notes.

AP and UPI often share reporters and tallying efforts in election coverage. This saves time, money, and duplication of effort. It also avoids the problem of disagreement: AP having one candidate ahead and UPI another.

Pooling by reporters is done when only several reporters have access to a news situation. The pool reporters share their notes with "the pack."

Patrick J. Sloyan, Washington correspondent for *Newsday*, tells of pooling he once did while covering the White House for UPI. President Johnson had brought a large group of Vietnam veterans to the White House to be decorated. Sloyan and Stuart Loory, reporter for the *Los Angeles Times*, each interviewed half of the GIs, then shared their notes.

That illustrates how rival reporters often work together on routine stories. But when reporters are working on something special, a story that can be an exclusive, all their competitive instincts well up. They guard their information jealously. They do not even hint to a rival that they are working on a big story.

Just how fierce rivalry can be among reporters was exemplified in Dallas the day President Kennedy was assassinated in 1963. The late Merriman Smith of UPI and Jack Bell of AP were riding in the Presidential motorcade. When the fatal shots exploded, Smith held the only phone in the car. Smith, with the biggest story of his career developing, refused to hand over the telephone to Bell. Smith kept dictating bulletins. Bell pummeled Smith black and blue during the ride to the hospital in a futile effort to get "Smitty" to give up the phone.

Ever since, the wire service car traveling with the President has two telephones—one for UPI and one for AP.

Be Precise

"Don't just tell us a church rally was feverish. Tell us, as one story did, that: 'Hands clapped, faces glistened, shirts and dresses darkened under the arms and across the backs, pulses throbbed, toes and heels tapped.'

"Don't just tell us that George Wallace is nervous. Tell us, as one story did, that: 'On one 40-minute flight he went through 21 sticks of chewing gum. He shuffled a deck of cards, counted them, shuffled them again. He glanced at the clouds above and below, tightened the seat belt, loosened it, counted the cards, chewed the gum, counted, shuffled, chewed.' "

—AP Log

Advice

- Always keep change in your pocket for a telephone call. You can never tell when an emergency will arise in newspapering.

SUGGESTION FOR INSTRUCTOR

- Have students visit the nearest bureau of the Associated Press or United Press International. Perhaps they can talk to the bureau chief. Assign feature story on the visit.

Chapter 35

Off the Record, Leaks, and Sources

Off the record means not for publication. If you agree to go off the record, you are ethically bound not to print the information.

Reporters avoid the commitment if at all possible. Some naïve sources often say, "Don't quote me, but. . ." or "This is off the record, but. . . ."

Cut such sources short. Explain firmly that your business is to go on the record, to get news. Talk people out of going off the record.

One of the problems is that some sources dealing with journalists do not really know what the term means. Once the late Marguerite Higgins and several other White House correspondents had a small, informal press conference with President Johnson. Higgins said later to Johnson that she was sorry she couldn't write a story about it. This dialogue ensued:

JOHNSON: Why can't you do a story?
HIGGINS: You said it was off the record.
JOHNSON: Yes. But I didn't mean you couldn't print it.

Establish ground rules at the start. Make clear your position. Whenever someone is introduced as a speaker at the Society of Professional Journalists,

SDX, meeting in Detroit, the moderator always makes clear that "everything is on the record."

A former United States ambassador to the United Nations once talked in Pittsburgh to 500 people who had bought tickets to hear him speak. He started his talk with the absurd announcement that he was speaking off the record.

Reporters can blithely ignore such requests. However, in small groups, reporters asked to go off the record can either agree and then keep the information in confidence, or leave the conference immediately so they are free to get the information elsewhere.

Once you have agreed to go off the record you have locked yourself in ethically. You are not even free to get the information elsewhere.

• REPEAT: Avoid going off the record. The occasions for going off the record will be extremely rare.

Private gatherings may be ethically troublesome. Alfred Friendly, former managing editor of the *Washington Post*, once wrote a memo to his staff laying out the situation:

If the reporter is at a private gathering as an individual and not because of his position and profession, politeness and decent social relations require that he specifically ask the person who discloses the information whether it may be published.

If the reporter has been invited to the gathering as a reporter, journalists may write what they learn, Friendly wrote.

Friendly concluded the memo with this admonition: "Remember that a cheap beat, won by cutting a corner, by a technicality, or by violating the spirit if not the letter of the understanding of the news source and of other newsmen, is empty."

BACKGROUNDERS

Whenever possible, use a clear, direct attribution to a specific source. That is the honest and just way. Readers can then judge the credibility of the source and the story.

However, sometimes it is impossible to name sources. Students should understand some terminology and ground rules.

A *backgrounder* is writing a story without attribution to a specific source. It is this kind of thing: "A high official in the Justice Department."

The backgrounder custom arose during World War II to allow reporters to know what President Roosevelt and other wartime leaders were thinking. They could report what they learned but without attribution to a specific source.

Since the war the device has been used by government officials to manage the news—to get out their side of the story, to push a measure or a program.

Another evil of this backgrounder is the *trial balloon*. This enables an official to announce something anonymously. If public and congressional reaction is favorable, the official can then make an announcement for attribution. If the reaction is hostile, the official can disavow any knowledge of the idea and withdraw it.

Reporters have gotten tougher about backgrounders. Some reporters have refused to play the game. They are revealing sources. That is a dubious ethical decision. A better way to fight backgrounders is to insist on a change in the rules.

Once a State Department official held a White House press briefing and told the reporters at the outset that he was speaking on background. Max Frankel, *New York Times* reporter, said: "There's no reason why most of this can't be on the record. The Times will not print this story unless it is on the record." The State Department official went on the record.

As Bill D. Moyers, former presidential press secretary, has asked, "Public officials should ask themselves that if they can make a statement anonymously, is there any good reason why they can't make it publicly?"

LEAKS

"The Ship of State is the only ship that leaks at the top," President Kennedy supposedly once remarked.

The fact is that government leaks are often deliberate. If they are not trial balloons, they can be deliberate leaks to undercut an official, perhaps forcing a resignation.

J. Edgar Hoover, the late FBI chief, would deliberately leak raw FBI files to the press if he wanted to destroy someone. He conducted a despicable vendetta against Martin Luther King by using leaks, innuendo, and lies.

Columnist Jack Anderson, revealing how Hoover had tried to use him in the vendetta against King, once wrote: "I have held back this story for more than seven years because of my rule against revealing sources. But Hoover is now fading . . . into history. His incredible attempt to panic King into committing suicide . . . also abrogates any right he may have to confidentiality."

No wonder Elie Abel, dean of the Columbia University journalism school, has suggested that leaks from government are not really leaks but deliberate handouts of news.

On the other hand, James Reston of the *New York Times* suggests that "the leak is the safety valve of democracy," that without leaks the country would get only government-controlled news.

Reston's colleague Tom Wicker has summed up the case for "leaks" perfectly:

Does anyone suppose that the Pentagon routinely discloses cost overruns on weapons systems, much less waste and inefficiency? Does the CIA or the FBI come forward voluntarily to tell Congress about opening the mail of American citizens or carrying out surveillance of political dissidents?

If the Interior Department is about to complete some sweetheart deal with an oil company or a strip-mining company, does it notify the press? Did John Ehrlichman own up to the Ellsberg break-in?

All such stories . . . come to Congress or the press from "leakers"—which is the term if you don't want the story to come out—or from public-spirited "whistle-blowers"—which is what you call them if you think the public has a right and a need to know about chicanery, waste, inefficiency, abuses of power, mistakes of judgment and plain ineptitude.

The *Times'* Seymour Hersh points out that a leak alone is usually not enough for a story. He notes that a leak must be investigated, confirmed, and supported until the reporter gets what Hersh calls the "one, final, all-important tip."

A *Washington Post* editorial put the whole government leakage problem in perspective: "The principal obligation to ensure that leaked information is not used unfairly or irresponsibly rests with the press."

CONFIDENTIALITY OF SOURCES

The confidentiality of sources should be inviolate. If a reporter promises not to reveal the identity of a source, he or she is honor-bound to keep the commitment.

That is why subpoenas and contempt citations directing journalists to reveal their sources should be fought. If reporters are forced to reveal their sources those sources will wither away.

Investigative reporting could not be done without confidentiality of sources.

Moreover, reporters feel that the courts are using them as an investigative arm of government if they are forced to reveal their sources.

Ideally, a law should be passed by Congress to provide the reporters with the same confidentiality of their sources as doctors have with patients, lawyers with clients, and clergy with parishioners.

The problem is that no consensus has been achieved on a national shield law: "Absolute or qualified?" . . . "Who is a reporter?" . . . "We [the press] don't need it—we have the First Amendment." . . . "If Congress gives it can take away."

The Supreme Court, in a 5-4 decision in 1972, said journalists have no First Amendment right to refuse to tell grand juries the names of their confidential sources.

Perhaps someday the court will reverse that precedent. But that someday appears to be at least twenty-five years away.

Justice Byron White, writing the majority opinion in that court decision, said journalists have the same duty as any other citizen to testify at grand jury proceedings.

However, Justice William Douglas dissented angrily. He wrote:

Forcing a reporter before a grand jury will have two retarding effects upon the ear and the pen of the press.

Fear of exposure will cause dissidents to communicate less openly to trusted reporters. And fear of accountability will cause editors and critics to write with more restrained pens. . . .

The press has a preferred position in our constitutional scheme not to enable it to make money, not to set newsmen apart as a favored class, but to bring fulfillment to the public's right to know.

Subsequent to that *Caldwell* decision several reporters—including Peter Bridge of the *Newark Evening News* and William Farr, then of the *Los Angeles Herald-Examiner*—went to jail over the issue.

Four journalists from the *Fresno Bee* went to jail because they refused to violate the confidentiality of their sources. The "Fresno Four" were cited for contempt and spent fifteen days in prison.

That, perhaps, is the answer. More reporters must be willing to go to jail over the issue.

John S. Knight, retired editor of Knight-Ridder newspapers, asked: "What's wrong with going to jail? People have gone to jail throughout history for their convictions."

Knight concluded that "maybe some of us will suffer" and "maybe some of us ought to suffer" to demonstrate the importance of protecting confidential sources.

"GAG ORDERS"

"Gag orders" are judicial restraining orders that forbid a reporter from publishing certain aspects of a case or a court proceeding. Failure to obey a court order can lead to a contempt citation. Contempt citations are potent weapons in a judge's arsenal.

While gag orders are usually overturned on appeal to a higher court, the ruling always comes too late for the press to print the information when it wants to.

A good example was the *Nebraska Press Association v. Stuart* case decided by the Supreme Court in 1976. The high court ruled that, in general, judges cannot impose gag orders on the press forbidding publication of information about criminal cases—even if judges think that such orders help assure the defendant a fair trial by preventing prejudicial publicity.

The case reached the high court after six people in one family were slain in

Sutherland, Nebraska. It was a lurid case of murder and sexual assault. A judge's order barred pretrial publication of certain aspects of the case.

In a majority opinion by Chief Justice Warren E. Burger, the Court refused to give the First Amendment (free press) priority over the Sixth Amendment (fair trial). But Burger held that the orders in the Nebraska case were presumptively unconstitutional.

The press "won"—but not in time to report the "gagged" aspects of the case.

Burger, in his ruling, lectured the press on its responsibilities:

The extraordinary protections afforded by the First Amendment carry with them something in the nature of a fiduciary duty to exercise the protected rights responsibly—a duty widely acknowledged but not always observed by editors and publishers.

It is not asking too much to suggest that those who exercise First Amendment rights in newspaper and broadcasting enterprises direct some effort to protect the rights of an accused to a fair trial by unbiased jurors.

It is not asking too much to suggest that the press be responsible. Nor can the press assert that the First Amendment is "greater" than the Sixth Amendment. The press should be aware of criminal defendants' rights. But on the other hand, freedom of the press is too precious a right to be gagged by the courts.

The press should fight, and fight, and fight against gag orders. The battle for freedom of the press is never won.

"Manipulating the Press"

William Beecher of the *Boston Globe* once did an interpretive piece on an oft-quoted "senior U.S. official" who could not be quoted by name and title because of press ground rules. Here is the beginning of that story:

WASHINGTON—This is a story about the mysterious "senior U.S. official" who for eight years has been globetrotting on Henry Kissinger's plane, issuing pronouncements and opinions.

His authoritative observations—on issues of the day, on the prospects of sensitive negotiations, indeed on chances of war and peace—are taken most seriously by world leaders and the public in general.

Thus he is one of the most powerful and influential men in the U.S. government. But ground rules imposed on the dozen or so newsmen who travel with him forbid unmasking him by name and title.

This self-same "senior U.S. official" was very much in evidence on Air Force Three, a specially fitted-out Boeing 707 when Secretary of State Kissinger made a recent eight-day overseas trip.

The official is to his accompanying press corps, informative, witty, charming, illusive, misleading, cunning, liked, distrusted, abused and protected, all in the course of a working trip abroad.

He has raised the practice of manipulating the press to an art form of diplomacy.

Letting in Light

The First Amendment is the most important of our precious freedoms. It serves to let in the light so necessary to the proper functioning of a democracy.

—U.S. Judge Harold Medina of New York

Recommended Conduct

Conduct yourself so that you can look your source in the eye the next day.

—Alfred Friendly, former managing editor of the *Washington Post*

Chapter 36

Sports and Other Specializations

If a man can write sports he can write anything.

Damon Runyon

Many city editors would hoot at the Runyon claim about the ability of sports writers. Indeed, there is a notion among some newspaper staffs that sports writers really belong to a subspecies of journalist. Sports writers are barely tolerated at some newspapers and are beneath contempt at others.

That attitude is as foolish as it is wrongheaded. Some of the best journalists in America are sports writers. There are bad sports writers as there are bad writers and bad reporters on the city side. But no journalists should automatically feel superior to sports writers.

Red Smith, Pulitzer-prize winning sports columnist of the *New York Times*, is one of the jewels of journalism. He has the proper cynical outlook on the sports business in general and on team owners in particular. But more important, Smith is one of the most literate journalists in America. His writing for thirty years has been so admirable that few journalists dare claim superiority.

The beginning of a Red Smith column in the *Times* puts the proper perspective on sports writers. It also says a lot about Red Smith while giving a small sample of his felicitous writing style:

Through the administrations of Richard Nixon and Gerald Ford, guys in this business kept encountering politicians who said: "Do you know the President? No? You'd enjoy meeting him, he's a real jock."

There are two reasons why this left the cockles as cool as a proper martini. One is the implication that because a guy writes about sports for a living he is a case of arrested development with no interests away from the playground and a mind too simple to entertain even small-talk of war or peace or books or plays or world affairs.

The other is the assumption that a sports writer, because he is a sports writer, regards enthusiasm for football or a grasp of the infield fly rule as a qualification for public office.

Newspaper staffers are also fond of sneering at the sports department as the "toy department." That, too, is wrong. Sports sections and sports writing are far, far better than they ever were, sometimes even better than the news sections.

Sports pages are coming up with more interpretive articles. They use much more serious sports copy and many more analytical pieces. They often deal with the social, economic, and political problems of sports.

Sports pages are producing more "whys" of winning and losing, providing more quotes and less dreary play-by-play of a game that many people saw on television.

Another thing positive about today's sports pages: Many of the good ones are no longer extensions of the publicity departments of sports teams. They offer unbiased accounts of various events and go above and beyond the actions on the playing field. The *Los Angeles Times* has been in the forefront of this sports-writing trend. The *New York Times*, particularly with Robert Lipsyte in the 1960s, has been stressing new breed sports writing—accenting the values and mores of society as much as writing sports.

Still, sports-writing fans with long memories will argue that the best sports writing in America was produced by the late *New York Herald Tribune* in the 1940s and 1950s.

It may be true that in the hinterland you will still find the clichéd and flowery sports prose in which a baseball is called "a spheroid," "a pill," "an apple," "a horsehide"—or anything but a baseball. The hope is that you don't find it.

Sports writing, like newspapering itself, has grown up.

One other trend in sports is worth noting. More and more newspapers are hiring women sports writers. Part of the reason is undoubtedly trendy—cashing in on women's liberation. But part of the reason is a belated realization that many people are interested in reading about women's sports and about all sports from a woman's point of view.

Anyway, many women who can write well—and who love sports—are no longer barred from sports departments.

As a matter of fact, women sports reporters are invading the men's inner sanctum—the locker room.

Laurie Mifflin, hockey writer for the New York *Daily News*, tells of being joyously hugged in the locker room after a game by a stark naked New York Ranger player.

Mifflin was unfazed. She is after all a professional reporter.

Stanley Cup Thriller

Here is a hard-news story, written under deadline, by a sports writer, Joe Lapointe, for the *Chicago Sun-Times*:

TORONTO—It was an unlikely Stanley Cup playoff game. It was fast-paced, sloppy, violent and thrilling.

And Darryl Sittler, the curly-haired, 25-year-old captain of the upstarts, roared into the record books last night with five goals to lead the Toronto Maple Leafs to a stunning 8-5 thrashing of the defending champion Philadelphia Flyers.

The result evened the quarter-final series at three games apiece and set up a Sunday showdown in Philadelphia.

The Leafs took advantage of a crisis moment in the National Hockey League to upstage the intimidators of the sport.

The Flyers insist that they were distracted by assault charges facing three teammates after a brawl here last week.

But fighting, continual flailing and pounding dominated last night's game.

Referee Wally Harris, trying valiantly to maintain some form of order amid a crackdown mood toward violence in the sport, kept control for only half the game.

Then the frustrated Flyers broke loose and countless slugfests produced a three-hour marathon that turned Maple Leaf Gardens into a pulsating madhouse.

Sittler's five goals, which tied a playoff record held for 28 years by Montreal's Maurice (Rocket) Richard, took the spotlight away briefly from the anti-violence crusade of Ontario Attorney General Roy McMurtry.

But his prosecution of Flyers Mel Bridgman, Don Saleski and Joe Watson has upset hockey's Hell's Angels and may jeopardize their effort for a third straight Stanley Cup.

"Look at it, look," the Flyers' Dave Schultz said, close to tears after the game. Schultz pointed to an ugly red gash on his neck and blamed it on Toronto's Dave (Tiger) Williams, one of many players and fans Philly's hatchetman battled.

"He bit me," Schultz said. "He bit me. He grabbed my hair. He butted me with his head.

"No, I don't think he should be charged under the law. But the league should do something."

Schultz fought with a fan who said he attacked him as he went to the dressing room following an earlier fight, this one with Toronto's Scott Garland.

His last brawl, a tag-team bout with teammate Bob Kelly, resulted in Schultz' expulsion from the game.

The man who epitomizes hockey rough stuff may face league suspension for his performance as he exited, goading the delirious crowd with gestures and shouts as they pelted him with debris. He may sit out the finale in the Spectrum.

The Leafs, undermatched in talent and brawn, were given little chance to win even a game against the champs when the series began.

Toronto coach Red Kelly, a veteran of both NHL and the Canadian Parliament, called the victory "another miracle."

Did he fear retribution when the Flyers got his Leafs back in Pennsylvania jurisdiction?

"No," Kelly said. "We'll win."

Flyer coach Fred Shero wasn't ready to praise Sittler, who tied an NHL regular-season record last winter with six goals in a game.

Shero blamed the high score on the prosecution atmosphere and said the series is "the worst in the history of hockey."

"They can't put (the legal problem) out of their minds," he said of the players who sat glumly around him. "They don't know how to play the game."

The Toronto fans, traditionally the most staid in hockey, taunted the Flyers with a mock "Bernie, Bernie" chant for goalie Bernie Parent, who never looked worse.

Now go back over the story. Note how the writer stressed the "whys" and major features of the game. Note how Lapointe used quotes from coaches and players rather than give the old-fashioned goal-by-goal account of the game. The story sparkles with color.

However, the story can be faulted for not giving the reader just a few paragraphs of when, why, and how Sittler got his record-tying goals. Were they "good goals" or "cheap goals"?

The story might also have told the reader when and how the tide of the game changed. Was it ever close? Whose goal put the Leafs ahead to stay?

The "new breed" of sports writers can go too far in abandonment of old-style sports reporting. They can forget that they are still *reporters* as well as writers.

WOMEN IN JOURNALISM

The whole field of journalism is more open to women today. It wasn't too long ago that a woman walking into a newsroom looking for a job was shunted to the women's department.

Today, more women are getting jobs as general assignment reporters, city desk assistants, and on the copy desk. One more barrier has fallen.

As for women's departments, most of them today are called something

TEAM REPORTERS—This trio of *Detroit News* reporters worked together to cover the bargaining talks between the United Auto Workers and the automobile industry. Left to right are Charlie Cain, Mark Lett, and Lou Mleczko. Photo was taken by Eddie Lombardo, photographer for the *Detroit News*. *(Photo by the* Detroit News.*)*

like "Accent." Most good papers have eschewed the old society news and wedding staples to produce much more germane stories. These stories are often on subjects that would have been taboo five years ago. This, too, is a change for the better.

BLACKS IN JOURNALISM

Most newspapers today are receptive to black journalists. The days of tokenism are over—almost. Yet, while most doors of newspapers are open to blacks, sometimes blacks seeking a media career are weak in language, grammar, and writing.

The fact is that most newspapers are anxious for blacks if for no other reason than the cynical one—they can get stories that white reporters cannot.

It is true that newspapers tolerate too many white mediocrities. But most of them got into newspapering before the doors were unlocked for blacks.

Talented black reporters can command a premium price. Still, according to the American Society of Newspaper Editors, city rooms average less than 1 percent minority employment in reporting and editing jobs.

TEAM REPORTING

One of the growing trends in newspapering is team reporting. This means assigning three or four reporters to one investigation or to one story. AP, for instance, has an urban affairs team.

Newspapers have long mobilized whole staffs to cover big stories. But now more credit is given to the team concept. Italicized boxes with the story will say something like this: "By The Detroit News auto talks coverage team of MARK LETT, CHARLIE CAIN and LOU MLECZKO."

The Detroit *Free Press* sometimes sets up a box this way:

WRITER: Helen Fogel
REPORTERS: Kathy Warbelow, Remer Tyson, Susan Watson, Jack Kresnak

SCIENCE AND MEDICINE

Most newspapers follow this rule: They want generalists first, specialists second. While there are exceptions, most newspapers will hire a reporter first who later can develop into a specialist. The reasoning is sound. Before you can be a specialist, you have to be a skilled general reporter. You will use those skills as a specialist.

Some specialists, such as *Detroit Free Press* medical writer Delores Katz, develop such expertise that, for instance, it is said of Katz that she knows more about medicine than many doctors. Specializing presents problems, however. Some music critics can write well, but do not know music. It is a rare music critic who writes felicitously and knows music, too.

The same problem prevails to a lesser extent with science and medicine writers. It is an unusual reporter in either field who can write as brightly as the news magazines do in the science and medical fields without distorting the science or medical facts.

For the longest time newspapers treated science almost as freak news. Scientists were burned so often by sensationalized newspaper accounts that they understandably grew to distrust and dislike reporters.

Whether it is science or medicine—or any other specialty writing—it boils down to good reporting and good writing. Here is the beginning of a medical story in the *Houston Post*, written by Mary Jane Schier:

Houston radiologist Dr. John Martin charged Wednesday that amended guidelines announced this week in Washington for the use of mammography to detect breast cancer in women under 50 are "so much more government gobbledygook."

The continuing controversy over performing mammograms in screening programs to find earlier breast cancer in younger women has caused "needless concern" among perhaps millions of American women, he said.

Martin is co-director of the Breast Cancer Detection Center at St. Joseph Hospital.

It is one of 27 such centers across the country funded by the National Cancer Institute (NCI) and the American Cancer Society (ACS).

In a three-page telegram Martin received Wednesday from NCI and ACS officials, he was advised that routine use of mammograms in screening asymptomatic women between 35 and 50 years is not recommended at this time.

But Martin said a major goal of the detection centers is to examine routinely women between 35 and about 70 to spot tiny tumors while they are much more curable than if left to grow until the lesions could be felt.

Martin said he has no intention of changing the screening procedures here because "the so-called 'risks' from mammograms are so minimal that they're not worth talking about in view of the potential lives that might be saved from the use of them."

Mammograms are low-dose X-ray tests of the structure of the breast. They are able to pick up pin-sized tumors which physicians cannot feel or detect any other way perhaps for another five years, Martin said.

"Repairing Mother Nature"

Here is the beginning of a science story feature in the *Chicago Tribune*, written by Ronald Kotulak:

WOODS HOLE, Mass.—They are repairing Mother Nature here.

But scientists at the Woods Hole Oceanographic Institution on the most southern point of Cape Cod are not so sure the world is ready to hear about what they have accomplished.

They have learned how to grow lobsters and clams twice as fast as normal while at the same time purifying polluted water to a nearly pristine condition.

Their only problem so far is an esthetic one. Will people eat the super shellfish raised on municipal sewage?

"Why not?" asked Dr. Roger Mann, a shellfish biologist. "They are already doing it without realizing it. Most of the big clam beds around the world are located near rivers that pour human sewage into the oceans."

The clams and other fish raised in the institution's pilot project have been given a clean bill of health so far as bacteria and viruses are concerned.

Watchword: Caution

Caution is the watchword for the science-medical stories, particularly those dealing with cures or breakthroughs. The *AP Log* relates that "it is mandatory that a health story making claims of cures, breakthroughs, dramatic new findings . . . be checked with the science staff BEFORE it goes to the wire."

AP science writer Alton Blakeslee put it this way:

An over-all guideline is that anything new has a long gauntlet to run to find its new place in the treatment of human ailments.

A brand new drug may show promise in the laboratory, but it will likely have unhappy side effects for some people. It may be too expensive.

We must include such cautions when indicated in order not to add to the burden of the sick and worried people ready to leap at any hint of a miracle.

CONSUMER AND ENVIRONMENTAL REPORTING

Consumer affairs and environmental reporting place a severe strain on reporter's objectivity. It is a natural inclination for most reporters to be on "the side of the angels" in covering such stories.

Reporters are against litter and against pollution. They are usually pro-consumer.

Yet their stories must be reported objectively—honestly and fairly. Reporters need to guard against writing stories that patently reveal their pro-ecology and pro-consumer biases.

The impact of a pipeline, the potential harm of offshore oil drilling, and the effect of a highway in an ecologically valuable swamp are invitations to bias.

Whatever their personal feelings, good reporters present the pros and cons of controversies. They give all sides of a dispute. In covering a strip-mining controversy, for instance, they report it objectively. They leave the side-taking to their paper's editorial writers.

In the mid-1960s, consumer and environmental beats were rarities. By the early 1970s, they had become the fastest-growing beats in the country. But newspapers, like people, are trendy. Today the rage for consumer and environmental reporting has, unfortunately, diminished.

Journalism students should understand two facts of newspaper life in regard to consumer and environmental reporting. Newspapers depend on advertisements. Too many papers—particularly smaller ones—when faced with a choice between tough consumer reporting and losing ads, will choose to retain advertising.

The other newspaper dilemma in environmental reporting is that business and "progress" are pitted against ecology. The newspaper will often side with business because newspaper owners tend to be conservative. Yet, in fairness, newspapers also face that perennial dilemma: jobs versus the environment.

Lou Mleczko, former consumer reporter for the *Detroit News*, is as scrupulously honest and fair a reporter who ever lived. Unlike some reporters, he refuses to shade facts to get "a better story" ·and hence better "play," or positioning, of his stories.

Mleczko's city editor, wondering whether his stories on auto repairs had been fair, once pulled a year's worth of Mleczko's auto-repair stories. The editor was astounded by Mleczko's objectivity.

"Sometimes I felt I was paralyzing my own efforts in trying to be too fair," Mleczko says. "I leaned over too far to be fair—to the point of being ridiculous.

"I made a great effort to allow the accused to have rebuttal space. In fact, sometimes I even put consumer critics on the defensive."

It is doubtful that reporters can be too fair. But Mleczko had the right approach to consumer reporting—indeed, all reporting.

Mleczko says the most difficult problem consumer writers face is "the clash with advertisers, writing what advertisers call 'negative stories.'" One other problem is that some papers are reluctant to name names, pulling the teeth from consumer stories.

It is obvious that consumer reporting requires firm backing from editors and publishers.

A final point on consumer reporting: Most newspapers feel that they don't have the time, money, and resources to get into comparison of products. Newspapers are not product-testing organizations. They leave that to *Consumer Reports*.

Carter versus Ford

One of the best environmental reporters in the country is Gladwin Hill of the *New York Times*. Here is an example of his work, a postelection comparison of the positions of Jimmy Carter and Gerald Ford on conservation.

NEW YORK—Jimmy Carter's election is viewed by conservationists as presaging a new era in the nation's quest for environmental quality.

The Ford administration, like the Nixon administration, has had a reputation among conservationists for inaction and obstruction on environmental matters. Carter, by contrast, won their support with his record as governor of Georgia and his subsequent policy positions.

Carter, who drew a League of Conservation Voters rating of "outstanding," had on his campaign staff a score of specialists assigned to environmental and natural resource questions.

His campaign declarations called for a wide and varied array of changes in federal environmental policies and organizational structures.

Foremost among these was his declared intention to overhaul the nation's diffuse and fragmented management of energy, centralizing it in a new cabinet-level department.

"I intend to abolish the Federal Energy Administration, the Federal Power Commission, the Energy Research and Development Administration and the Energy Resources Council," Carter said.

While any such sweeping realignment would probably encounter congressional resistance, Carter has projected other basic administrative changes.

As governor, he battled the Army Corps of Engineers and the Agriculture Department's Soil Conservation Service over the dam-building and stream channelization projects, vowing to curb these activities if he got the chance.

In his campaign, he said, "A great reduction must be made in these activities," adding, "The federal government's dam-building era is coming to an end."

On the controversial question of nuclear power development, Carter differed sharply with the Nixon and Ford policies, recommending the subordination of nuclear power to other energy sources, such as coal, and increased emphasis on more advanced technologies, such as the harnessing of solar energy.

The most fundamental difference between Carter and President Ford is in their over-all philosophies.

Ford's expressed attitude has been that there is an intrinsic conflict between environmental improvement and economic development.

Carter has said repeatedly, "There is no incompatibility between careful planning and economic progress on the one hand and environmental quality on the other."

Promising to "renew the nation's commitment to clean air," Carter has charged that automobile manufacturers have "dragged their feet" in reducing car emissions.

He said that he would press for preservation of air quality in areas where it now surpassed federal requirements. . . .

Ford's two vetoes of strip-mining control legislation were described by Carter as "serious environmental insults."

OTHER SPECIALITIES

An exasperated financial officer of American Telephone and Telegraph once complained about an interviewing reporter who did not know the difference between stocks and bonds.

It is probably obvious, but it must be said: All specialty writers should know their fields thoroughly. Religion and education writers need to know the problems and controversies in their field—local, national, and international. The same can be said about any other specialty writer.

One of the hardest things to do as a specialist is to avoid becoming a captive of a special-interest group. Reporters need sources. But to maintain credibility with all sides, specialists must be tough and impartial.

Business and financial writers, for instance, often get too cozy with the business and financial interests of their community. Such writers tend to play up good business news and play down bad business news. This is good for the interests but not for the public.

On the other hand, some newspapers have printed critical stories about business, prompting charges that the press is antibusiness. Arthur Ochs Sulzberger, publisher of the *New York Times*, answered that accusation in a speech to the Economic Club of Detroit.

"Is the press anti-business?" Sulzberger asked. "The answer is no. Is the press anti-dullness, anti-stuffiness, anti-corporate secrecy? The answer is yes. Is a probing, skeptical, searching press coverage good for business? I think so."

Labor writers have to tightrope walk a thin line of fairness. They cannot be partial to either side without forfeiting the respect of the other side.

Newspapers have become much fairer about labor disputes. There was a day when management was all pure and labor all evil. As press critic A. J. Liebling once wrote, "What newspapers call pig-headedness in a railroad conductor is what they call devotion to principle in a railroad president."

Lou Mleczko of the *Detroit News* tells of writing a story on labor negotiations between the United Auto Workers and the Ford Motor Company.

"Both the union and management were mad at me," Mleczko says. "Each side felt that I was being unfair."

That kind of reporting is a good indication that the reporter has been fair. Yet some journalism professors disparagingly refer to such reporting as "the theory of balanced incompetence."

In any case, impartial reporting is what all good journalists strive for.

GROUP JOURNALISM

Reporting in one of the bureaus of national news magazines can be frustrating especially if a writer's ego is easily bruised. Field correspondents for the news weeklies file long dispatches to the home office. They feel themselves lucky sometimes if one of the quotes they garnered makes "the book."

Still, the prestige of working for *Time* or *Newsweek*—and larger salaries than the average newspaper slave gets—makes the jobs desirable.

News magazines generally hire reporters who have first gotten experience with newspapers or on radio and TV.

FOREIGN CORRESPONDENCE

Foreign reporting is one of the most glamorous and desirable jobs in news-papering. Most papers do not have overseas bureaus. Those that do have them usually insist that a reporter first earn his or her spurs as a general assignment staffer. This means "working your way" overseas.

A typical pattern goes something like this: Reporters start on the police beat; next they work on general assignment or a "beat": then, perhaps, they cover the city-county building; and, maybe, the next assignment is as the number one political writer, or a posting to the state capital or the Washington bureau.

The pattern varies. In any case, a foreign reporting job will not fall into your lap—unless you marry the publisher's son or daughter.

THE GUILD

The American Newspaper Guild is a living monument to Heywood Broun. The Guild, spurred by Broun, was founded in 1933. It enabled journalists for the first time to begin working for more than "the romance of the game."

Before the Guild, journalists and teachers were the two lowest-paid professionals. The Guild changed that, although it took decades to do it. The Guild did not really develop muscles until the 1960s. Today, thanks to the Guild, many journalists are getting pay commensurate with their skills, knowledge, and responsibility.

But the Guild must recognize one important fact: Reporters are not 8-to-3 factory workers. Journalists, despite the semantic and legal arguments over definition, are professionals. They do not always work a straight seven-and-a-half hour day.

One young reporter tells of the shop steward at a Chicago newspaper who loomed over his desk at 5 P.M., pointed to his watch, and asked, "What are you doing here at 5 o'clock?"

That attitude annoys even staunch Guild supporters. Good journalists do not "punch a time-clock." They are hustling, enterprising, and individualistic reporters and writers. They are professionals.

Business-Finance Story

Here is the top of a business-finance story from *The Miami Herald* written by Jane Scholz:

As a wage earner who has to cut corners to save $20 a week, you probably feel that you're a pretty insignificant part of the multimillion-dollar savings and loan association where your nest egg is socked away.

But one of these days, Mr. Depositor, you may get a letter from the president of that big financial institution, asking you how that business should be run.

It's not as outlandish as it sounds.

The 50,000 Floridians who save with American Savings and Loan of Miami Beach have already had to decide whether the institution should convert from a mutual association to a capital stock company.

It's likely that before very long depositors of at least half a dozen more savings institutions in the state will be asked to make that same decision.

American Savings went public in April and immediately sold out all publicly offered shares of its stock at $14.50 each.

Today a share of American Savings stock sells for roughly $16.

Since the American Savings conversion, three more Miami savings and loans have applied to the Federal Home Loan Bank Board for permission to become stock companies. . . .

So what difference does it make to you—as a saver, as someone who might someday go to your savings and loan for a home mortgage loan or as someone who might have a chance to buy stock in your savings and loan—whether your savings and loan is a mutual association or a stock company?

Both critics and supporters of stock conversion plans agree that it could make a big difference.

Religion Story

Here is the beginning of a religion story in the *Washington Post*, written by Marjorie Hyer:

Roman Catholic leaders on two continents have sharply protested the action of Ecuador's military government last week in which police broke up a church conference that included 17 bishops and held them prisoner for 27 hours.

Speaking for the National Conference of Catholic Bishops, which he heads as president, Archbishop Joseph L. Bernardin of Cincinnati issued a "strong protest" of the incident in which four United States bishops, a priest and a lay official of the U.S. Catholic Conference were involved.

The Latin American Bishop's Council and the U.S. Catholic Conference were involved.

The Latin American Bishop's Council and the Roman Catholic bishops of Ecuador have also condemned the action.

The disruption of the conference at a church retreat center near Riobamba, Ecuador, Aug. 12, made front page headlines in both North and South America.

Archbishop Bernardin, who was joined in his protest by Bishop John J. Fitzpatrick of Brownsville, Tex., chairman of the Latin America committee for the U.S. bishops' conference, called the Ecuadorian government action "an unwarranted and unjustifiable intrusion by a state in the legitimate exercise of the pastoral ministry of the Church."

Chapter 37

Grammar, Language, and Student Errors

I am still committed to the idea that the ability to think for one's self depends upon one's mastery of the language."

Joan Didion in *Slouching towards Bethlehem**

Anyone who teaches journalism also teaches English—grammar, spelling, and composition. Anyone who wants to be a journalist should strive to master the language.

Sadly, the national illiteracy rate is rising. Journalists, of all people, should be part of the solution, not the problem. Many electronic journalism majors feel that they don't need to learn the language because they are "going into radio and television anyway."

They are wrong. They must know the language just as much as print students must.

Two of the most frequent major student errors are inaccuracy and lack of attribution. Students make mistakes for the same reasons that professionals do: carelessness, haste, and human shortcomings.

*Dell Publishing Co., Inc., New York, 1968.

The other major failing in student copy is lack of attribution. Incriminating and opinionated sentences must have attribution. In a crime story you cannot simply write, "Jones stabbed Smith." You must make it: "Jones stabbed Smith, police said"—as long as the police did say it.

You cannot just write: "Smathers was killed when his car was struck by an auto driven by Robert X. Zelma." It must have "police-said" attribution.

If you have a long police account, you can avoid having attribution with practically every sentence by setting up your recapitulation of events with a colon. For example: "Police gave this account:.."

PEEVES AND PREDILECTIONS

Some of the points in this chapter may have been made before. But even if they have been, they bear repeating.

- Avoid the stuffy or pedantic-sounding word or phrase. Make it "before" rather than "prior to."
- Avoid the explanation point (screamer). Screamers brand a writer as immature. They are bogus efforts to add punch to copy.
- Avoid turning a noun into a verb: "But Stargis *postcards* from San Francisco." Nouns do get turned into verbs, but reporters should make sure that they are acceptable usage. This will not pass: "The secretary said she had all those files to be 'liaised.' "

On the other hand, don't tamper with colorful quotes like baseball player Yogi Berra's comment on missing a fly ball, "I nonchalanted it."

- Make it "people" not "persons" in this context: "Seven people were killed in the crash." "Persons" sounds stiff and affected. However, it is only fair to warn you that some editors will have apoplexy if you use "people" instead of "persons."
- Make it "about," not "approximately." It is less fancy-sounding, means the same thing, and is more than twice as terse.
- Every "currently" and "presently" you eliminate from your copy will place you closer to reporters' Elysium. "He is currently writing a book." Is there any need for currently?
- Avoid academicese, educationese, legalese, and sociologese. That means avoiding pretentious, polysyllabic writing. That means avoiding words like "finalize," "maximize," and "structured." That means not using ponderous, Kantian prose like this: "This phase utilized multiple regression which optimizes prediction of the dependent variable by deriving weights for each independent variable and a constant weight."
- Avoid paired negatives: "not improbable," "not infrequently." Say it positively. Make it "frequently."
- Misplaced modifier. For example: "Wearing silk-stocking masks, the Ford Fairlane sped away with the bandits."
- Non sequitur. This offender is usually found in obituaries. "Born in Brooklyn, she began writing poetry at 15." Does being born in Brooklyn have anything to do with writing poetry?

- Switching tenses when using partial quotations. This: "Baker said in an interview yesterday that 'I wouldn't rule out the possibility.' " Since you cannot change the direct quote, recast the sentence or paraphrase the idea. This way: "Baker said he 'wouldn't rule out the possibility.' " One more example: "Ford accepted the Butz resignation, saying it was 'one of the saddest decisions of my presidency.' " It could be written this way: "Ford accepted the Butz resignation, saying it was 'one of the saddest decisions' of his presidency." Or it could be written this way: "It was 'one of the saddest decisions of my presidency,' Ford said." Switching from third to first person leaves your syntax showing.

- Avoid "mishap" in writing about fatalities. "Six were killed in the mishap." Make it "accident." "Mishap" sounds too trivial.

- Hyphenate compound adjectives modifying a noun as in "blue-black sedan." Hyphens are ghastly things. When in doubt, check the dictionary. The tendency is to write words solid. Generally write words solid unless confusion would result. For example, it is better to hyphenate "co-op" because "coop" is easily misread.

- "Rushed to the hospital." How else are injured people taken to hospitals?

MORE FREQUENT THAN "FREQUENT ERRORS"

Be conscious of the following mistakes:

- "Armed gunman." What else is a gunman but armed?
- Effect and affect. Usually "effect" is a noun, "affect" a verb. The one exception is, "the union effected a settlement." A reporter wrote: "The decision began to effect schools outside the South." Wrong. It should be "affect." This is correct: "What effect will the ruling have?"
- Podium. Usually misued, even in the *New York Times*. "Carter took his place behind the podium." It should be "lectern." Conductors stand on podiums. Speakers stand on a dais behind a lectern.
- Wrong number. Disagreement between subject and verb. "The coach said each of the runners were outstanding." It should be "was" outstanding. "Neither Smith nor Jones are going." It should be "is." "The target of the demonstrators' ire were Carter and Mondale." It should be "was."
- "Winstons taste good like a cigarette should." "As" is required in place of "like."

WOMEN'S LIBERATION

Sexism should be routed from the language. Do not write: "Housewives will be chagrined to learn that the price of bread has gone up two cents." Write "consumer" or some other word that includes men, who also buy bread.

Avoid sexual stereotypes and phrases that degrade women. Do not write that "the girl" handles the files. Make it "the secretary handles the files." Avoid sneering and leering references to women. Do not write "lady lawyer." Say "the woman is a lawyer" if it is germane to the story.

Recast sentences to avoid unnecessary masculine genders. Rather than write, "the average Russian likes his vodka," make it, "the average Russian drinks vodka."

After that plea for women's equality, however, another plea is necessary: Do not distort the language. The use of "person" instead of "man" has a jarring, ugly sound in such expressions as "spokesperson" or "chairperson." Instead of writing "salespersons" to avoid "salesmen," make it "sales people."

One of the more ridiculous efforts to "liberate" the language is the use of "freshperson" for "freshman." Writing "Jacqueline Gladstone, chairman," is not sexism. "Man" in this case is used in the generic sense. Nor should you seriously write, "Barbara Tuchman is a great herstorian."

The following lead sounds so obviously liberated—and so linguistically grating:

Alphonse H. Kelton, 66, former chairperson of the Rutgers history department, was stricken with what a spokesperson termed a heart attack.

VOGUE WORDS

Vogue words are words and phrases that "everyone" is writing or speaking. They are "in." The words might have had an impact originally. But when everyone starts using them, they become clichés. "Scenario," "bottom line," "game plan," "super," "right on"—all get hopelessly worked to death by writers.

Reporters easily slip into the habit of using vogue words. Two perpetual offenders are "quietly" and "massive." Everything is massive—a report, an attack, a building. Obviously quiet actions are taken "quietly." For example:

WASHINGTON—The administration's top civil rights lawyer has quietly cut ties with an all-white club here.

Would he sever such ties with a press conference and a press release?

"The senator quietly closed his eyes." How else?

Reporters also overwork such words as "controversial" and "confrontation." Reporters must choose words carefully. They are writers, too.

SPLIT INFINITIVES

Split infinitives are not really the horrors your high school English teacher may have suggested. In some cases sentences read smoother if an infinitive is split.

Sometimes avoiding a split will leave an awkward sentence. "To really grasp the situation" may be preferable to such avoidances as, "to grasp the situation really," or "really to grasp the situation."

In most cases splits can be avoided. There is no need to write: "She urged Congress to sharply reduce" because you can write "to reduce sharply."

One more example: "Men are likely to openly criticize their partners" is a split infinitive. But you certainly would not write it, "Men are likely openly to criticize their partners." A better but still awkward way would be, "Men are likely to criticize openly their partners." The best way of all is to write, "Men are likely to criticize their partners openly."

Question: Is it really worth the bother?

MORE CROTCHETS

Be aware of the following subtleties:

- "Smith was stabbed during an argument." Properly, he was stabbed during a "quarrel." "The professors had an *argument* over the meaning of life."
- "Beaten about the head." No, "beaten *on* the head."
- Too-late information. A lead might say "two university professors died over the weekend." Then the writer forces the reader to go through twelve paragraphs to find out how the second professor died.
- Redundancies. "At about 2 P.M." You don't need both prepositions any more than you need "new" in a "new record." Guard against redundancies in writing: "He plans to shuttle *back and forth* between New York and Washington"; "She said she feared the strike may resume *again*"; "*true* facts."; "*private* yacht."
- Clichés. One of the seventy-seven deadly sins of writing: "It beggars description," et al.
- Avoid "we," "our," and "us" in referring to the United States. Make it "the nation," "the country," "the United States." "Our" and "we" are all right in quotations.
- Avoid "it was learned," "told the Daily Bladder," or "told this reporter." That is all puffery for the reporter and the newspaper. It is the job of reporters to learn and to be told.
- Question marks with quotations depend on the sense of the sentence. This way: "Whatever happened to 'Tricky Dick'?" But: " 'What do you take me for?' she asked."
- Student failings: Forgetting to name the court in court stories and leaving out the news peg in feature and speech stories (telling the reader the reason for writing the story). Avoid vague, meaningless adjective modifiers such as "somewhat," "rather," "sort of." Don't write, "he alleged he was innocent."

TWO WRITING MISTAKES

The mayor is quoted as saying, "He's talking about the same things I've been saying for three years." Then the reporter adds, "The mayor also hopes. . . ." Properly it should read, "The mayor also *said* he hopes. . . ."

Another frequent mistake by reporters is failure to link up someone mentioned in the lead with the person named in the second paragraph. The reporter assumes it is understood who is referred to. For example:

The director of the Health Department has denied charges that she refused to aid a welfare investigation.

Kathleen Myer said that "on the contrary, the Health Department has been a tower of strength in the investigation."

Properly, there should be a direct link between the lead and the second paragraph. This way: "Kathleen Myer, the *director*, ..."

Thirteen Commandments

An editor of the late *Chicago American* once wrote thirteen grammatical commandments. They provide a smile, perhaps, while they make grammatical points:

1   Don't use no double negatives.
2   Make each pronoun agree with their antecedents.
3   Join clauses good, like a conjunction should.
4   About them sentence fragments.
5   When dangling, watch your participles.
6   Verbs has got to agree with their subjects.
7   Just between you and I, case is important, too.
8   Don't write run-on sentences they are hard to read.
9   Don't use commas, which aren't necessary.
10 Try to not ever split infinitives.
11 It is important to use your apostrophe's correctly.
12 Proofread your writing to see if you any words out.
13 Corect speling is esential.

"American Fat"

Russell Baker, humor columnist of the *New York Times*, has neatly skewered fat writing. Here is the beginning of his column on "American Fat":

WASHINGTON—Americans don't like plain talk anymore. Nowadays they like fat talk. Show them a lean, plain word that cuts to the bone and watch them lard it with thick greasy syllables front and back until it wheezes and gasps for breath as it comes lumbering down upon some poor threadbare sentence like a sack of iron on a swayback horse.

"Facilitate" is typical of the case. A generation ago only sissies and bureaucrats would have said "facilitate" in public. Nowadays we are a nation of "facilitate" utterers.

"Facilitate" is nothing more than a gout-ridden, overstuffed "ease." Why has "ease" fallen into disuse among us? It is a lovely little bright snake of a word which comes hissing quietly off the tongue and carries us on, without fuss and French horns, to the object which is being eased.

This is English at its very best. Easing is not one of the great events of life; it does not call for Beethoven; it is not an idea to get drunk on, to wallow in, to encase in multiple oleaginous syllabification until it becomes a pompous ass of a word like "facilitate."

Abused and Misused Words

Unique—One of a kind. It cannot be modified as in the frequent expression, "somewhat unique."

Refute—To prove wrong. The word probably wanted is "rebut," to answer or reply to.

Marshal—Field and fire marshal have one "l." John Marshall and Thurgood Marshall are associated with the Supreme Court.

All right—Two words. Not "alright" as some students insist on spelling it.

Under way—Two words.

Over and more than—It is incorrect to write "he weighed over 250 pounds." But the battle for the correct "more than" is lost.

Hopefully—Another lost battle.

Transpire—Ditto.

Its and it's—"Its" is a possessive adjective. ("Its first win of the year.") "It's" is a contraction, meaning "it is." ("It's a beautiful day.") Never are the twain interchangeable.

That and *which*—"That" is defining and is needed in this construction: "The home run that Bench hit won the game." Nondefining: "The home run, which was Bench's twenty-fifth of the season, came in the third inning."

Due to and *owing to*—Avoid both. Better to write "because of": "He couldn't attend because of a headache."

Cite-site-sight—Look them up if you are unsure.

Infer-imply—Speakers imply, listeners infer.

Lie-lay—Lie (recline) and lay (put or place).

Uninterested-disinterested—Uninterested (not interested) and disinterested (impartial).

Further-farther—"Farther" is used for physical distances. "Further" refers to time distance. Correct: "Jupiter is farther from the earth than Mercury." Correct: "You have to go back further in time for its origins."

Accommodate—The most misspelled word in the English language?

Clarity, Clarity, Clarity

Reporters often write something that is clear to them—*they* know what they mean. Unfortunately, the reader does not.

For instance, a reporter for a metropolitan newspaper wrote: "In the six-year race for the State Supreme Court. . . ." It is obvious that the reporter meant to write, "In the race for a six-year term. . . ."

It is essential for reporters' prose to be perfectly clear, as a former President used to say.

Parts of Speech

If you never learned—really learned—the parts of speech in grammar school or high school, get a grammar book and spend one month of your life studying the parts of speech. You may need to know them in the course of a newspaper career.

Journalists are writers. Writers should know the parts of speech.

SUGGESTION TO INSTRUCTOR

- Instructors can render a great service to journalism by constantly stressing accuracy. One way is for instructors in role-playing or with handouts to give wrong spellings of names or facts that readers should know. The purpose is not to be able to say, "See, I tricked you." The purpose is to drum into students the necessity for accuracy. Teach them to look suspiciously at handout "facts." Teach them to be wary of something they *thought* they could trust to be accurate.

Chapter 38

Reflections on Newspapering

To the foundation of a school for publishers, failing which, no school of journalism can have meaning.

A. J. Liebling

Of all the institutions in our inordinately complacent society, none is so addicted as the press to self-righteousness, self-satisfaction and self-congratulation.

A. H. Raskin of the *New York Times*

Newspapers routinely criticize everything in society. They rarely criticize themselves. The press criticism there is seldom reaches a wide audience.

The situation has improved. Newspapers are readier to admit error than they used to be. Some papers are not only franker about the mistakes they make, but give corrections and "skin-backs"—stories correcting error—much more prominent play.

The rise of journalism reviews, which criticize media coverage, has been a welcome development. Moreover, some newspapers have confessed to fallibility by naming ombudsmen.

Ombudsmen handle reader's complaints. They also criticize their own paper professionally and ethically.

A *Washington Post* ombudsman put it this way: "My job is mainly monitoring the paper for fairness, balance and perspective. If I see something wrong, and they (the publisher and top editors) agree with it, they put out a memo and fix it."

Wonder of wonders, sometimes the *Post* publishes criticism of its own reporting and treatment of news.

But still, as press critic A. J. Liebling once wrote, "newspapers write about themselves with awe, and only after mature reflection." The air of infallibility still hovers over too many newspapers.

NEWSPAPER: BUSINESS OR PUBLIC SERVICE?

No ethical discussion can ignore one recurring problem: the publishers. Certainly most publishers have high ethical standards. But the problem is that most publishers are interested in making money first, putting out a good newspaper second. At too many papers, putting out a good newspaper is a distant second.

Naturally newspapers have to make a profit. But Liebling's crack about journalism schools for publishers is valid. Too many publishers are spineless. Their dead hands are on too many newspapers.

Publishers, as business people, tend to be conservative politically, socially, and journalistically. One reason is that they need advertising. Another is that, as business people, pubishers tend to protect the conservative interests and institutions in society.

As a rule, the smaller the newspaper, the greater the fear of offending advertisers and subscribers.

It is easier for a big-city newspaper to ignore the feelings of a single advertiser. For a small newspaper, however, a single advertiser might be important to the paper's financial health.

Often the publisher's predilections run through the whole editorial side: from publisher, to editor, to managing editor, to city editor, to staffer.

The sad refrain too often is, "How does the Chief want this played?" Editors lean toward their publishers' biases.

As Oswald Garrison Villard wrote in *The Disappearing Daily*: "Reporters, as well as editors, take the color of their employers unconsciously when they do not do so consciously."*

Many papers are burdened with "sacred cows" and policy stories. A "sacred cow" is a story handled with kid gloves because the editor and/or publisher has a special interest in it. A policy story is one played up or down, reflecting the whims of the publisher and/or editor.

Sometimes news stories are killed (not run) because they are critical of

*Alfred A. Knopf, Inc., New York, 1944.

people, the hometown, or local institutions. Reporters, finding this anguishing and frustrating, have quit over the issue.

But after a sad litany of gutless journalism that reporters recite over their after-work drinks, someone will cite courageous editors and publishers. Courageous editors and publishers are those who pursue stories at the risk of advertising and circulation loss, at the risk of rocking the seats of the mighty.

Two who deserve canonization for courage are Katharine Graham, publisher of the *Washington Post*, and Harry Ashmore, former editor of the *Arkansas Gazette*. Graham had the courage to push the Watergate investigation when most of the nation's press was not interested and the powerful were sneering at a "third-rate burglary." Ashmore courageously defied Southern mores on race in the 1950s at the cost of readers and advertisers.

CHARACTER

Character is as important in newspapers as it is in people. A. M. Rosenthal, *New York Times* executive editor, wrote a memo to his staff that made the point. The memo said:

It is the character of the paper that has made its readers trust it. . . .
That character rests on:
The belief that although total objectivity may be impossible because every story is written by a human being, the duty of every reporter and editor is to strive for as much objectivity as humanly possible.
The belief that no matter how engaged the reporter is emotionally, he tries as best he can to disengage himself when he sits down to write.
The belief that presenting both sides of the issue is not hedging but the essence of responsible journalism.

Those are high standards and high ideals. Most journalists strive for them. Sometimes they fail, as all human beings err. But their eyes are on the stars.

THE MAKING OF GREAT NEWSPAPERS

What makes a great newspaper? Sports writer Red Smith has given the best answer:

No matter what one may read in the textbooks or hear in journalism schools, only one ingredient can make a great newspaper: great journalists. The truth should be self-evident and yet it escapes many publishers that a newspaper cannot possibly be better than the journalists who put it out.

How do you get great journalists?

By paying top salaries. But even more important, by giving reporters freedom to dig, roam, write, and report without handholding and suppression. Reporters must have freedom to write stories honestly, without slanting. Reporters must be free to write stories on the basis of facts they discover—not be sent out to find support for the preconceptions of the editor.

Finally, reporters must have the support and backing of their editors. Good editors are essential for good reporters. Good editors give guidance, help, advice, and direction on the basis of their wisdom and experience.

Freedom of the Press . . .

Freedom of the press is guaranteed only to those who own one.

—A. J. Liebling

Role of the Press

The function of the press in society is to inform, but its role is to make money.

—A. J. Liebling

Index

Index